To the Instructor

Thank you for your interest in the Townsend Press vocabulary series—the most widely used vocabulary books on the college market today. Our goal in this series has been to produce nothing less than excellent books at nothing more than reasonable prices.

About the Book

Notice that the introduction to students (page 1) immediately makes clear to them just why vocabulary study is important. Students are motivated to learn by the four compelling kinds of evidence for word study. The back cover as well convinces students that "a solid vocabulary is a source of power."

You may want to look then at the preface, starting on page vii, which describes in detail the nine distinctive features of the book.

You'll see that a second color is used in the text to make the material as inviting as possible. You'll note, too, that while each chapter takes up only four pages, those pages contain a great deal of hands-on practice to help ensure that students master each word. And you'll find that the practice materials themselves are far more carefully done, and more appealing, than the run-of-the-mill items you typically find in a skills text. The quality and interest level of the content will help students truly learn the words, without either boring them or insulting their intelligence.

Supplements to the Book

Adding to the value of *Advanced Word Power* is the quality of the supplements:

- An *Instructor's Edition*, which you hold in your hand. The Instructor's Edition is identical to the student text except that it includes the answers to all of the practices and tests.

- A combined *Instructor's Manual and Test Bank*, free with adoptions of 20 or more copies. This booklet contains a pretest and a posttest for the book and for each of the six units in the text. It also includes teaching guidelines, suggested syllabi, an answer key, and an additional mastery test for each chapter.

- *Computer software*, in IBM (DOS or Windows) or Macintosh format, which provides additional tests for each vocabulary chapter in the book. Free with adoptions of 20 or more copies, the software contains a number of user- and instructor-friendly features, including brief explanations of answers, a sound option, frequent mention of the user's first name, a running score at the bottom of the screen, and a record-keeping file.

Adopters of the book can obtain any of these supplements by calling our toll-free number, 1-800-772-6410; by faxing Townsend Press at 1-800-225-8894; or by writing to us at the address shown on page iv.

(Continues on next page)

A Comprehensive Vocabulary Program

There are nine books in the Townsend Press vocabulary series:

- *Vocabulary Basics* (reading level 4–6)
- *Groundwork for a Better Vocabulary, 2/e* (reading level 5–8)
- *Building Vocabulary Skills, 2/e* (reading level 7–9)
- *Building Vocabulary Skills, Short Version, 2/e* (reading level 7–9)
- *Improving Vocabulary Skills, 2/e* (reading level 9–11)
- *Improving Vocabulary Skills, Short Version, 2/e* (reading level 9–11)
- *Advancing Vocabulary Skills, 2/e* (reading level 11–13)
- *Advancing Vocabulary Skills, Short Version, 2/e* (reading level 11–13)
- *Advanced Word Power* (reading level 12–14)

Note that the short versions of *Building Vocabulary Skills, Improving Vocabulary Skills,* and *Advancing Vocabulary Skills* are limited to 200 words, as opposed to the 260 words and 40 word parts in each of the long versions. For some students and classes, the short versions of the book will provide an easier, more manageable approach to vocabulary development.

ADVANCED
WORD
POWER

BETH JOHNSON

SUSAN GAMER

TOWNSEND PRESS   Marlton, NJ 08053

Books in the Townsend Press Reading Series:

Groundwork for College Reading
Ten Steps to Building College Reading Skills
Ten Steps to Improving College Reading Skills
Ten Steps to Advancing College Reading Skills

Books in the Townsend Press Vocabulary Series:

Vocabulary Basics
Groundwork for a Better Vocabulary
Building Vocabulary Skills
Building Vocabulary Skills, Short Version
Improving Vocabulary Skills
Improving Vocabulary Skills, Short Version
Advancing Vocabulary Skills
Advancing Vocabulary Skills, Short Version
Advanced Word Power

Supplements Available for Most Books:

Instructor's Edition
Instructor's Manual, Test Bank and Computer Guide
Computer Software (MS-DOS, Windows, or Macintosh)

Copyright © 1999 by Townsend Press, Inc.
Printed in the United States of America
9 8 7 6 5 4 3 2 1

All rights reserved. No part of this work may be reproduced in any form without permission in writing from the publisher. Send requests to Townsend Press at the address below.

Send book orders and requests for desk copies or supplements to:

Townsend Press
1038 Industrial Drive
West Berlin, New Jersey 08091-9164

For even faster service, call us at our toll-free number:
1-800-772-6410

Or FAX your request to:
1-800-225-8894

Or you may send us E-mail at:
textbooktp@aol.com

For more information about Townsend Press, visit our website:
www.townsendpress.com

ISBN 0-944210-46-5

Contents

Note: For ease of reference, the title of the selection that closes each chapter is included.

Preface   vii

Introduction   **1**

UNIT ONE

Chapter 1   Blue Jeans   **8**
Chapter 2   Do Opposites Attract?   **12**
Chapter 3   What Are You Stingy About?   **16**
Chapter 4   Loony but True   **20**
Chapter 5   Writing a Better Paper   **24**

Unit One Review   *(Crossword Puzzle)*   **28**
Unit One Tests   **29**

UNIT TWO

Chapter 6   Bad Translations   **36**
Chapter 7   Memory Aids   **40**
Chapter 8   A Formula for Teaching   **44**
Chapter 9   The One-Room Schoolhouse   **48**
Chapter 10   Galileo   **52**

Unit Two Review   *(Crossword Puzzle)*   **56**
Unit Two Tests   **57**

UNIT THREE

Chapter 11   Isadora Duncan   **64**
Chapter 12   Miles Standish   **68**
Chapter 13   Men, Women, and Talk   **72**
Chapter 14   Is Human Nature Good or Evil?   **76**
Chapter 15   The Strange Case of X   **80**

Unit Three Review   *(Crossword Puzzle)*   **84**
Unit Three Tests   **85**

UNIT FOUR

Chapter 16   The Salem Witches   **92**
Chapter 17   Fashion Show   **96**
Chapter 18   Math Anxiety   **100**
Chapter 19   The Gypsies   **104**
Chapter 20   The Jonestown Tragedy   **108**

Unit Four Review   *(Crossword Puzzle)*   **112**
Unit Four Tests   113

UNIT FIVE

Chapter 21   Helen Keller   **120**
Chapter 22   Figures of Speech   **124**
Chapter 23   When Is a Treatment Therapy?   **128**
Chapter 24   Hawks and Doves   **132**
Chapter 25   New Year's Resolutions   **136**

Unit Five Review   *(Crossword Puzzle)*   **140**
Unit Five Tests   141

UNIT SIX

Chapter 26   Weird Facts   **148**
Chapter 27   The Scholar   **152**
Chapter 28   A Case of Depression   **156**
Chapter 29   Scientific Discoveries   **160**
Chapter 30   Saint Francis of Assisi   **164**

Unit Six Review   *(Crossword Puzzle)*   **168**
Unit Six Tests   169

APPENDIXES

A   Limited Answer Key   **175**

B   Dictionary Use   **179**

C   Word List   **181**

Preface

The problem is all too familiar: *students just don't know enough words.* Reading, writing, and content teachers agree that many students' vocabularies are inadequate for the demands of courses. Weak vocabularies limit students' understanding of what they read and the clarity and depth of what they write. In addition, students with weak vocabularies do not perform well on either the vocabulary *or* the reading comprehension parts of such standardized tests as the SAT.

The purpose of *Advanced Word Power*—and the other books in the Townsend Press vocabulary series—is to provide a solid, workable solution to the vocabulary problem. In the course of 30 chapters, *Advanced Word Power* teaches 300 important words, all of which are part of a solid college vocabulary and all of which occur with high frequency on standardized college-admission tests. Here are the book's distinctive features:

1 **An intensive words-in-context approach.** Studies show that students learn words best by reading them repeatedly in different contexts, not through rote memorization. The book gives students an intensive in-context experience by presenting each word in six different contexts. Each chapter takes students through a productive sequence of steps:

   • Students infer the meaning of each word by considering two sentences in which it appears and then choosing from multiple-choice options.
   • On the basis of their inferences, students identify each word's meaning in a matching test. They are then in a solid position to deepen their knowledge of a word.
   • Finally, they strengthen their understanding of a word by applying it three times: in two sentence practices and in a selection practice.

   Each encounter with a word brings it closer to becoming part of the student's permanent word bank.

2 **Abundant practice.** Along with extensive practice in each chapter, there are a crossword puzzle and a set of unit tests at the end of every five-chapter unit. The puzzle and tests reinforce students' knowledge of the words in each chapter. In addition, Chapters 2 through 30 repeat words from earlier chapters (such repeated words are marked with small circles like this°), allowing for even more reinforcement. Last, there are supplementary tests in the *Test Bank* and the computer software that accompany the book. All this practice means that students learn in the surest possible way: by working closely and repeatedly with each word.

3 **Controlled feedback.** The opening activity in each chapter gives students three multiple-choice options to help them decide on the meaning of a given word. The multiple-choice options also help students to complete the matching test that is the second activity of each chapter. A limited answer key at the back of the book then provides answers for the third activity in the chapter. All these features enable students to take an active role in their own learning.

4 **Focus on essential words.** A good deal of time and research went into selecting the 300 words featured in the book. Word frequency lists were consulted, along with lists in a wide range of vocabulary and SAT preparation books. In addition, the authors and editors each prepared their own sets of words. A computer was then used to help in the consolidation of the many word lists.

Finally, a long process of group discussion led to decisions about the words that would be most helpful for students.

5 **Appealing content.** Dull practice materials work against learning. On the other hand, meaningful, lively, and at times even funny sentences and selections can spark students' attention and thus enhance their grasp of the material. For this reason, a great deal of effort was put into creating sentences and selections with both widespread appeal and solid context support. We have tried throughout to make the practice materials truly enjoyable for teachers and students alike. Look, for example, at the selection on page 23 that closes the fourth chapter of this book.

6 **Clear format.** The book has been designed so that the format itself contributes to the learning process. Each chapter consists of two two-page spreads. In the first two-page spread (the first such spread is on pages 8–9), students can easily refer to all ten words in context while working on the matching test, which provides a clear meaning for each word. In the second two-page spread, students can refer to a box that shows all ten words while they work through the fill-in activities on these pages.

7 **Supplementary materials.**

a A convenient *Instructor's Edition* is available at no charge to instructors using the book. It is identical to the student book except that it contains answers to all of the activities and tests.

b A combined *Instructor's Manual and Test Bank* is also offered at no charge to instructors who have adopted the book. This booklet contains a pretest and a posttest for the book and for each of the six units in the text. It also includes teaching guidelines, suggested syllabi, an answer key, and an additional mastery test for each chapter.

c *Comprehensive computer software* also accompanies the book. Free to adopters, this software provides two additional tests for each vocabulary chapter in the book. The program includes a number of user- and instructor-friendly features: brief explanations of answers, a sound option, frequent mention of the user's first name, a running score at the bottom of the screen, a record-keeping file, and actual pronunciation of each word.

Probably in no other area of reading instruction is the computer more useful than in reinforcing vocabulary. This vocabulary program takes full advantage of the computer's unique capabilities and motivational appeal. Here's how the program works:

- Students are tested on the ten words in a chapter, with each word in a sentence context different from any in the book itself.

- After students answer each question, they receive immediate feedback: The computer tells if a student is right or wrong and why, frequently using the student's first name and providing a running score.

- When the test is over, the computer supplies a test score and a chance to take a retest on the ten words. Students then receive a score for this retest. What is so valuable about this, of course, is that the computer gives students immediate additional practice with the words they need to review.

- In addition, the computer offers a second, more challenging test in which students must identify the meanings of the chapter words without the benefit of context. This test is a final check that students have really learned the words. And, again, there is the option of a retest, with its own score.

By the end of this program, students' knowledge of each word in the chapter will have been carefully reinforced. And this reinforcement will be the more effective for having occurred in an electronic medium that especially engages today's students.

To obtain a copy of any of the above materials, instructors may write to the Reading Editor, Townsend Press, 1038 Industrial Drive, West Berlin, NJ 08091. Alternatively, instructors may call our toll-free number, 1-800-772-6410, or fax us at 1-800-225-8894.

8 **Realistic pricing.** As with other Townsend Press books, the goal has been to offer the highest possible quality at the best possible price. While *Advanced Word Power* is comprehensive enough to serve as a primary text, its modest price also makes it an inexpensive supplement.

9 **One in a sequence of books.** *Vocabulary Basics* is the most fundamental book in the Townsend Press vocabulary series. It is followed by *Groundwork for a Better Vocabulary* (a slightly more advanced basic text), and then by the three main books in the series: *Building Vocabulary Skills* (also a basic text), *Improving Vocabulary Skills* (an intermediate text), and *Advancing Vocabulary Skills* (a more advanced text). There are also short versions of these three books. *Advanced Word Power* is the most challenging book in the TP vocabulary series. Suggested grade levels for all these books are included in the Instructor's Manual. Together, the books can help create a vocabulary foundation that will make any student a better reader, writer, and thinker.

ACKNOWLEDGMENTS

We are grateful to the teachers and editors who helped us determine the final list of words for this book: Donald J. Goodman, John Langan, Paul Langan, Carole Mohr, and Sherrie L. Nist. And we much appreciate the design, editing, and proofreading skills of the multi-talented Janet M. Goldstein.

Beth Johnson   *Susan Gamer*

Introduction

WHY VOCABULARY DEVELOPMENT COUNTS

You have probably often heard it said, "Building vocabulary is important." Maybe you've politely nodded in agreement and then forgotten the matter. But it would be fair for you to ask, "*Why* is vocabulary development important? Provide some evidence." Here are four compelling kinds of evidence.

1 Common sense tells you what many research studies have shown as well: vocabulary is a basic part of reading comprehension. Simply put, if you don't know enough words, you are going to have trouble understanding what you read. An occasional word may not stop you, but if there are too many words you don't know, comprehension will suffer. The content of textbooks is often challenging enough; you don't want to work as well on understanding the words that express that content.

2 Vocabulary is a major part of almost every standardized test, including reading achievement tests, college and graduate school entrance exams, and armed forces and vocational placement tests. Test developers know that vocabulary is a key measure of both one's learning and one's ability to learn. It is for this reason that they include a separate vocabulary section as well as a reading comprehension section. The more words you know, then, the better you are likely to do on these important tests.

3 Studies have indicated that students with strong vocabularies are more successful in school. And one widely known study found that a good vocabulary, more than any other factor, was common to people enjoying successful careers in life. Words are in fact the tools not just of better reading, but of better writing, speaking, listening, and thinking as well. The more words you have at your command, the more effective your communication can be, and the more influence you can have on the people around you.

4 In today's world, a good vocabulary counts more than ever. Far fewer people work on farms or in factories. Far more are in jobs that provide services or process information. More than ever, words are the tools of our trade: words we use in reading, writing, listening, and speaking. Furthermore, experts say that workers of tomorrow will be called on to change jobs and learn new skills at an ever-increasing pace. The keys to survival and success will be the abilities to communicate skillfully and to learn quickly. A solid vocabulary is essential for both of these skills.

Clearly, the evidence is overwhelming that building vocabulary is crucial. The question then becomes, "What is the best way of going about it?"

WORDS IN CONTEXT: THE KEY TO VOCABULARY DEVELOPMENT

Memorizing lists of words is a traditional method of vocabulary development. However, a person is likely to forget such memorized lists quickly. Studies show that to master a word, you must see and use it in various contexts. By working actively and repeatedly with a word, you greatly increase the chance of really learning it.

The following activity will make clear how this book is organized and how it uses a words-in-context approach. Answer the questions or fill in the missing words in the spaces provided.

Inside Front Cover and Contents

Turn to the inside front cover.

- The inside front cover provides a _____*pronunciation guide*_____ that will help you pronounce all the vocabulary words in the book.

Now turn to the table of contents on pages v–vi.

- How many chapters are in the book? ____*30*____

- What two sections conclude each unit? _____*A unit review (crossword puzzle) and a set of unit tests*_____

- Three short sections follow the last chapter. The first of these sections provides a limited answer key, the second gives helpful information on using _____*the dictionary*_____, and the third is an index of the 300 words in the book.

Vocabulary Chapters

Turn to Chapter 1 on pages 8–11. This chapter, like all the others, consists of five parts:

- The ***first part*** of the chapter, on pages 8–9, is titled _____*Ten Words in Context*_____.

The left-hand column lists the ten words. Under each **boldfaced** word is its _____*pronunciation*_____ (in parentheses). For example, the pronunciation of *affinity* is _____ə-fĭn′ĭ-tē_____. For a guide to pronunciation, see the inside front cover as well as "Dictionary Use" on page 179.

Below the pronunciation guide for each word is its part of speech. The part of speech shown for *affinity* is _____*noun*_____. The vocabulary words in this book are mostly nouns, adjectives, and verbs. **Nouns** are words used to name something—a person, place, thing, or idea. Familiar nouns include *boyfriend, city, hat,* and *truth*. **Adjectives** are words that describe nouns, as in the following word pairs: *former* boyfriend, *large* city, *red* hat, *whole* truth. All of the **verbs** in this book express an action of some sort. They tell what someone or something is doing. Common verbs include *sing, separate, support,* and *imagine*.

To the right of each word are two sentences that will help you understand its meaning. In each sentence, the **context**—the words surrounding the boldfaced word—provides clues you can use to figure out the definition. There are four common types of context clues: examples, synonyms, antonyms, and the general sense of the sentence. Each is briefly described below.

1 Examples

A sentence may include examples that reveal what an unfamiliar word means. For instance, take a look at the following sentence from Chapter 1 for the word *incessant*:

The children nearly drove their parents crazy on the long car trip with their **incessant** demands: "Are we there yet? Is it much further? How much longer?"

The sentence provides three examples of incessant demands: "Are we there yet?", "Is it much further?", and "How much longer?" What do these three examples have in common? The answer to that question will tell you what *incessant* means. Look at the answer choices below, and in the answer space provided, write the letter of the one you feel is correct.

   <u>c</u> *Incessant* means   a. silent.   b. wise.   c. nonstop.

All of the examples given in the sentence are questions that young children on car trips ask over and over. So if you wrote *c*, you chose the correct answer.

2 Synonyms

Synonyms are words that mean the same or almost the same as another word. For example, the words *joyful, happy*, and *delighted* are synonyms—they all mean about the same thing. Synonyms serve as context clues by providing the meaning of an unknown word that is nearby. The sentence below from Chapter 2 provides a synonym clue for *dispassionate*.

> The surgeon's voice was **dispassionate** when he told the patient's family that the operation had failed, but despite his calm tone, his eyes looked very sad.

Instead of using *dispassionate* twice, the author used a synonym in the second part of the sentence. Find that synonym, and then choose the letter of the correct answer from the choices below.

   <u>b</u> *Dispassionate* means   a. unreasonable.   b. unemotional.   c. disturbing.

The author uses two terms to describe the surgeon's tone of voice: *dispassionate* and *calm*. Therefore, *dispassionate* must be another way of saying *calm*. (The author could have written, "The surgeon's voice was *calm*.") Since *calm* can also mean *unemotional*, the correct answer is *b*.

3 Antonyms

Antonyms are words with opposite meanings. For example, *help* and *harm* are antonyms, as are *work* and *rest*. Antonyms serve as context clues by providing the opposite meaning of an unknown word. For instance, the sentence below from Chapter 1 provides an antonym clue for the word *opulence*.

> The **opulence** of the magnificent, luxurious resort was in stark contrast to the poverty of the little fishing village at its gates.

The author is contrasting the resort and the fishing village, so we can assume that *opulence* and *poverty* have opposite, or contrasting, meanings. Using that contrast as a clue, write the letter of the answer that you think best defines *opulence*.

   <u>b</u> *Opulence* means   a. closeness.   b. riches.   c. permanence.

The correct answer is *b*. Because *opulence* is the opposite of *poverty*, it must mean "riches."

4 General Sense of the Sentence

Even when there is no example, synonym, or antonym clue in a sentence, you can still deduce the meaning of an unfamiliar word. For example, look at the sentence from Chapter 1 for the word *affinity*.

> My cat has an **affinity** for small, dark hiding places—I've found her asleep in my dresser drawer, under the footstool, and inside my suitcase.

After studying the context carefully, you should be able to figure out the connection between the cat and small, dark hiding places. That will be the meaning of *affinity*. Write the letter of your choice.

   <u>a</u> *Affinity* means   a. a preference.   b. a fear.   c. ignorance.

Since the sentence says that the cat is often found in these places, it is logical to conclude that the cat has a preference for them. Thus answer *a* is correct.

By looking closely at the pair of sentences provided for each word, as well as the answer choices, you should be able to decide on the meaning of a word. As you figure out each meaning, you are working actively with the word. You are creating the groundwork you need to understand and to remember the word. *Getting involved with the word and developing a feel for it, based upon its use in context, is the key to word mastery.*

It is with good reason, then, that the directions at the top of page 8 tell you to use the context to figure out each word's _____ *meaning* _____. Doing so deepens your sense of the word and prepares you for the next activity.

• The ***second part*** of the chapter, on page 9, is titled _____ *Matching Words with Definitions* _____.

According to research, it is not enough to see a word in context. At a certain point, it is helpful as well to see the meaning of a word. The matching test provides that meaning, but it also makes you look for and think about that meaning. In other words, it continues the active learning that is your surest route to learning and remembering a word.

Note the caution that follows the test. Do not proceed any further until you are sure that you know the correct meaning of each word as used in context.

Keep in mind that a word may have more than one meaning. In fact, some words have quite a few meanings—and may even be more than one part of speech. (If you doubt it, try looking up in a dictionary, for example, the word *draw* or *fast*.) In this book, you will focus on one common meaning for each vocabulary word. However, many of the words have additional meanings. For example, in Chapter 1, you will learn that *fledgling* is an adjective meaning "inexperienced," as in the sentence "Myra and her sisters are excited about their fledgling catering service." If you then look up *fledgling* in the dictionary, you will discover that it has another meaning as a noun—"a young bird that has recently acquired its flight feathers," as in "We watched a robin giving flying lessons to her three fledglings." After you learn one common meaning of a word, you will find yourself gradually learning its other meanings in the course of your school and personal reading.

• The ***third part*** of the chapter, on page 10, is titled _____ *Sentence Check 1* _____.

Here are ten sentences that give you an opportunity to apply your understanding of the ten words. After inserting the words, check your answers in the limited key at the back of the book. Be sure to use the answer key as a learning tool only. Doing so will help you to master the words and to prepare for the last two activities and the unit tests, for which answers are not provided.

• The ***fourth and fifth parts*** of the chapter, on pages 10–11, are titled _____ *Sentence Check 2* _____ and _____ *Final Check* _____.

Each practice tests you on all ten words, giving you two more chances to deepen your mastery. In the fifth part, you have the context of an entire passage in which you can practice applying the words.

At the bottom of the last page of this chapter is a box where you can enter your score for the final two checks. These scores should also be entered into the vocabulary performance chart located on the inside back page of the book. To get your score, take 10% off for each item wrong. For example, 0 wrong = 100%, 1 wrong = 90%, 2 wrong = 80%, 3 wrong = 70%, 4 wrong = 60%, and so on.

You now know, in a nutshell, how to proceed with the words in each chapter. Make sure that you do each page very carefully. *Remember that as you work through the activities, you are learning the words.*

How many times in all will you use each word? If you look, you'll see that each chapter gives you the opportunity to work with each word six times. Each "impression" adds to the likelihood that the word will become part of your active vocabulary. You will have further opportunities to use the word in the crossword puzzle and unit tests that end each unit and on the computer disk that is available with the book.

In addition, many of the words are repeated in context in later chapters of the book. Such repeated words are marked with small circles (°). For example, which words from Chapter 1 are repeated in the Final Check on page 15 of Chapter 2?

_____ *affinity* _____   _____ *sagacious* _____

A FINAL THOUGHT

The facts are in. A strong vocabulary is a source of power. Words can make you a better reader, writer, speaker, thinker, and learner. They can dramatically increase your chances of success in school and in your job.

But words will not come automatically. They must be learned in a program of regular study. If you commit yourself to learning words, and if you work actively and honestly with the chapters in this book, you will not only enrich your vocabulary—you will enrich your life as well.

Unit One

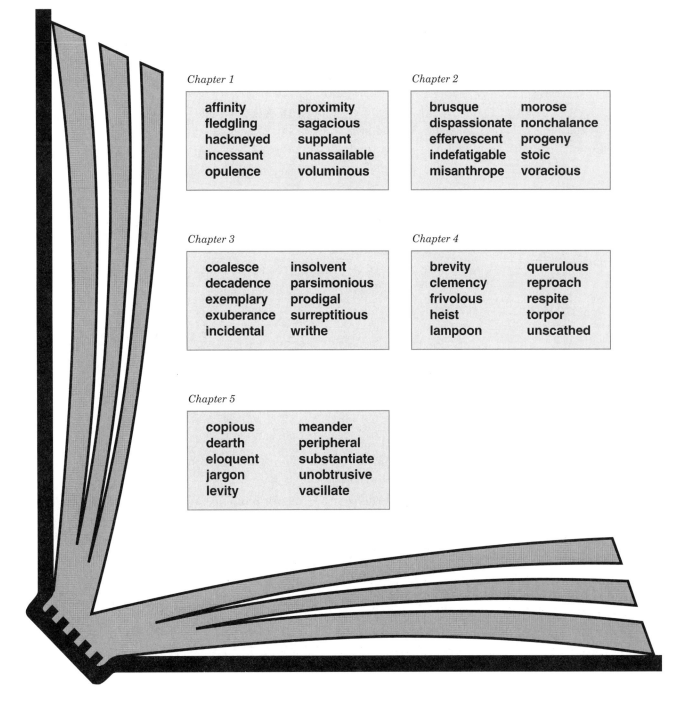

Chapter 1

affinity	proximity
fledgling	sagacious
hackneyed	supplant
incessant	unassailable
opulence	voluminous

Chapter 2

brusque	morose
dispassionate	nonchalance
effervescent	progeny
indefatigable	stoic
misanthrope	voracious

Chapter 3

coalesce	insolvent
decadence	parsimonious
exemplary	prodigal
exuberance	surreptitious
incidental	writhe

Chapter 4

brevity	querulous
clemency	reproach
frivolous	respite
heist	torpor
lampoon	unscathed

Chapter 5

copious	meander
dearth	peripheral
eloquent	substantiate
jargon	unobtrusive
levity	vacillate

affinity	proximity
fledgling	sagacious
hackneyed	supplant
incessant	unassailable
opulence	voluminous

Ten Words in Context

In the space provided, write the letter of the meaning closest to that of each **boldfaced** word. Use the context of the sentences to help you figure out each word's meaning.

1 **affinity**
(ə-fĭn′ĭ-tē)
-noun

- It is hard for someone with an **affinity** for warm weather to be happy living in Alaska.
- My cat has an **affinity** for small, dark hiding places—I've often found her asleep in my dresser drawer, under the footstool, and inside my suitcase.

<u>a</u> *Affinity* means   a. a preference.   b. a fear.   c. ignorance.

2 **fledgling**
(flĕj′lĭng)
-adjective

- The short-story class is full of **fledgling** writers. They're all enthusiastic, but since they're beginners, they're shy about sharing their work.
- Myra and her sisters are excited about their **fledgling** catering service, which was booked for three parties during its first week of business.

<u>b</u> *Fledgling* means   a. old.   b. new.   c. different.

3 **hackneyed**
(hăk′nēd)
-adjective

- The **hackneyed** phrase "Have a nice day!" is heard so often that it has become almost meaningless.
- The worst part of our family reunions is hearing my uncle's **hackneyed** jokes—the ones he's been telling since about 1950.

<u>a</u> *Hackneyed* means   a. worn-out.   b. insulting.   c. funny.

4 **incessant**
(ĭn-sĕs′ənt)
-adjective

- Mrs. Raglan finally insisted that her husband see a doctor about his **incessant** snoring—it didn't bother him, but she wasn't getting any sleep.
- The children nearly drove their parents crazy on the long car trip with their **incessant** demands: "Are we there yet? Is it much further? How much longer?"

<u>c</u> *Incessant* means   a. silent.   b. wise.   c. nonstop.

5 **opulence**
(ŏp′yə-ləns)
-noun

- The **opulence** of the magnificent, luxurious resort was in stark contrast to the poverty of the little fishing village at its gates.
- The writer Thoreau had no liking for **opulence**. He wrote in his journal, "That man is richest whose pleasures are the cheapest."

<u>b</u> *Opulence* means   a. closeness.   b. riches.   c. permanence.

6 **proximity**
(prŏk-sĭm′ĭ-tē)
-noun

- The **proximity** of the railroad tracks worries neighborhood parents when their children play outside.
- I don't drive a car, so when I was apartment hunting, I had to consider the **proximity** of public transportation.

<u>c</u> *Proximity* means   a. similarity.   b. contrast.   c. nearness.

7 **sagacious**
(sə-gā′shəs)
-adjective

- The Bible tells the story of King Solomon, who was so **sagacious** that he knew what to do when two women came to him, both claiming to be the mother of the same child.
- Often when you are faced with a difficult situation, the **sagacious** thing is to do nothing right away, but wait to see what happens.

_b_ *Sagacious* means   a. silly.   b. intelligent.   c. strong.

8 **supplant**
(sə-plănt′)
-verb

- Acme Company fired its entire accounting staff today. It intends to **supplant** these employees with part-time workers.
- An idealistic young revolutionary overthrew the dictator and set up a democratic government. But he too was soon **supplanted** when a military strongman seized power.

_a_ *Supplant* means   a. to replace.   b. to restore.   c. to support.

9 **unassailable**
(ŭn′ə-sā′lə-bəl)
-adjective

- The Evanses' claim that their house is the oldest in town is **unassailable**. They have a deed dated 1804, and a copy was filed in the county courthouse that same year.
- "My opponent may try to attack me," said the candidate, "but my record is **unassailable**. On every issue, I've voted for the benefit of this city."

_b_ *Unassailable* means   a. untrue.   b. undeniable.   c. unimportant.

10 **voluminous**
(və-loo′mə-nəs)
-adjective

- Denise chose a wedding dress in a "Southern belle" style, with a long, **voluminous** skirt. Now she's worried she'll trip over all those yards of material.
- In the weeks before Christmas, each issue of our newspaper is **voluminous**, swollen enormously by all the ads. After the holidays, the paper shrinks back to its normal size.

_c_ *Voluminous* means   a. valuable.   b. cut short.   c. large.

Matching Words with Definitions

Following are definitions of the ten words. Clearly write or print each word next to its definition. The sentences above and on the previous page will help you decide on the meaning of each word.

1. _fledgling_ — New and untried; inexperienced; newly hatched
2. _opulence_ — Luxury
3. _proximity_ — Closeness
4. _hackneyed_ — Overused; stale; trite
5. _unassailable_ — Impossible to deny
6. _voluminous_ — Big; bulky
7. _supplant_ — To take the place of
8. _affinity_ — A natural attraction or liking
9. _sagacious_ — Wise; sensible
10. _incessant_ — Constant; without stopping

CAUTION: Do not go any further until you are sure the above answers are correct. Then you can use the definitions to help you in the following practices. Your goal is eventually to know the words well enough so that you don't need to check the definitions at all.

➤ *Sentence Check 1*

Using the answer line, complete each item below with the correct word from the box. Use each word once.

| a. **affinity** | b. **fledgling** | c. **hackneyed** | d. **incessant** | e. **opulence** |
| f. **proximity** | g. **sagacious** | h. **supplant** | i. **unassailable** | j. **voluminous** |

_____ *opulence* _____ 1. Irene knew her roommate's family was wealthy, but nothing had prepared her for the ___ of their home—it was like a palace.

_____ *unassailable* _____ 2. During the 1960s, the Beatles held an ___ position as the world's most popular rock group They sold more records and won more fame than any other band.

_____ *voluminous* _____ 3. In her ___ tote bag, my mother carries money, credit cards, photos, makeup, a mirror, running shoes, and an amazing quantity of other stuff.

_____ *sagacious* _____ 4. It would not be ___ to go out today without an umbrella—look at those black clouds!

_____ *affinity* _____ 5. Crows have a(n) ___ for bright, shiny things, so they sometimes pick up bits of mirrors, metal, or jewelry and carry them back to their nests.

_____ *supplant* _____ 6. "You'll always be my best friend," Christy told Carole when Carole moved away. "I may have other friends, but no one will ever ___ you in my heart."

_____ *incessant* _____ 7. Mr. Engelhardt finally told his daughter to stop jogging in place in her upstairs bedroom; the ___ pounding noise was giving him a headache.

_____ *proximity* _____ 8. While visiting Hollywood, Sayda was excited by the ___ of movie stars. "You could be standing right beside one and never know it!" she said.

_____ *fledgling* _____ 9. I get my hair done cheaply by going to a beauty school, where ___ hairdressers do cuts and coloring for half of what more experienced beauticians charge.

_____ *hackneyed* _____ 10. Allie has decided to stop saying the ___ word "Hello!" when she answers the phone. Instead, she says "Greetings!"

NOTE: Now check your answers to these questions by turning to page 175. Going over the answers carefully will help you prepare for the next two practices, for which answers are not given.

➤ *Sentence Check 2*

Using the answer lines, complete each item below with **two** words from the box. Use each word once.

_____ *affinity* _____
_____ *hackneyed* _____ 1–2. The instructor told me, "You have an unfortunate ___ for ___ phrases. To improve your writing, you'll need to get over your fondness for stale, worn-out expressions."

_____ *fledgling* _____
_____ *sagacious* _____ 3–4. Though only a(n) ___ politician, our new young senator made very ___ decisions during her first year in office. Her wisdom suggests that she has a promising future.

_____proximity_____   5–6. The luxury hotel stands in close ___ to a shabby, run-down housing
_____opulence_____   project, and the ___ of the one is a striking contrast to the poverty of
                                 the other.

_____voluminous_____   7–8. The report on child abuse was ___—over a thousand pages—and filled
_____unassailable_____   with ___ evidence that child abuse is a widespread problem today.

_____incessant_____   9–10. After receiving ___ complaints for weeks that its telephone operators
_____supplant_____   were rude and careless, the mail-order company decided to ___ them
                                 with a computerized ordering system.

➤ *Final Check:* Blue Jeans

Here is a final opportunity for you to strengthen your knowledge of the ten words. First read the following selection carefully. Then fill in each blank with a word from the box at the top of the previous page. (Context clues will help you figure out which word goes in which blank.) Use each word once.

"An American classic" is a(n) (1)_____*hackneyed*_____ phrase, overused to describe everything from meatloaf to the latest hairstyle. But at least one thing has a(n) (2)_____*unassailable*_____ right to be called an American classic. Blue jeans were born in the United States during the great California gold rush of 1849. They were created by Levi Strauss, a German who sold dry-goods to the cowboys and gold miners of San Francisco. Strauss realized that the (3)_____*proximity*_____ of all those workingmen created an opportunity for him. He considered what all those miners and cowboys would be likely to buy, and he was (4)_____*sagacious*_____ enough to realize that they needed tough, inexpensive pants. He founded the Levi Strauss Company to manufacture what he called "waist trousers." At first, the (5)_____*fledgling*_____ company did make a few mistakes. For instance, it placed a copper rivet at the jeans' crotch, where the main seams came together. When cowboys wearing the jeans sat around the campfire, that copper rivet heated up, making getting back into the saddle a painful experience. But such mistakes were few, and Levi Strauss's pants became so popular that they soon (6)_____*supplant*_____(e)d almost every other kind of pants among the workingmen of the West. Strauss was able to retire and live in (7)_____*opulence*_____. Since then, the general public has developed such a(n) (8)_____*affinity*_____ for blue jeans that they have never gone out of style. However, they have been constantly changed by the (9)_____*incessant*_____, never-ending tides of fashion. During the 1950s, teenagers wore them straight and tight. In the 1960s, the look was (10)_____*voluminous*_____ bell-bottoms that swept the ground. Since then jeans have been tie-dyed, acid-washed, ripped, cut off, and made of every imaginable material. Still, they all have a common ancestor: the tough "waist trousers" invented by Strauss a century and a half ago.

Scores	Sentence Check 2 _____%	Final Check _____%

Enter your scores above and in the vocabulary performance chart on the inside back cover of the book.

CHAPTER

2

brusque	morose
dispassionate	nonchalance
effervescent	progeny
indefatigable	stoic
misanthrope	voracious

Ten Words in Context

In the space provided, write the letter of the meaning closest to that of each **boldfaced** word. Use the context of the sentences to help you figure out each word's meaning.

1 **brusque**
(brŭsk)
-*adjective*

- Rose lost her job as a receptionist because she was so **brusque** with people who called. The office replaced her with someone who spoke more politely.
- Although Maria seems **brusque** when you first meet her, she's really just shy with people she doesn't know well. After you talk with her awhile, she becomes more relaxed and friendly.

_a_ *Brusque* means   a. blunt.   b. admirable.   c. silly.

2 **dispassionate**
(dĭs-păsh′ə-nĭt)
-*adjective*

- The surgeon's voice was **dispassionate** when he told the patient's family that the operation had failed, but despite his calm tone, his eyes looked very sad.
- "Historians are supposed to be **dispassionate**," the lecturer apologized, "but when my topic is the horrors of slavery, I find it hard to keep my feelings hidden."

_b_ *Dispassionate* means   a. unreasonable.   b. unemotional.   c. disturbing.

3 **effervescent**
(ĕf′ər-vĕs′ənt)
-*adjective*

- The lecturer could hardly be described as **effervescent**. She droned on about the Federal Reserve in a dreary voice, never looking up from her notes.
- Marnie is on the way to stardom. When her play opened last night, the critics raved about her "**effervescent** charm," saying that she "lit up the stage."

_c_ *Effervescent* means   a. hard-working.   b. nervous.   c. lively.

4 **indefatigable**
(ĭn′dĭ-făt′ĭ-gə-bəl)
-*adjective*

- When Mona and her friend Patty get together, they are **indefatigable** talkers. They talk endlessly and tirelessly about everything.
- The great athlete seemed **indefatigable**. After running a marathon, swimming for miles, and biking up steep hills, she was still energetic.

_b_ *Indefatigable* means   a. easily tired.   b. never getting tired.   c. depressed.

5 **misanthrope**
(mĭs′ən-thrōp′)
-*noun*

- Molière's play *The Misanthrope* is about a man, Alceste, who is enraged and disgusted by his fellow humans. To put it briefly, Alceste hates everyone.
- One of our neighbors is a true **misanthrope**. She hasn't a friend in the world; in fact, she looks on everyone as an enemy.

_a_ *Misanthrope* means   a. an antisocial person.   b. a criminal.   c. a lunatic.

6 **morose**
(mə-rōs′)
-*adjective*

- On the first workday of the year, everyone at the office seemed **morose**. No wonder we felt low; after the holidays, it's always a letdown to get back to work.
- Larry always becomes **morose** when he drinks. Since alcohol makes him feel so dreary and blue, you'd think he'd give it up.

_c_ *Morose* means   a. confused.   b. frantic.   c. gloomy.

12

7 **nonchalance**
(nŏn′shə-läns′)
-*noun*

- **Nonchalance** is not appropriate behind the wheel of a car. An automobile is not a toy to be played with casually—it is a dangerous machine to be handled with concentration.
- Trying to create an impression of **nonchalance** despite his nervousness, Hari strolled to the speaker's stand smiling and whistling a little tune.

_b_ *Nonchalance* means   a. uneasiness.   b. lack of concern.   c. lack of awareness.

8 **progeny**
(prŏj′ə-nē)
-*noun*

- In the wonderful children's book *Charlotte's Web,* Charlotte, the spider, dies, but several of her **progeny** stay to befriend Charlotte's beloved Wilbur, the pig.
- Grandfather worked at two jobs in order to provide food and clothing for his many **progeny**.

_c_ *Progeny* means   a. enemies.   b. leaders.   c. offspring.

9 **stoic**
(stō′ĭk)
-*adjective*

- My dog's reaction to getting his yearly shots is hardly **stoic**. It takes the vet and two assistants to hold him down, and he howls as if he's being torn to pieces.
- "Some patients' **stoic** response to illness or injury is truly amazing," the doctor said. "Come what may, they remain calm and courageous."

_b_ *Stoic* means   a. emotional.   b. showing no distress.   c. planned.

10 **voracious**
(vô-rā′shəs)
-*adjective*

- Beagles are **voracious** eaters—their owners say they will eat anything that's not nailed down—so they tend to become fat unless they get enough exercise.
- Ginny has a **voracious** appetite for news. She gets a morning and an evening newspaper, listens to an "all news, all the time" radio station, and watches the TV newscast every night.

_a_ *Voracious* means   a. greedy.   b. small.   c. unconcerned.

Matching Words with Definitions

Following are definitions of the ten words. Clearly write or print each word next to its definition. The sentences above and on the previous page will help you decide on the meaning of each word.

1. _____misanthrope_____   A person who hates or distrusts humankind
2. _____progeny_____   Children; descendants
3. _____effervescent_____   Bubbling with high spirits; exhilarated
4. _____dispassionate_____   Not influenced by emotion; impartial
5. _____brusque_____   Rudely abrupt; curt
6. _____nonchalance_____   Casual indifference; lack of concern
7. _____indefatigable_____   Untiring
8. _____stoic_____   Seemingly unaffected by pain or discomfort
9. _____voracious_____   Ravenous; consuming or eager to consume large amounts; insatiable
10. _____morose_____   Very gloomy or sullen

CAUTION: Do not go any further until you are sure the above answers are correct. Then you can use the definitions to help you in the following practices. Your goal is eventually to know the words well enough so that you don't need to check the definitions at all.

➤ *Sentence Check 1*

Using the answer line, complete each item below with the correct word from the box. Use each word once.

a. **brusque**	b. **dispassionate**	c. **effervescent**	d. **indefatigable**	e. **misanthrope**
f. **morose**	g. **nonchalance**	h. **progeny**	i. **stoic**	j. **voracious**

_____ *brusque* _____   1. It's difficult to ask Professor Henderson a question. His typical response is a(n) ___ "What? What kind of question is that?"

_____ *indefatigable* _____   2. Dad was a(n) ___ walker. He could hike for mile after mile, never seeming to get weary.

_____ *nonchalance* _____   3. When they feel nervous and ill at ease, many people try to achieve an air of ___ by putting their hands in their pockets and humming.

_____ *morose* _____   4. The kids were sulky and ___ on the first day of school. They hated to face the fact that summer had ended.

_____ *stoic* _____   5. "I intend to bear this with ___ courage," Eileen vowed as she set forth for the dentist's office. "And also with plenty of Novocain."

_____ *effervescent* _____   6. At the end of the day, the second-graders were as ___ as they had been when it began, telling jokes and giggling. Their teacher envied their high spirits.

_____ *progeny* _____   7. The funny book *Cheaper by the Dozen* tells the story of the Gilbreth clan, which consisted of a mother, a father, and twelve red-haired ___.

_____ *voracious* _____   8. Although they are small, most rodents are ___ eaters. Mice, gerbils, and hamsters nibble almost constantly.

_____ *misanthrope* _____   9. Will Rogers was the exact opposite of a(n) ___. He once said, "I never met a man I didn't like."

_____ *dispassionate* _____   10. I find this editorial convincing, partly because it is so ___. I like it when a writer reasons with readers, rather than trying to manipulate their feelings.

NOTE: Now check your answers to these questions by turning to page 175. Going over the answers carefully will help you prepare for the next two practices, for which answers are not given.

➤ *Sentence Check 2*

Using the answer lines, complete each item below with **two** words from the box. Use each word once.

_____ *dispassionate* _____
_____ *stoic* _____   1–2. The English have the reputation of being ___, with ice water in their veins, and ___— dry-eyed in the face of tragedy. But their emotional reaction to the death of Princess Diana cast doubt on that hackneyed° stereotype.

_____ *effervescent* _____
_____ *brusque* _____   3–4. Simon, who is enthusiastic and ___, was brimming over with excitement as he presented his idea in class. But the professor, a blunt, curt type, gave it a(n) ___ one-word dismissal: "Wrong."

morose	5–6. Our ___, gloomy uncle is utterly friendless, but he insists he is not a(n)
misanthrope	___. "I don't hate people," he claims. "I just haven't met any that I like."
voracious	7–8. Jill is a sensation-seeker who has a(n) ___ appetite for excitement and
indefatigable	is ___ in looking for it. She is tireless in her quest for thrilling, risky experiences.
nonchalance	9–10. Marian approached parenthood with a certain ___, taking it all lightly.
progeny	But her husband, who was awed by the thought of having ___, felt very solemn about it.

➤ *Final Check:* **Do Opposites Attract?**

Here is a final opportunity for you to strengthen your knowledge of the ten words. First read the following selection carefully. Then fill in each blank with a word from the box at the top of the previous page. (Context clues will help you figure out which word goes in which blank.) Use each word once.

With regard to romance, it is widely believed that "opposites attract," but psychologists tell us that lovers usually resemble each other in many ways. Let us hope the psychologists are right, because it seems likely that a marriage between opposites would be a bumpy road.

If Joe is (1)___*indefatigable*___, ready to jog a few miles after sawing a cord of firewood, while Ann needs to lie down and rest for an hour after dusting the piano, how happy can they be together? If Jordan has a(n) (2)___*voracious*___ appetite while Amy "eats like a bird," imagine a typical meal: he's on his third helping before she has even taken a bite. If Julio is sad and (3)___*morose*___ while Assunta is bubbly, bouncy, and (4)___*effervescent*___, how long can it be before one of them starts to get on the other's nerves? What about Jerrold, who takes to his bed with the sniffles while his (5)___*stoic*___ wife Abbie bravely hobbles off to work on a broken leg? What about (6)___*dispassionate*___ Jan, whose attitude toward life is one of casual (7)___*nonchalance*___, and his wife Alice, who is intensely committed to every cause from AIDS to humane zoos?

No, the outlook is not bright for these couples. And what of their (8)___*progeny*___? Children are supposed to "take after" their parents, but that would be a problem for someone whose father is a(n) (9)___*misanthrope*___ and whose mother "loves everyone," or for the offspring of a(n) (10)___*brusque*___, blunt, no-nonsense mother and an easygoing, soft-spoken father.

Opposites may attract, then, but, despite their affinity° for each other, it might not be sagacious° for opposites to marry.

Scores	Sentence Check 2 _____%	Final Check _____%	

Enter your scores above and in the vocabulary performance chart on the inside back cover of the book.

coalesce	insolvent
decadence	parsimonious
exemplary	prodigal
exuberance	surreptitious
incidental	writhe

Ten Words in Context

In the space provided, write the letter of the meaning closest to that of each **boldfaced** word. Use the context of the sentences to help you figure out each word's meaning.

1 coalesce
(kō′ə-lĕs′)
-verb

- Four block associations in our neighborhood will **coalesce** to form a single task force.
- When I got caught in a rainstorm, I learned that the dyes in my new shirt weren't waterproof. The red and blue stripes ran and **coalesced** into purple smears.

a *Coalesce* means   a. to join.   b. to produce.   c. to come into being.

2 decadence
(dĕk′ə-dəns)
-noun

- The older generation always seems to see **decadence** among young people, groaning that "kids today" are spoiled, lazy, and extravagant.
- Grandfather considers the internal combustion engine a sign of the **decadence** of Western civilization. "Stop the decay before it's too late!" he says. "Get out of your cars, get on your feet, and walk!"

b *Decadence* means   a. a disappointment.   b. a decline.   c. disapproval.

3 exemplary
(ĭg-zĕm′plə-rē)
-adjective

- Christine has a glowing letter of recommendation from her former boss, in which he says, "She is an **exemplary** employee who always does more than is asked."
- This year, the "Teacher of the Year" award was given to not one but two **exemplary** instructors.

a *Exemplary* means   a. excellent.   b. extra.   c. exotic.

4 exuberance
(ĭg-zoo′bər-əns)
-noun

- Jenny called all her friends, shrieking with **exuberance** over being accepted at her first-choice college.
- Children may believe they are the only ones who are happy to see summer vacation arrive, but their teachers feel some **exuberance**, too!

c *Exuberance* means   a. fear.   b. boredom.   c. joy.

5 incidental
(ĭn′sĭ-dĕn′tl)
-adjective

- Selma chose her college because it has such a good nursing program, but an **incidental** reason was that it is located in a beautiful town.
- Rita and Jen moved in together so they could split the rent, but an **incidental** effect is that they can borrow each other's clothes.

a *Incidental* means   a. secondary.   b. incorrect.   c. secret.

6 insolvent
(ĭn-sŏl′vənt)
-adjective

- Barry lost his head when he got his first credit card. He went on a spending spree, couldn't pay his bills, and ended up **insolvent**.
- Compulsive gamblers often lose so much money that they become **insolvent**, but they can't control their urge, and their debt keeps growing.

a *Insolvent* means   a. without money.   b. without friends.   c. without goals.

7 parsimonious
(pär′sə-mō′nē-əs)
-adjective

- The boss, a **parsimonious** man, insists that we save old memos and letters and use the backs of pages as note paper.
- Elena is a **parsimonious** cook. She creates cheap meals from old cheese rinds, stale bread, and wilted vegetables. They taste awful.

_a_ *Parsimonious* means   a. stingy.   b. mischievous.   c. talented.

8 prodigal
(prŏd′ĭ-gəl)
-adjective

- Mary and Kim both make decent salaries. They could live comfortably on what they make if they weren't such **prodigal** spenders.
- I don't think it's **prodigal** to spend some extra money to get well-made shoes. Cheap ones fall apart so fast that you soon end up buying another pair.

_b_ *Prodigal* means   a. useful.   b. extravagant.   c. careful.

9 surreptitious
(sŭr′əp-tĭsh′əs)
-adjective

- Students naturally want to know what will be covered on a test. Instead of trying to find out by **surreptitious** means, it is better simply to ask the instructor, who is often willing to provide at least a rough idea.
- As the wedding reception ended, several guests made **surreptitious** trips to the parking lot, where they tied tin cans and crepe paper to the newlyweds' car.

_c_ *Surreptitious* means   a. straightforward.   b. useless.   c. secret.

10 writhe
(rīth)
-verb

- Grandpa remembers the scratchy long underwear he wore to school in the winter: "It was so itchy that I would **writhe** and wriggle at my desk all day long."
- The children **writhed** with impatience as they waited to board the plane. "Stop fidgeting before you drive me nuts," their weary father begged them.

_c_ *Writhe* means   a. freeze.   b. squeeze.   c. squirm.

Matching Words with Definitions

Following are definitions of the ten words. Clearly write or print each word next to its definition. The sentences above and on the previous page will help you decide on the meaning of each word.

1. _____parsimonious_____   Too thrifty; stingy; miserly

2. _____prodigal_____   Wasteful and reckless with money

3. _____exuberance_____   High-spirited enthusiasm

4. _____writhe_____   To twist and turn, as in pain or discomfort

5. _____decadence_____   A condition of moral deterioration; decay

6. _____exemplary_____   Worthy of imitation; praiseworthy

7. _____insolvent_____   Unable to pay debts; penniless

8. _____coalesce_____   To merge to form one whole

9. _____surreptitious_____   Done in a secret or sly way; stealthy

10. _____incidental_____   Occurring as a minor consequence of something more important

CAUTION: Do not go any further until you are sure the above answers are correct. Then you can use the definitions to help you in the following practices. Your goal is eventually to know the words well enough so that you don't need to check the definitions at all.

➤ *Sentence Check 1*

Using the answer line, complete each item below with the correct word from the box. Use each word once.

| a. **coalesce** | b. **decadence** | c. **exemplary** | d. **exuberance** | e. **incidental** |
| f. **insolvent** | g. **parsimonious** | h. **prodigal** | i. **surreptitious** | j. **writhe** |

coalesce   1. Three high schools in the county have ___(e)d to create a centralized "magnet" school.

exemplary   2. Although the local newspaper is small, it has an excellent reputation. In fact, every year it wins statewide awards for its ___ reporting.

incidental   3. "Stopping smoking can save your life," said the doctor. "And there are some ___ benefits as well: you won't have stained teeth, yellow fingers, or bad breath."

parsimonious   4. The school's ___ administration decided to save money by dimming all the lights. The students, who could barely see to read, protested angrily.

decadence   5. "When the rich get richer and the poor get poorer," the economist warned, "that is a sign of ___: the society is starting to weaken."

surreptitious 6. Smoking is forbidden in the office, but some employees keep sneaking off for ___ trips to the fire stairs, where they light up.

writhe   7. Trying to scratch an itchy spot on its back, the pig ___(e)d and twisted as it rubbed against the fence.

prodigal   8. When stories came out about the senator's lavish offices, his many trips to luxury resorts, and his huge staff of underworked employees, taxpayers complained about such a(n) ___ waste of their money.

insolvent   9. The shelter for the homeless has made an urgent appeal for donations. Without more contributions to pay its bills, it will soon be ___.

exuberance   10. As soon as Tony came in the door, I knew he had good news. His ___ showed all over his face.

NOTE: Now check your answers to these questions by turning to page 175. Going over the answers carefully will help you prepare for the next two practices, for which answers are not given.

➤ *Sentence Check 2*

Using the answer lines, complete each item below with **two** words from the box. Use each word once.

surreptitious
coalesce   1–2. When it comes to food, most of us have some private, ___ pleasures. Liz stirs honey and mashed potatoes together until they ___, then eats the goo with a spoon.

exuberance
writhe   3–4. In their ___ over knowing a secret, children often blurt it out—"My daddy's hair comes *off!*"—while their parents ___ with embarrassment.

_____ *insolvent* _____ 5–6. Vann will never end up ___; he's far too ___ ever to overspend. On

_____ *parsimonious* _____   Halloween, he gave each trick-or-treater a penny.

_____ *Prodigal* _____ 7–8. ___ spending is sometimes considered a sign of ___. People who love

_____ *decadence* _____   opulence° and fling their money around senselessly are seen as
deteriorating morally.

_____ *exemplary* _____ 9–10. "Virtue is its own reward," is an old saying, meaning that ___ behavior

_____ *incidental* _____   is valuable for its own sake. Other benefits, such as praise, are merely
___.

➤ *Final Check:* What Are You Stingy About?

Here is a final opportunity for you to strengthen your knowledge of the ten words. First read the following selection carefully. Then fill in each blank with a word from the box at the top of the previous page. (Context clues will help you figure out which word goes in which blank.) Use each word once.

Few people like to think of themselves as cheap, but almost everyone seems to be (1)_____ *parsimonious* _____ about something. Even rich, extravagant people who are (2)_____ *prodigal* _____ in most ways are likely to be thrifty about, say, toothpaste. My father, who has taken business trips with many fat-cat executives, reports that even they will squeeze the last little bit out of a tube of toothpaste by shutting a window or a door on it, rather than throw it away. Many of us are stingy with soap, using a bar until it is reduced to a tiny sliver and then squeezing a few of the soap fragments together in the hope they will (3)_____ *coalesce* _____. Nearly anyone will (4)_____ *writhe* _____ and crawl to get a dropped nickel out from under the bed.

I fold and save used aluminum foil to reuse again and again. And when a bottle of shampoo is nearly empty, I add water to get a few more washes out of it. Countless people reuse tea bags. My sagacious° mother-in-law taught us a thrifty trick: When a bottle of beer or soda looks empty, lay it on its side for a while—a few drinkable drops will soon collect.

Why do we do these things? We aren't really afraid that taking a new tea bag or a new piece of foil is a sign of moral (5)_____ *decadence* _____, or that it will make us (6)_____ *insolvent* _____. Nor do we think our thrift is (7)_____ *exemplary* _____, because it's often (8)_____ *surreptitious* _____; we do it on the sly rather than holding ourselves up as a model. Since the actual saving is so small, it must be (9)_____ *incidental* _____ to the main benefit: the feeling of satisfaction we get. This is like the (10)_____ *exuberance* _____ we feel when we find a dime or a quarter on the street— or even a penny, if it's heads up.

Scores   Sentence Check 2 _____ %   Final Check _____ %

Enter your scores above and in the vocabulary performance chart on the inside back cover of the book.

CHAPTER

4

brevity	querulous
clemency	reproach
frivolous	respite
heist	torpor
lampoon	unscathed

Ten Words in Context

In the space provided, write the letter of the meaning closest to that of each **boldfaced** word. Use the context of the sentences to help you figure out each word's meaning.

1 **brevity**
(brĕv′ĭ-tē)
-*noun*

- Everyone was surprised by the **brevity** of the principal's speech at graduation. He spoke for less than five minutes.
- President Calvin Coolidge was famous for the **brevity** of his remarks. When a woman told him, "I have a bet that I can get you to say three words to me!" his response was, "You lose."

 _c_ *Brevity* means   a. strength.   b. intelligence.   c. briefness.

2 **clemency**
(klĕm′ən-sē)
-*noun*

- A good teacher knows when to show **clemency**. For instance, if a student has been working very hard but does poorly on one quiz, the teacher might offer not to count that score.
- The convicted murderer was executed, even though religious leaders around the world asked the court to show **clemency** and reduce his sentence to life in prison.

 _a_ *Clemency* means   a. mercy.   b. haste.   c. strength.

3 **frivolous**
(frĭv′ə-ləs)
-*adjective*

- Do you feel like seeing a serious movie, or something more **frivolous**?
- One moment we were laughing over some ridiculous joke, but then the news of our friend's injury put an end to our **frivolous** mood.

 _a_ *Frivolous* means   a. lighthearted.   b. cold-hearted.   c. brokenhearted.

4 **heist**
(hīst)
-*noun*

- The house was unlocked, empty, and full of wedding presents—a perfect target for a **heist**.
- The action movie was about the attempted **heist** of a famous painting, Leonardo da Vinci's "Mona Lisa."

 _c_ *Heist* means   a. a purchase.   b. an imitation.   c. a burglary.

5 **lampoon**
(lăm-pōōn′)
-*verb*

- Someone in our office **lampooned** all our paperwork by circulating a six-page form to be submitted, in triplicate, by anyone who wanted a pencil. Several humorless employees actually filled it out.
- *Forbidden Broadway* is a comedy show consisting of takeoffs on plays running in New York. Each theater season it **lampoons** a new crop of victims.

 _b_ *Lampoon* means   a. to summarize.   b. to make fun of.   c. to praise.

6 **querulous**
(kwĕr′ə-ləs)
-*adjective*

- People who work in the "Complaints" department of a store must get used to dealing with lots of **querulous** customers.
- The spoiled little boy looked at his pile of birthday presents and said in a **querulous** voice, "None of them are very big, are they?"

 _c_ *Querulous* means   a. shaky.   b. dishonest.   c. discontented.

7 **reproach**
   (rĭ-prōch′)
   -noun

- The kids deserve a **reproach** for making such a mess of the house while their parents were away.
- During the campaign, both candidates drew a **reproach** from the newspapers for making untruthful statements and generally behaving very badly.

_b_ *Reproach* means

    a. an expression   b. an expression   c. an expression
       of thanks.   of disapproval.   of respect.

8 **respite**
   (rĕs′pĭt)
   -noun

- Emergency-room doctors work long shifts. Their only **respite** is a short nap on a couch.
- Twice a week, a nurse spends an afternoon at the Hendersons' house, so that Mrs. Henderson can have a **respite** from caring for her sick husband.

_a_ *Respite* means

    a. time off.   b. a salary.   c. a mark of respect.

9 **torpor**
   (tôr′pər)
   -noun

- When Dermot took a midwinter vacation in Florida, the unaccustomed heat drained his energy. His **torpor** was so overwhelming that all he wanted to do was lie in a hammock.
- The sleepy little town seemed to doze peacefully through the summer afternoon. It looked as if nothing could rouse it from its **torpor**.

_c_ *Torpor* means

    a. hostility.   b. curiosity.   c. drowsiness.

10 **unscathed**
   (ŭn-skāthd′)
   -adjective

- "Thanks to my seat belt," said Frankie, "I was able to walk away from the collision **unscathed**. Without it, I would probably have been badly injured."
- When her husband left her, Mimi lamented, "I wish I could say that this has left me **unscathed**. But the truth is that I've been deeply wounded."

_c_ *Unscathed* means

    a. strengthened.   b. angry.   c. unhurt.

Matching Words with Definitions

Following are definitions of the ten words. Clearly write or print each word next to its definition. The sentences above and on the previous page will help you decide on the meaning of each word.

1. _querulous_   Complaining; whining
2. _lampoon_   To attack or ridicule through humorous imitation
3. _reproach_   Blame; a rebuke
4. _brevity_   Briefness; shortness of duration
5. _torpor_   A state of mental or physical inactivity; sluggishness
6. _heist_   A theft
7. _frivolous_   Not sensible; not properly serious; silly
8. _clemency_   Mercy in judging; leniency
9. _unscathed_   Not harmed or injured
10. _respite_   A short period of rest or relief; time out

CAUTION: Do not go any further until you are sure the above answers are correct. Then you can use the definitions to help you in the following practices. Your goal is eventually to know the words well enough so that you don't need to check the definitions at all.

➤ *Sentence Check 1*

Using the answer line, complete each item below with the correct word from the box. Use each word once.

a. **brevity**	b. **clemency**	c. **frivolous**	d. **heist**	e. **lampoon**
f. **querulous**	g. **reproach**	h. **respite**	i. **torpor**	j. **unscathed**

frivolous   1. Feeling ___ on a sunny Saturday morning, I treated myself to a manicure rather than doing the housework that was waiting for me.

heist   2. The police believe at least three people were involved in the jewelry-store ___: one to be a lookout, one to do the actual stealing, and one to drive the getaway car.

clemency   3. Since the shoplifting incident was James's first such offense, the court showed ___ and only fined him rather than sending him to jail.

brevity   4. Professor Mazzeo's lectures are noted for their ___. He frequently finishes speaking before even half the hour is up.

querulous   5. Although Mr. Hackman frequently says, "I don't like to complain," his conversation is full of ___ comments about all the things that upset him.

torpor   6. After a snake eats, it generally falls into a state of ___ for a day or more, barely moving or even breathing.

unscathed   7. Our cat fell out of an attic window but walked away ___.

lampoon   8. Some very funny movies are takeoffs on certain types of serious movies. For instance, *Airplane* ___s disaster movies, while *Love at First Bite* makes fun of vampire films.

respite   9. I spend Thursday mornings at my sister's house, giving her some ___ from her very active two-year-old twins.

reproach   10. Sheila is a very forgiving person. Although she had every right to be angry at me for what I did, she accepted my apology without a word of ___.

NOTE: Now check your answers to these questions by turning to page 175. Going over the answers carefully will help you prepare for the next two practices, for which answers are not given.

➤ *Sentence Check 2*

Using the answer lines, complete each item below with **two** words from the box. Use each word once.

lampoon
frivolous   1–2. Political cartoons ___ public figures, but this mockery is not ___; rather than being merely funny, it is meant to reveal and comment on social problems and wrongdoing.

unscathed
respite   3–4. Caring for a loved one during a long illness does not leave even an exemplary° caregiver ___. In fact, "burnout" is very likely if the caregiver does not have a(n) ___ from time to time.

brevity
reproach   5–6. According to Shakespeare, "___ is the soul of wit." If so, the one-line joke is beyond ___, since it could hardly be briefer.

_____heist_____   7–8. The thief who was responsible for the ___ pleaded for ___, claiming

_____clemency_____   that he was a modern-day Robin Hood. "I steal from the rich and give to the poor," he said.

_____torpor_____   9–10. Champagne makes many people sleepy. But others, rather than being

_____querulous_____   overcome by ___, feel irritable and ___ after drinking it.

➤ _Final Check:_ Loony but True

Here is a final opportunity for you to strengthen your knowledge of the ten words. First read the following selection carefully. Then fill in each blank with a word from the box at the top of the previous page. (Context clues will help you figure out which word goes in which blank.) Use each word once.

One reason why people watch TV and movies is to laugh at fictional characters and the goofy things they do. But guess what, folks—real people are every bit as silly, and just as easy to (1)_____lampoon_____. Here are some stories from the files of "Incredible but True . . ."

An insolvent° homeless man walked into a bank in Michigan and asked a teller for fifty cents. She didn't understand what he'd said and thought he was trying to rob her. So she handed over all the cash in her drawer—about $1,300. He thanked her and left. When the police caught up with the man, they didn't charge him with a crime. They had to show (2)_____clemency_____, they said, because he hadn't done anything illegal or surreptitious°—he had just openly asked for money.

A real bank robber was captured within a few minutes of his (3)_____heist_____. The (4)_____brevity_____ of his freedom was easily explained. He had written his holdup note on the back of his own pay stub, complete with his name and address. When he got home, the cops were already there, waiting for him.

When police in Florida noticed a car weaving in and out of its lane, they pulled it over. Imagine their surprise when they found a three-and-a-half-foot-long iguana at the wheel. The large lizard was sitting on the lap of its sleeping owner, who was taking a short (5)_____respite_____ from driving. Fortunately, he and the lizard were both (6)_____unscathed_____; of the two, however, the lizard made out better. It got a nice new home, while the man went to jail for drunk driving. The judge didn't pay much attention to the man's (7)_____querulous_____ complaint that it was the iguana who had actually been driving.

A fishing ship in the Sea of Japan sank, and its crew claimed it had been struck by a cow that fell out of the sky. Everyone assumed that the sailors had made up this (8)_____frivolous_____ story to escape (9)_____reproach_____ for some mistake of their own. But then the crew of a Russian cargo plane admitted they had stolen a cow they'd found wandering on an airfield and put it aboard the plane. Now, cows are generally extremely calm animals. But cruising at 30,000 feet shook even a calm cow out of her usual (10)_____torpor_____. The terrified animal panicked, dived out of the plane, and, well, there was the ship. . . .

Scores	Sentence Check 2 _____%	Final Check _____%

Enter your scores above and in the vocabulary performance chart on the inside back cover of the book.

copious	meander
dearth	peripheral
eloquent	substantiate
jargon	unobtrusive
levity	vacillate

Ten Words in Context

In the space provided, write the letter of the meaning closest to that of each **boldfaced** word. Use the context of the sentences to help you figure out each word's meaning.

1 **copious**
(kō′pē-əs)
-*adjective*

- The food at the party was too **copious**; the guests stuffed themselves, but there were still platters and bowls of food left over.
- Weeds are **copious** in Charlene's garden, but flowers are few.

__b__ *Copious* means   a. of poor quality.   b. plentiful.   c. persuasive.

2 **dearth**
(dûrth)
-*noun*

- The director of the Class Night show said gloomily, "We have a **dearth** of talent this year. Not one of these acts is worth putting on stage."
- The **dearth** of snow this winter disappointed my children. They had received new sleds for Christmas but never got a chance to use them.

__c__ *Dearth* means   a. a surplus.   b. a sufficient amount.   c. a shortage.

3 **eloquent**
(ĕl′ə-kwənt)
-*adjective*

- Lincoln's Gettysburg Address is considered one of the most **eloquent** speeches of all time, but on the day he gave it, many in the audience were insulted. They thought it was too short.
- The director of the shelter for battered women wrote an **eloquent** letter to the newspapers, movingly describing the victims' plight and pleading for donations.

__a__ *Eloquent* means   a. stirring.   b. confusing.   c. simple.

4 **jargon**
(jär′gən)
-*noun*

- "It's essential that you learn the vocabulary of this subject," the instructor warned us, "or the **jargon**, if you prefer. Whatever you call it, it will be on the test."
- Bernice wanted to make a home-cooked meal for her friends but was puzzled by all the **jargon** in the cookbook. What did *braise* mean? Or *sauté*? Or *mince*?

__b__ *Jargon* means   a. grammatical errors.   b. technical language.   c. humor.

5 **levity**
(lĕv′ĭ-tē)
-*noun*

- The playwright George Bernard Shaw once remarked that his method was to say very serious things, but with "the utmost **levity**." He wanted to convey weighty ideas through wit and humor.
- The guidance counselor thought Kirk's attitude showed too much **levity**. "You should laugh less and spend more time thinking about serious things," she said.

__c__ *Levity* means   a. seriousness.   b. surprise.   c. lightheartedness.

6 **meander**
(mē-ăn′dər)
-*verb*

- "Come straight home from school," Mom always said to us. "Don't **meander**."
- The brook **meandered** through the valley, disappearing into the underbrush, then coming into view again, and here and there even turning back on itself.

__a__ *Meander* means   a. to wander.   b. to hurry.   c. to fall.

7 **peripheral**
(pə-rĭf′ər-əl)
-*adjective*

- The meeting to discuss the new road went slowly because the committee kept bringing up **peripheral** issues, such as the need for traffic lights on the old road.
- The lecturer kept getting sidetracked, because audience members repeatedly asked questions about **peripheral** matters that had little to do with her topic.

_b_ *Peripheral* means   a. essential.   b. of little importance.   c. doubtful.

8 **substantiate**
(səb-stăn′shē-āt′)
-*verb*

- If you seek damages under a "lemon law," be prepared to **substantiate** your claim that your car is a lemon. You'll need to show all your repair bills and correspondence.
- A man in our town claims to be 125 years old, but he's unable to **substantiate** this. He has no birth certificate, baptismal certificate, court records, or witnesses.

_c_ *Substantiate* means   a. to report.   b. to repeat.   c. to prove.

9 **unobtrusive**
(ŭn′əb-trōō′sĭv)
-*adjective*

- Jared arrived late for class. Hoping to remain **unobtrusive**, he quickly slid into a seat at the end of the last row.
- When his favorite author autographed books at the mall, Desmond expected to see a dazzling celebrity. Instead, she turned out to be a small, colorless, **unobtrusive** person with a timid smile.

_a_ *Unobtrusive* means   a. not noticeable.   b. not easily forgotten.   c. not important.

10 **vacillate**
(văs′ə-lāt′)
-*verb*

- Anand reaches decisions very slowly. For instance, when we went to get ice cream last night, he **vacillated** for fifteen minutes between vanilla and chocolate.
- Should he call Shelley or Robin? Thinking it over at the phone booth, Andy **vacillated** as the moments ticked by and the people waiting for the phone got more and more impatient.

_b_ *Vacillate* means   a. to speak.   b. to hesitate.   c. to select.

Matching Words with Definitions

Following are definitions of the ten words. Clearly write or print each word next to its definition. The sentences above and on the previous page will help you decide on the meaning of each word.

1. _____levity_____   Lightness of manner or speech
2. _____meander_____   To move aimlessly; wander lazily; stray
3. _____peripheral_____   Of minor importance or relevance; only slightly connected with what is essential; irrelevant
4. _____vacillate_____   To sway indecisively between two opinions
5. _____eloquent_____   Extremely expressive and persuasive
6. _____unobtrusive_____   Not readily noticeable or eye-catching; inconspicuous
7. _____jargon_____   The specialized language of people in the same profession
8. _____substantiate_____   To prove the truth of; confirm; verify
9. _____dearth_____   A scarcity; lack
10. _____copious_____   Abundant; in plentiful supply

CAUTION: Do not go any further until you are sure the above answers are correct. Then you can use the definitions to help you in the following practices. Your goal is eventually to know the words well enough so that you don't need to check the definitions at all.

➤ *Sentence Check 1*

Using the answer line, complete each item below with the correct word from the box. Use each word once.

a. **copious**	b. **dearth**	c. **eloquent**	d. **jargon**	e. **levity**
f. **meander**	g. **peripheral**	h. **substantiate**	i. **unobtrusive**	j. **vacillate**

_____ *jargon* _____   1. It took Andre all night to put together the wagon he had bought for his daughter. The instructions were written in a strange ___, such as "Attach flange B to sprocket C and secure with Permacaps."

_____ *levity* _____   2. I got an unfortunate case of the giggles during the boss's speech. "This is no time for ___," a colleague hissed at me.

_____ *substantiate* _____   3. "Can you ___ your story that the dog ate your homework?" the teacher asked Kay. "Yes!" Kay said, and showed her the veterinarian's X-rays.

_____ *eloquent* _____   4. The defense attorney's closing argument seemed both ___ and convincing, but the jury convicted his client anyway.

_____ *peripheral* _____   5. "We're supposed to be discussing the death penalty," the moderator reminded the panel. "Let's not get into ___ issues like conditions in prisons."

_____ *vacillate* _____   6. As she thought about what to wear to her job interview, Amy ___(e)d between a conservative navy-blue suit and a more stylish floral dress.

_____ *dearth* _____   7. Remy's vegetable garden yielded an uneven crop. There was a(n) ___ of tomatoes—three, to be exact—and about a ton of zucchini.

_____ *meander* _____   8. During the exam, the instructor ___(e)d through the test room, up and down the aisles, left and then right, apparently with no particular purpose—but the students knew she was keeping a sharp eye on them.

_____ *unobtrusive* _____   9. "The costumes must be ___," the playwright urged. "I want the audience to focus on what the actors are saying, not what they're wearing."

_____ *copious* _____   10. Van took ___ notes—they filled three notebooks—but they were so badly organized that they didn't do him much good.

NOTE: Now check your answers to these questions by turning to page 175. Going over the answers carefully will help you prepare for the next two practices, for which answers are not given.

➤ *Sentence Check 2*

Using the answer lines, complete each item below with **two** words from the box. Use each word once.

_____ *copious* _____
_____ *dearth* _____   1–2. "I'm hearing ___ complaints here, " said Mom at our family meeting, "but there's a(n) ___ of constructive ideas. For the next few minutes, I'd like everyone to keep quiet unless you have something sagacious° to say."

_____ *eloquent* _____
_____ *jargon* _____   3–4. Some of the most ___ language is also the most simple. For example, Martin Luther King's famous "I have a dream" speech is something a child could understand, free of high-flown language or technical ___.

_____ *meander* _____ 5–6. After our picnic, the kids and I ___(e)d lazily through the woods,

_____ *unobtrusive* _____ taking delight in the tiny ___ wildflowers that we found half-hidden under the dead leaves.

_____ *peripheral* _____ 7–8. "Alice's Restaurant" is a great song by Arlo Guthrie. It begins with

_____ *levity* _____ Guthrie and his friends having Thanksgiving dinner, then veers off into a very funny ___ story about being arrested for littering. Despite its ___, it ends up making a serious statement about the absurdity of war.

_____ *substantiate* _____ 9–10. Although the suspect said he could ___ his story about being out of town

_____ *vacillate* _____ on the night of the crime, he was not very convincing, as he continued to ___ about whether he'd been in Maine or Georgia at the time.

➤ *Final Check:* Writing a Better Paper

Here is a final opportunity for you to strengthen your knowledge of the ten words. First read the following selection carefully. Then fill in each blank with a word from the box at the top of the previous page. (Context clues will help you figure out which word goes in which blank.) Use each word once.

Many students know enough about grammar and spelling to write a paper that's reasonably correct, but they may need some additional guidelines to produce a paper that will be above average—perhaps even (1)_____ *eloquent* _____. Here are three rules that can help.

First, choose your topic with care. If a general topic has already been assigned (such as baseball), choose with care what aspect of it you will discuss (watching it? playing it? hating it? loving it?). You may assume that topics are scarce, but in fact it's just the opposite. There's no (2)_____ *dearth* _____ of potential topics: your problem is to select, from the (3)_____ *copious* _____ possibilities, the one that's best for your purpose.

Second, decide what tone you will use, and stick to it. If your subject is technical, it's fine to use (4)_____ *jargon* _____. If your subject lends itself to (5)_____ *levity* _____, then you can be witty. Decide whether you're going to write in your own voice or remain in the background, (6)_____ *unobtrusive* _____ and dispassionate°. Be sure your tone is appropriate for your topic: if you're discussing suicide, say, or capital punishment, don't try to be funny or frivolous°. Whatever tone you decide on, be consistent: don't (7)_____ *vacillate* _____ between tones. Don't be unbuttoned and slangy in one sentence but formal in the next—your paper will sound awkward and inconsistent.

Third, decide what your point is, support it, and stick to it. You need to (8)_____ *substantiate* _____ it with solid, unassailable° evidence. And don't (9)_____ *meander* _____ along, wandering off into (10)_____ *peripheral* _____ issues. You may think that throwing in a few additional topics will fascinate your readers, but it's more likely to confuse them.

In sum, then, to be sure of an exemplary° paper, focus on your topic, your tone, and your point.

Scores	Sentence Check 2 _____ %	Final Check _____ %

Enter your scores above and in the vocabulary performance chart on the inside back cover of the book.

UNIT ONE: *Review*

The box at the right lists twenty-five words from Unit One. Using the clues at the bottom of the page, fill in these words to complete the puzzle that follows.

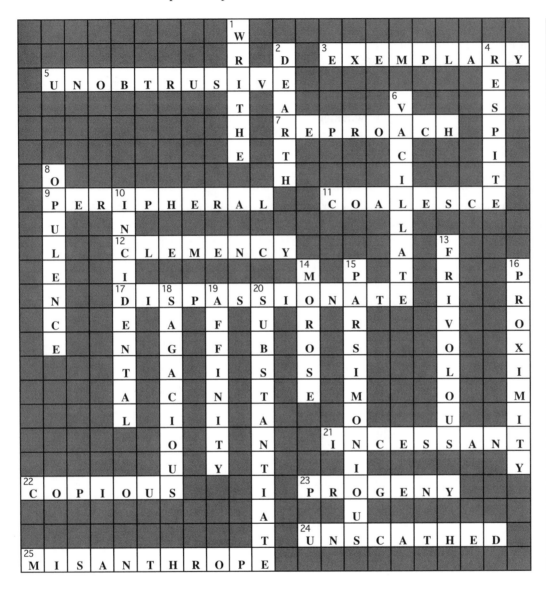

affinity
clemency
coalesce
copious
dearth
dispassionate
exemplary
frivolous
incessant
incidental
misanthrope
morose
opulence
parsimonious
peripheral
progeny
proximity
reproach
respite
sagacious
substantiate
unobtrusive
unscathed
vacillate
writhe

ACROSS

3. Worthy of imitation or praise
5. Not readily noticeable
7. Blame; a rebuke
9. Of minor importance or relevance
11. To merge to form one whole
12. Mercy in judging
17. Not influenced by emotion; impartial
21. Constant; without stopping
22. Abundant; in plentiful supply
23. Descendants
24. Not harmed or injured
25. A person who hates or distrusts humankind

DOWN

1. To twist and turn, as in pain or discomfort
2. A scarcity; lack
4. A short period of rest or relief
6. To sway indecisively between two opinions
8. Luxury
10. Occurring as a minor consequence of something more important
13. Silly
14. Very gloomy or sullen
15. Stingy
16. Closeness
18. Wise; sensible
19. A natural attraction or liking
20. To prove; confirm

UNIT ONE: Test 1

PART A

Choose the word that best completes each item and write it in the space provided.

_____frivolous_____ 1. When you fill out your income tax form, don't put in any jokes or wise-cracks. That is called filing a(n) ___ return, and it can land you in trouble.

    a. unobtrusive   b. incessant   c. frivolous   d. voracious

_____torpor_____ 2. A heat wave makes most of us feel drowsy and lazy. But did you know that people who freeze to death are also overcome by ___?

    a. jargon   b. torpor   c. clemency   d. affinity

_____Proximity_____ 3. ___ is a factor in friendship and romance. We are most likely to form a relationship with someone who lives next door, sits next to us in class, or works in the next cubicle.

    a. Decadence   b. Levity   c. Opulence   d. Proximity

_____clemency_____ 4. Do you think juvenile offenders should receive ___ because they are so young? Or should they be punished as harshly as adult lawbreakers?

    a. decadence   b. levity   c. progeny   d. clemency

_____voracious_____ 5. A teenage boy often has a ___ appetite. He may drink half a gallon of milk a day, and after he raids the refrigerator, there's usually not a crumb left.

    a. voracious   b. sagacious   c. peripheral   d. brusque

_____morose_____ 6. "Gloomy Gus" is a traditional name for a(n) ___ person.

    a. sagacious   b. eloquent   c. morose   d. effervescent

_____Incidental_____ 7. "___" music is another term for background music in a play or movie. It isn't a direct result of the plot but is just a minor element to set the mood.

    a. Querulous   b. Insolvent   c. Incidental   d. Indefatigable

_____hackneyed_____ 8. Robert feels that the old traditional "Welcome" mat is ___. So on his doorstep, he has a mat that says "Go Away."

    a. stoic   b. hackneyed   c. brusque   d. copious

_____nonchalance_____ 9. In the musical _The King and I_ is the song "I Whistle a Happy Tune." The singer says that when she feels scared, she whistles to achieve an air of ___.

    a. nonchalance   b. decadence   c. brevity   d. torpor

_____meander_____ 10. The verb "to ___" comes from the actual name of a river in Greece, famous for its winding course.

    a. supplant   b. meander   c. lampoon   d. substantiate

_____peripheral_____ 11. The strikers say that their main demand is higher pay. The other issues, such as working conditions and hours, are just ___.

    a. voluminous   b. unscathed   c. incessant   d. peripheral

(Continues on next page)

_____ *stoic* _____ 12. Dion bore his toothache in ___ silence for a week before he gave in and went to the dentist.

a. voracious   b. copious   c. frivolous   d. stoic

_____ *supplant* _____ 13. "Swear to me," whispered Juliet, "that no one else will ever ___ me in your heart." Romeo said, "Er, um, well . . ."

a. supplant   b. meander   c. substantiate   d. lampoon

PART B
Write **C** if the italicized word is used **correctly**. Write **I** if the word is used **incorrectly**.

___C___ 14. Tired of the same old writing assignments, Pia decided to *lampoon* the whole idea of the student essay. Her title was "Ten Ways to Produce a Paper Without Saying Anything."

___C___ 15. Grandfather needs home health care, but six nurses have quit because he is so *querulous*. He never stops complaining and making demands.

___I___ 16. As Marina's wedding gifts started to arrive, her mother reminded her, "Be sure to send everyone a note of *reproach*."

___I___ 17. Belinda was *unscathed* by the tragedy that struck her family. She became more and more despondent and eventually committed suicide.

___I___ 18. Food was so *copious* in the war-torn, ravaged city that the people were reduced to eating rats and boiled shoe leather.

___I___ 19. "Our fine library," the college catalogue boasted, "offers a *dearth* of material on every important subject."

___C___ 20. In theater *jargon,* "to fly" means to pull scenery up into the fly loft, the area above the stage.

___I___ 21. The speaker at the funeral said, "I am so overwhelmed by the *levity* of this sad occasion that I cannot find words to express my grief."

___C___ 22. The airline lost Vera's suitcase, but she had thrown away her baggage check, so she could not *substantiate* her claim.

___C___ 23. Denyse wanted a rock band to play at her wedding, but her husband-to-be insisted on soft, *unobtrusive* music so that the guests could talk without shouting.

___I___ 24. As he arrived at "Frosty Feast—1,001 Fabulous Flavors," Alex made up his mind to *vacillate*. He strode up to the counter and said firmly, "Vanilla, please."

___I___ 25. The *decadence* of the pioneer settlement was striking. Every man, woman, and child worked long and hard to build a new community in the wilderness.

Score (Number correct) _____ × 4 = _____%

Enter your score above and in the vocabulary performance chart on the inside back cover of the book.

UNIT ONE: *Test 2*

PART A

Complete each item with a word from the box. Use each word once.

a. **affinity**	b. **brevity**	c. **brusque**	d. **coalesce**	e. **eloquent**
f. **heist**	g. **incessant**	h. **opulence**	i. **parsimonious**	j. **prodigal**
k. **progeny**	l. **respite**	m. **writhe**		

_____ *affinity* _____ 1. Some writers have a(n) ___ for long, unusual words. They love to send the reader scurrying to the dictionary every few lines.

_____ *parsimonious* _____ 2. It's good sense to check the bill in a restaurant, to be sure you haven't been overcharged. But many people are embarrassed to do this because they don't want to look ___.

_____ *prodigal* _____ 3. The "___ son" in the Bible recklessly squanders his entire fortune and then limps back to his father's home, penniless, ragged, and starving.

_____ *progeny* _____ 4. The famous author had no children. When asked if this saddened her, she said no and pointed to a shelf full of her books. "These are my___," she said.

_____ *brusque* _____ 5. The boss likes to come across as a hardheaded, tough, ___, no-nonsense type. As a result, many of the staff are afraid of him.

_____ *writhe* _____ 6. In the limbo, a dance from the West Indies, the dancers must ___ and bend over backward to get under a low pole.

_____ *incessant* _____ 7. After an afternoon of hearing his kids' nonstop quarrels, Matt yelled, "Stop that ___ squabbling before I go out of my mind!"

_____ *opulence* _____ 8. The ___ of the theater lobby took our breath away. We were surrounded by gold draperies, crystal chandeliers, gleaming mirrors, velvet carpeting, and marble pillars.

_____ *brevity* _____ 9. A famous author once apologized for sending a friend a very long letter, saying that the reason was "I didn't have time to write a short one." This suggests that ___ requires considerable work.

_____ *heist* _____ 10. Julia was innocently shopping when the store was robbed. But the police suspected that she had taken part in the ___ and arrested her along with the real thieves.

_____ *respite* _____ 11. Some elementary schools no longer have recess. This troubles many parents and teachers, who feel that children need a(n) ___ during the school day.

_____ *eloquent* _____ 12. The speaker's appeal for the victims of the famine was so ___ that it moved the audience to tears—and to donate generously.

_____ *coalesce* _____ 13. Hiding the children's Easter basket behind the radiator was not a good idea. I should have realized that all the jellybeans would ___ into one sticky lump.

(Continues on next page)

PART B
Write **C** if the italicized word is used **correctly**. Write **I** if the word is used **incorrectly**.

_C_ 14. "Your essay is *exemplary*," the professor said. "With your permission, I would like to include it in the next edition of my textbook, as a model research paper."

_I_ 15. The *exuberance* of the children in the hospital was sad to see. Thin, pale, and exhausted, many were too weak even to look up as visitors arrived.

_C_ 16. "I've won the million-dollar lottery!" Felice shrieked with joy. "I'm rich! I'll never be *insolvent* again!"

_C_ 17. Roy, who was supposed to be on a diet, kept making *surreptitious* trips to the kitchen to nibble on this and that, whenever he thought no one would notice.

_I_ 18. The *fledgling* company has an excellent reputation—which is understandable, since it's been in business for twenty years and has thousands of satisfied customers.

_I_ 19. Ty made the *sagacious* decision to bet a month's salary at the racetrack. He lost, and now he can't pay his rent.

_I_ 20. "We have an *unassailable* defense," Henry's lawyer said, "so I advise you to plead guilty and throw yourself on the mercy of the court."

_C_ 21. One model in a high-fashion show wore a hat so *voluminous* that it had to be supported with four poles carried by four attendants.

_C_ 22. The author took a *dispassionate* approach to the topic. He presented both sides of the issue evenhandedly and did not let his own feelings intrude.

_I_ 23. The symphony's second movement—slow, mournful, and *effervescent*—is based on a funeral march.

_I_ 24. Reba is *indefatigable*. She can't walk a block without having to stop and rest awhile, and after climbing one flight of stairs she has to lie down to recover.

_I_ 25. The story is about a kindly, generous, cheerful *misanthrope* who loves and is loved by everyone.

Score (Number correct) _____ × 4 = _____ %

Enter your score above and in the vocabulary performance chart on the inside back cover of the book.

UNIT ONE: Test 3

PART A: Synonyms

In the space provided, write the letter of the choice that is most nearly the **same** in meaning as the **boldfaced** word.

_a_   1. **brusque**   **a)** gruff   **b)** bright   **c)** brainy   **d)** polite

_d_   2. **clemency**   **a)** hopelessness   **b)** unhappiness   **b)** cleverness   **d)** forgiveness

_b_   3. **decadence**   **a)** decency   **b)** corruption   **c)** confidence   **d)** defense

_a_   4. **eloquent**   **a)** moving   **b)** boring   **c)** frightening   **d)** disappointing

_a_   5. **exemplary**   **a)** excellent   **b)** extinct   **c)** excessive   **d)** external

_c_   6. **fledgling**   **a)** flying   **b)** needed   **c)** new   **d)** failing

_a_   7. **heist**   **a)** a burglary   **b)** a charity   **c)** a mistake   **d)** an imitation

_b_   8. **incessant**   **a)** incompetent   **b)** ceaseless   **c)** careless   **d)** rare

_b_   9. **incidental**   **a)** major   **b)** minor   **c)** memorable   **d)** incredible

_d_   10. **indefatigable**   **a)** satisfied   **b)** dishonest   **c)** uncaring   **d)** untiring

_b_   11. **jargon**   **a)** humor   **b)** specialized language   **c)** history   **d)** drama

_c_   12. **lampoon**   **a)** to learn   **b)** to teach   **c)** to spoof   **d)** to admire

_a_   13. **levity**   **a)** merriness   **b)** weariness   **c)** sickness   **d)** envy

_a_   14. **misanthrope**   **a)** a hater   **b)** a lover   **c)** a wanderer   **d)** an entertainer

_b_   15. **nonchalance**   **a)** passion   **b)** coolness   **c)** nonexistence   **d)** stupidity

_d_   16. **progeny**   **a)** friends   **b)** enemies   **c)** defendants   **d)** descendants

_b_   17. **querulous**   **a)** cheery   **b)** cross   **c)** shy   **d)** helpful

_a_   18. **reproach**   **a)** condemnation   **b)** praise   **c)** deceit   **d)** imitation

_b_   19. **respite**   **a)** an assignment   **b)** a vacation   **c)** a career   **d)** a skill

_c_   20. **stoic**   **a)** insane   **b)** irresponsible   **c)** unflinching   **d)** disrespectful

_a_   21. **substantiate**   **a)** to support   **b)** to attack   **c)** to conceal   **d)** to ignore

_a_   22. **supplant**   **a)** to displace   **b)** to summarize   **c)** to supervise   **d)** to dislike

_c_   23. **vacillate**   **a)** to leave   **b)** to return   **c)** to waver   **d)** to understand

_b_   24. **voracious**   **a)** tired   **b)** hungry   **c)** busy   **d)** cautious

_a_   25. **writhe**   **a)** to bend   **b)** to blend   **c)** to carry   **d)** to wear

(Continues on next page)

PART B: Antonyms

In the space provided, write the letter of the choice that is most nearly the **opposite** in meaning to the **boldfaced** word.

_d_ 26. **affinity**   a) fondness   b) happiness   c) satisfaction   d) dislike

_a_ 27. **brevity**   a) length   b) shortness   c) knowledge   d) fame

_c_ 28. **coalesce**   a) to come across   b) to come home   c) to come apart   d) to come between

_d_ 29. **copious**   a) abundant   b) cooperative   c) uncooperative   d) few

_a_ 30. **dearth**   a) abundance   b) pleasure   c) sadness   d) fear

_a_ 31. **dispassionate**   a) prejudiced   b) disappointing   c) disastrous   d) predictable

_d_ 32. **effervescent**   a) evil   b) eager   c) bouncy   d) dull

_a_ 33. **exuberance**   a) apathy   b) excitement   c) wealth   d) poverty

_d_ 34. **frivolous**   a) amused   b) witty   c) silly   d) serious

_a_ 35. **hackneyed**   a) original   b) true   c) false   d) predictable

_b_ 36. **insolvent**   a) healthy   b) wealthy   c) wise   d) handsome

_b_ 37. **meander**   a) to go slowly   b) to go directly   c) to stop   d) to start

_a_ 38. **morose**   a) happy   b) puzzled   c) depressed   d) bereaved

_c_ 39. **opulence**   a) affluence   b) influence   c) poverty   d) obedience

_c_ 40. **parsimonious**   a) skillful   b) patient   c) generous   d) impatient

_a_ 41. **peripheral**   a) central   b) untrue   c) numerous   d) few

_c_ 42. **prodigal**   a) angry   b) sleepy   c) thrifty   d) lonely

_d_ 43. **proximity**   a) pronunciation   b) process   c) appearance   d) distance

_c_ 44. **sagacious**   a) sensible   b) sensory   c) foolish   d) fearless

_a_ 45. **surreptitious**   a) forthright   b) secret   c) superfluous   d) inadequate

_c_ 46. **torpor**   a) relevance   b) irrelevance   c) energy   d) money

_b_ 47. **unassailable**   a) strong   b) weak   c) rare   d) common

_a_ 48. **unobtrusive**   a) glaring   b) obscure   c) subtle   d) dim

_b_ 49. **unscathed**   a) wrong   b) wounded   c) unarmed   d) unharmed

_d_ 50. **voluminous**   a) constant   b) towering   c) variable   d) tiny

---

Score   (Number correct) _____ × 2 = _____%

Enter your score above and in the vocabulary performance chart on the inside back cover of the book.

Unit Two

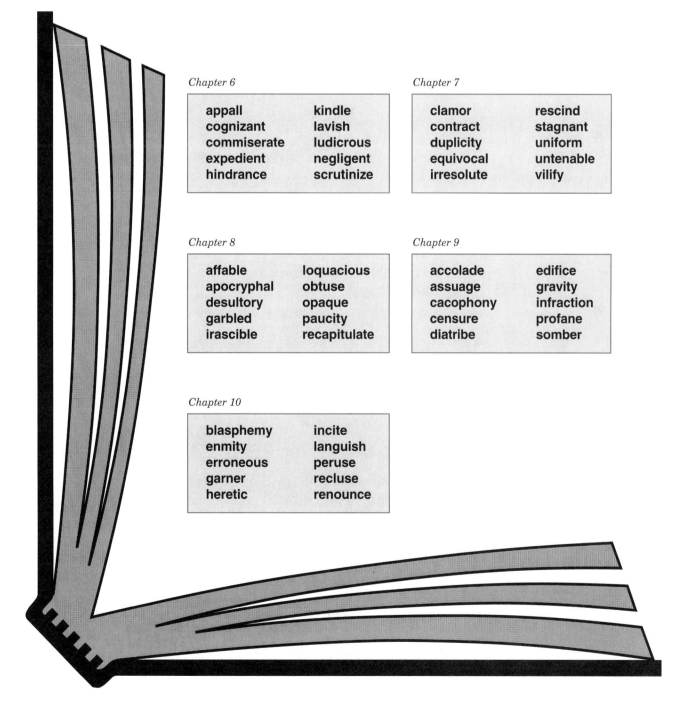

Chapter 6

appall	kindle
cognizant	lavish
commiserate	ludicrous
expedient	negligent
hindrance	scrutinize

Chapter 7

clamor	rescind
contract	stagnant
duplicity	uniform
equivocal	untenable
irresolute	vilify

Chapter 8

affable	loquacious
apocryphal	obtuse
desultory	opaque
garbled	paucity
irascible	recapitulate

Chapter 9

accolade	edifice
assuage	gravity
cacophony	infraction
censure	profane
diatribe	somber

Chapter 10

blasphemy	incite
enmity	languish
erroneous	peruse
garner	recluse
heretic	renounce

appall	kindle
cognizant	lavish
commiserate	ludicrous
expedient	negligent
hindrance	scrutinize

Ten Words in Context

In the space provided, write the letter of the meaning closest to that of each **boldfaced** word. Use the context of the sentences to help you figure out each word's meaning.

1 appall
(ə-pôl′)
-*verb*

- At the end of World War II, the facts that emerged about the Nazi concentration camps and death camps **appalled** the whole world.
- "When the facts about this awful crime are disclosed," said the lawyer, "they will **appall** you and show clearly that the defendant is a monster."

b Appall means   a. to appeal to.   b. to shock.   c. to bore.

2 cognizant
(kŏg′nĭ-zənt)
-*adjective*

- After a picnic in the woods, Shawn found a tick on his ankle and then developed a rash. **Cognizant** of the risk of Lyme disease, he saw his doctor right away.
- Many Americans have diabetes without being **cognizant** of their condition.

b Cognizant means   a. confused by.   b. conscious of.   c. careless about.

3 commiserate
(kə-mĭz′ə-rāt′)
-*verb*

- Mom was disappointed with the widows' support group. The members just wanted to **commiserate** with each other, but she wanted to learn about positive steps to take, not just get sympathy.
- When my dog died, my roommate tried to **commiserate** with me, but he didn't really understand how I was feeling.

a Commiserate means   a. to express sorrow.   b. to draw a comparison.   c. to complain.

4 expedient
(ĭk-spē′dē-ənt)
-*adjective*

- Marty's interest in Elaine seems entirely **expedient**; he knows she has money, and he wants someone wealthy who will support him.
- In order to sell his old car for the highest possible price, Jim did the **expedient** thing: he slapped a new coat of paint on it and didn't mention that it needed new brakes and an exhaust system.

c Expedient means   a. unbelievable.   b. admirable.   c. self-interested.

5 hindrance
(hĭn′drəns)
-*noun*

- The biggest **hindrance** to peace in the Middle East may be the acts of terrorism committed by both sides.
- Some people seem perfectly willing to lie if the truth would be a **hindrance** to getting what they want.

c Hindrance means   a. a cause.   b. an effect.   c. a barrier.

6 kindle
(kĭn′dl)
-*verb*

- Before Tyrone joined the navy, Kate had thought of him as "just a friend." But his warm, affectionate letters began to **kindle** her love for him.
- The senator's lifelong devotion to politics was **kindled** early, when she was elected president of her high-school senior class.

b Kindle means   a. to stop.   b. to inspire.   c. to change.

7 **lavish**
(lăv′ĭsh)
-adjective

- The **lavish** new offices looked very impressive, but behind all that splendor, the company was going broke.
- Avery celebrated his promotion by taking his friends out for a **lavish** dinner. "The best of everything!" he told the waiter, "and it's all on me."

_a_ _Lavish_ means   a. overly luxurious.   b. subtle.   c. amusing.

8 **ludicrous**
(loo′dĭ-krəs)
-adjective

- Struggling in the wind and rain with my umbrella, which had turned inside out, while my dog tugged wildly at his leash and my bag of groceries burst and spilled, I must have been a **ludicrous** sight.
- "Diet Tips from Space Aliens"; "Five-Year-Old Gives Birth to Basketball Team"; "Florida Floating Out to Sea"—no idea seems too **ludicrous** to be reported in the supermarket tabloids.

_b_ _Ludicrous_ means   a. horrifying.   b. ridiculous.   c. inspiring.

9 **negligent**
(nĕg′lĭ-jənt)
-adjective

- While Hester may be a **negligent** housekeeper—her apartment is dusty and untidy—she makes up for it by being a loving, conscientious mother.
- It's not surprising that Rich flunked out of college. His attitude toward studying has always been **negligent**.

_c_ _Negligent_ means   a. anxious.   b. amusing.   c. careless.

10 **scrutinize**
(skroot′n-īz′)
-verb

- The detectives **scrutinized** the crime scene for fingerprints and other clues.
- Before handing in his report, Dan was told to **scrutinize** it for misspellings and other errors.

_a_ _Scrutinize_ means   a. to inspect.   b. to describe.   c. to add to.

Matching Words with Definitions

Following are definitions of the ten words. Clearly write or print each word next to its definition. The sentences above and on the previous page will help you decide on the meaning of each word.

1. _hindrance_   An obstacle; impediment
2. _cognizant_   Aware
3. _expedient_   Self-serving; convenient
4. _lavish_   Extravagant
5. _negligent_   Careless
6. _scrutinize_   To examine
7. _kindle_   To stir up; arouse
8. _appall_   To horrify; dismay
9. _ludicrous_   Laughable
10. _commiserate_   To sympathize; express compassion

CAUTION: Do not go any further until you are sure the above answers are correct. Then you can use the definitions to help you in the following practices. Your goal is eventually to know the words well enough so that you don't need to check the definitions at all.

➢ *Sentence Check 1*

Using the answer line, complete each item below with the correct word from the box. Use each word once.

a. **appall**	b. **cognizant**	c. **commiserate**	d. **expedient**	e. **hindrance**
f. **kindle**	g. **lavish**	h. **ludicrous**	i. **negligent**	j. **scrutinize**

_____cognizant_____ 1. Janna's parents were ___ of her problems at school, but they did not know the cause until a psychologist diagnosed a learning disability.

_____hindrance_____ 2. It's OK not to have a car in the city, where public transportation is available, but the lack of a car is a real ___ to getting around in the country.

_____lavish_____ 3. We exclaimed with delight over our ___ hotel room, with its thick rug, brocade curtains, and gorgeous furniture.

_____appall_____ 4. The amount of food that's wasted in the school cafeteria ___(s) me—surely there must be some way to share all that extra food with people who need it.

_____negligent_____ 5. Julie is ___ about nutrition. She eats mostly junk food, when she bothers to eat at all.

_____commiserate_____ 6. "Laugh and the world laughs with you; cry and you cry alone" is an old saying. It means that others would rather share your happiness than ___ with you over your sorrows.

_____scrutinize_____ 7. Handwriting experts ___ letters, notes, and signatures to identify the writers.

_____kindle_____ 8. We hope that letting our children have a puppy will ___ their sense of responsibility and help them develop respect for animals.

_____expedient_____ 9. It was ___ for James to tell his new girlfriend, "I attended a very prestigious college," without mentioning that he'd flunked out.

_____ludicrous_____ 10. In the funny movie *All of Me*, Steve Martin and Lily Tomlin are in a(n) ___ situation—they have to share the same body.

NOTE: Now check your answers to these questions by turning to page 175. Going over the answers carefully will help you prepare for the next two practices, for which answers are not given.

➢ *Sentence Check 2*

Using the answer lines, complete each item below with **two** words from the box. Use each word once.

_____lavish_____
_____ludicrous_____ 1–2. Milly gave a(n) ___ birthday party for her dog, complete with an expensive cake, candles, and fancy decorations. The poor animal wore a party hat and a huge satin ribbon and looked ___.

_____expedient_____
_____commiserate_____ 3–4. The mayor found it politically ___ to close the school, but then visited it to ___ with the teachers and students. Everyone felt that his expressions of sympathy were phony.

_____kindle_____
_____hindrance_____ 5–6. Parents who want to ___ a love of reading in their kids often complain that TV is a serious ___. The kids would rather watch the tube than open a book.

_____ *negligent* _____   7–8. "The boss hates ___ work," Rasheed was told on his first day at his new
_____ *scrutinize* _____   job. "You can expect her to ___ all your letters and memos, looking for
                                      careless errors."

_____ *cognizant* _____   9–10. Explaining her decision to give up smoking, Celia said, "I am ___ of
_____ *appall* _____   the statistics on smoking and cancer. The facts are unassailable°, and
                                      they ___ me."

➤ *Final Check:* Bad Translations

Here is a final opportunity for you to strengthen your knowledge of the ten words. First read the following selection carefully. Then fill in each blank with a word from the box at the top of the previous page. (Context clues will help you figure out which word goes in which blank.) Use each word once.

When a company introduces a product into a new country, it should (1)_____ *scrutinize* _____ the promotional materials carefully. Sometimes a company is not (2)_____ *cognizant* _____ of how ads will be read in a foreign language. The results can be (3)_____ *ludicrous* _____, making would-be customers writhe° with laughter—or with shock—instead of making them want to buy the product. Here are a few examples.

When Coca-Cola was introduced in China, the company mounted a(n) (4)_____ *lavish* _____ advertising campaign that featured thousands of billboards with the Chinese phrase *Ke-kou-ke-la.* Unfortunately, the company had been (5)_____ *negligent* _____ about learning just what *Ke-kou-ke-la* meant in Chinese. It translated into something like "Bite the wax tadpole." That phrase did not exactly (6)_____ *kindle* _____ anyone's desire to buy Coke.

Maybe soft-drink companies tend to have special problems with Chinese. It certainly would have been (7)_____ *expedient* _____ for the Pepsi company to test-market its slogan before going into China. The translation of the slogan "Come alive with the Pepsi generation" shocked and (8)_____ *appall* _____(e)d Chinese shoppers. What it said was, "Pepsi will bring your ancestors back from the dead."

But problems arise with other languages, too. The Chevy Nova didn't sell very well in South America. Finally company officials realized that the (9)_____ *hindrance* _____ was the car's name. In Spanish, the phrase *No va* means "It won't go."

When the Pope visited Miami, a fledgling° businessman, perhaps counting on beginner's luck, made thousands of T-shirts that were supposed to say in Spanish, "I saw the Pope." You have to (10)_____ *commiserate* _____ with the poor guy—he got stuck with a copious° supply of unsold shirts. What the Spanish phrase really said was, "I saw the potato."

Scores	Sentence Check 2 _____%	Final Check _____%

Enter your scores above and in the vocabulary performance chart on the inside back cover of the book.

CHAPTER

7

clamor	rescind
contract	stagnant
duplicity	uniform
equivocal	untenable
irresolute	vilify

Ten Words in Context

In the space provided, write the letter of the meaning closest to that of each **boldfaced** word. Use the context of the sentences to help you figure out each word's meaning.

1 **clamor**
(klăm′ər)
-noun

- By the time I left the nightclub, I had an awful headache from the **clamor** of the crowd and the music.
- The hungry parakeets set up an excited **clamor** when they saw their owner enter the room.

<u>a</u> *Clamor* means   a. loud noise.   b. tense silence.   c. whispers.

2 **contract**
(kŭn-trăkt′)
-verb

- Our company can't seem to decide whether to grow or to **contract**. First it hired a hundred extra workers; then it laid off two hundred.
- The universe is expanding, but scientists do not know whether this will continue forever, or whether eventually it will start to **contract**, becoming more and more dense until it collapses on itself.

<u>b</u> *Contract* means   a. to become visible.   b. to become smaller.   c. to become weaker.

3 **duplicity**
(do͞o-plĭs′ĭ-tē)
-noun

- "I can't tolerate **duplicity**," said the professor. "If you didn't get around to writing your paper on time, say so. Don't make up some story about death or illness in your family."
- Dogs seem incapable of **duplicity**. If a dog soils the rug, he will slink around guiltily. He won't try to pretend that the cat did it.

<u>c</u> *Duplicity* means   a. repetition.   b. exaggeration.   c. deceit.

4 **equivocal**
(ĭ-kwĭv′ə-kəl)
-adjective

- Keith seemed **equivocal** about whether he'd gotten the job or not. First he said it was "a sure thing," but then he added that he had to go back for another interview.
- After her first date with Chris, Karen was **equivocal** about how she felt toward him. She said he was "interesting," which could mean almost anything.

<u>a</u> *Equivocal* means   a. vague.   b. the same.   c. discouraged.

5 **irresolute**
(ĭ-rĕz′ə-lo͞ot′)
-adjective

- In *Hamlet,* why doesn't Hamlet kill Claudius sooner? Is it because he is too **irresolute** to act, or because he is prevented from carrying out his purpose?
- Carleton is **irresolute** about marrying Tania. He's sure they are in love, but they seem to have far too many fights.

<u>a</u> *Irresolute* means   a. unable to decide.   b. lacking self-control.   c. unknowing.

6 **rescind**
(rĭ-sĭnd′)
-verb

- The state can **rescind** the licenses of people arrested for driving while drunk.
- It's very rude to **rescind** your invitation to one date just because you've met someone you'd prefer to invite.

<u>b</u> *Rescind* means   a. to renew.   b. to cancel.   c. to abuse.

40

7 **stagnant**
(stăg′nənt)
-*adjective*

- At age forty, Ira is considering a midlife career change. He feels that his present career is **stagnant**: he's going nowhere in his job.
- The pond was **stagnant**, and algae and weeds were growing so thickly that they covered the still water underneath.

_b_ *Stagnant* means   a. out of control.   b. motionless.   c. spread thin.

8 **uniform**
(yōō′nə-fôrm′)
-*adjective*

- To give hand-sewing a professional appearance, it's important to make the stitches **uniform**. Take the trouble to make them all the same size—the result will be worth it.
- People whose teeth are unevenly spaced and discolored may benefit from a dental technique called bonding, which makes teeth look more **uniform**.

_a_ *Uniform* means   a. unvarying.   b. different.   c. insupportable.

9 **untenable**
(ŭn-tĕn′ə-bəl)
-*adjective*

- In the exam room, the instructor looked grimly at the math formulas penciled on my shirt cuffs. "Your story that you don't know how they got there is **untenable**," she said. "You can't expect me to believe you!"
- Jocelyn's theory that the explorers missing at the South Pole had been eaten by polar bears was interesting but **untenable**. Polar bears live at the North Pole.

_b_ *Untenable* means   a. uninteresting.   b. unable to be defended.   c. unclear.

10 **vilify**
(vĭl′ə-fī)
-*verb*

- Most of Professor Jones's students praise him, but a few **vilify** him. It's strange that he should be so respected by some and so harshly criticized by others.
- "I don't think it's fair to **vilify** the entire college just because one fraternity has behaved badly," said Liam. "People should aim their dislike at the right target."

_c_ *Vilify* means   a. to argue with.   b. to assault physically.   c. to speak evil of.

Matching Words with Definitions

Following are definitions of the ten words. Clearly write or print each word next to its definition. The sentences above and on the previous page will help you decide on the meaning of each word.

1. _____duplicity_____   Deliberate deceptiveness; deceit
2. _____equivocal_____   Open to more than one interpretation and often intended to mislead
3. _____uniform_____   All or always the same; without variety
4. _____contract_____   To reduce in size; become compressed
5. _____clamor_____   A loud outcry; hubbub
6. _____untenable_____   Unable to be held or defended; insupportable
7. _____stagnant_____   Not moving; not flowing; motionless
8. _____vilify_____   To make abusive statements about
9. _____rescind_____   To repeal; take back
10. _____irresolute_____   Uncertain how to think or act; undecided

CAUTION: Do not go any further until you are sure the above answers are correct. Then you can use the definitions to help you in the following practices. Your goal is eventually to know the words well enough so that you don't need to check the definitions at all.

➤ *Sentence Check 1*

Using the answer line, complete each item below with the correct word from the box. Use each word once.

a. **clamor**	b. **contract**	c. **duplicity**	d. **equivocal**	e. **irresolute**
f. **rescind**	g. **stagnant**	h. **uniform**	i. **untenable**	j. **vilify**

Irresolute   1. ___ about whether to take the subway or catch a bus, I hesitated too long and managed to miss both.

untenable   2. Lenore insisted that she had paid all the rent she owed, but her claim was ___. She was unable to produce any canceled checks or receipts.

contract   3. Bodily movement results when our muscles first ___ and then relax.

vilify   4. The candidate's voice shook as he showed reporters an ugly cartoon attacking his wife. "___ me if you like—I can take abuse," he said. "But leave my family alone."

clamor   5. It seems that every courtroom drama includes a scene in which a(n) ___ erupts, with the judge pounding the gavel and shouting "Order in the court!"

equivocal   6. When Ben asked Jenna if she loved him, her ___ response—"Oh, Ben, I love everybody"—left him more confused than ever.

rescind   7. Angry over a council member's racist statements, a citizens' group decided to ___ its invitation to have him speak at the annual fundraising dinner.

duplicity   8. City supervisors said the repairs to our street would take a month, but they took almost a year. We don't know if this was ___ on the city's part, or an honest miscalculation.

stagnant   9. Sales had been ___ for months, so the company began an aggressive new ad campaign in the hope that merchandise would begin moving again.

uniform   10. "No longer will each department handle billing its own way," the boss announced. "From now on we will all use the same set of ___ procedures."

NOTE: Now check your answers to these questions by turning to page 175. Going over the answers carefully will help you prepare for the next two practices, for which answers are not given.

➤ *Sentence Check 2*

Using the answer lines, complete each item below with **two** words from the box. Use each word once.

irresolute / *untenable*   1–2. Eddie paused, ___, outside the professor's office. He wanted to argue about his poor grade, but he hesitated because he was afraid she would consider his reasons ___.

vilify / *stagnant*   3–4. "Don't expect me to ___ the mayor," said the opposing candidate. "He's a decent, honest man. But our city has grown sluggish and ___ during his administration. It's time to move forward again!"

_____ contract _____   5–6. Asked whether the college should expand or ___, the president gave
_____ equivocal _____   a(n) ___ answer: "Growth is positive, but we may need to draw inward
                                   and sharpen our focus."

_____ uniform _____   7–8. The American "melting pot" was seen as taking foreign immigrants
_____ clamor _____   and blending them so they would coalesce° into a(n) ___ mixture. This
                                   idea is now so unpopular that it often raises a(n) ___ of protest.

_____ rescind _____   9–10. The new office manager promised to ___ some pointless rules about
_____ duplicity _____   using the copier, but he seems to have been guilty of ___. The silly
                                    rules are still in place.

➤ _Final Check:_ Memory Aids

Here is a final opportunity for you to strengthen your knowledge of the ten words. First read the following selection carefully. Then fill in each blank with a word from the box at the top of the previous page. (Context clues will help you figure out which word goes in which blank.) Use each word once.

If you've ever said "Thirty days hath September . . . ," you know how helpful mnemonic devices—memory aids—can be. You can also use them to remember new words.

How can you remember (1)_____ vilify _____? Think of saying something _vile,_ and there you are: "to speak e_vil_ of." For (2)_____ stagnant _____, you could think of _st-_ as in _st_anding _st_ill—not moving. And (3)_____ clamor _____ is easier to remember if you think of a _claim,_ which is also a demand, though not necessarily a loud one. If you've ever used a duplicating machine—a copier—to make double copies, you'll have no trouble remembering that (4)_____ duplicity _____ means double-dealing, or dishonesty. To remember the adjective (5)_____ uniform _____, just think of what people in the Air Force or the Navy wear so that they all look the same.

A prefix—a word part at the beginning of a longer word—can also be a memory aid. Remember that the prefix _ir-_ means "not" and _resolve_ means "make up your mind," and you won't forget that (6)_____ irresolute _____ means "not having made up your mind." To remember (7)_____ untenable _____, think of holding something with your _ten_ fingers. Add the prefix _un,_ which also means "not," and you have it: "not holdable." The prefix _con-,_ meaning "together," will help you recall what (8)_____ contract _____ means: think of making something smaller by pulling or pushing its parts closer _together._ And one meaning of the prefix _re-_ is "back" or "backward," which can remind you of (which means "take your mind _back_ to") the fact that (9)_____ rescind _____ means "take back" or repeal.

Sometimes the best way to learn a word is to cut it in half and see what it says. Think of _equal_ and _voice_ to remember that (10)_____ equivocal _____ describes something which can be understood in more than one way—as if _equal voices_ were speaking.

Try making up your own mnemonic devices. Even if they sound frivolous° or ludicrous°, you'll find that they're a powerful tool and an exemplary° learning aid.

Scores   Sentence Check 2 _____%   Final Check _____%

Enter your scores above and in the vocabulary performance chart on the inside back cover of the book.

affable	loquacious
apocryphal	obtuse
desultory	opaque
garbled	paucity
irascible	recapitulate

Ten Words in Context

In the space provided, write the letter of the meaning closest to that of each **boldfaced** word. Use the context of the sentences to help you figure out each word's meaning.

1 **affable**
(ăf′ə-bəl)
-adjective

- Dobermans and pit bulls are often thought of as unfriendly dogs, while golden retrievers and Labradors are seen as **affable**.
- I wish my new boss were more **affable**. She seems so stern that I'm afraid to ask her a question when I don't understand something.

_b_ *Affable* means   a. bad-tempered.   b. good-natured.   c. intelligent.

2 **apocryphal**
(ə-pŏk′rə-fəl)
-adjective

- A hero of American folklore is the giant lumberjack Paul Bunyan, whose footprints supposedly formed the Great Lakes. Clearly, this story is **apocryphal**.
- There is a story in our family that my great-great-grandfather was a train robber, but I think the story is probably **apocryphal**.

_a_ *Apocryphal* means   a. fictitious.   b. difficult to understand.   c. true.

3 **desultory**
(dĕs′əl-tôr′ē)
-adjective

- When the shoe repair shop lost my boots, the clerk's search was so **desultory** and disorganized that I had to go through the shelves and find them myself.
- Darrin went to the emergency room with a severe stomachache, but the doctor on duty gave him only a quick, **desultory** examination and sent him home.

_b_ *Desultory* means   a. fake.   b. random.   c. intensive.

4 **garbled**
(gär′bəld)
-adjective

- When Tim printed his essay, a computer error made it come out **garbled**. Only meaningless symbols and numbers appeared on the page.
- The children played a game in which each one whispered a message to the next child in line. The first child whispered, "My favorite color is purple," but the message the last child heard was **garbled**: "You shouldn't holler at your uncle."

_c_ *Garbled* means   a. lengthy.   b. shortened.   c. distorted.

5 **irascible**
(ĭ-răs′ə-bəl)
-adjective

- "The holidays are supposed to be a happy time," sighed Martine. "But with all the extra work and guests, I find myself becoming **irascible**—I'm a real grouch."
- "I know my patients are improving when they become grumpy," said Dr. Imiri. "An **irascible** patient is on the road to recovery."

_a_ *Irascible* means   a. bad-tempered.   b. nervous.   c. depressed.

6 **loquacious**
(lō-kwā′shəs)
-adjective

- Kyle, who prefers to sleep or read on a long plane trip, says it never fails: he always ends up with a **loquacious** seat companion who wants to chat nonstop.
- The English have an amusing phrase for **loquacious** people: they say that such a person can "talk the hind leg off a donkey."

_a_ *Loquacious* means   a. talking too much.   b. aggressive.   c. irritable.

7 **obtuse**
(ŏb-tōōs′)
-adjective

- Harvey started to tell an offensive joke at the office holiday lunch. I kicked him under the table, hoping to shut him up, but he was too **obtuse** to get the message.
- Children can be remarkably **obtuse** about understanding school subjects like math, but their wits sharpen amazingly when they're learning a new video game.

_b_ *Obtuse* means   a. angry.   b. dimwitted.   c. thoughtful.

8 **opaque**
(ō-pāk′)
-adjective

- We attempted to follow the movie's complex plot, but the characters' motives and reactions remained **opaque**. We finally gave up trying to understand it.
- Articles on Einstein's theory of relativity usually start reassuringly, noting that there is no reason why it should be **opaque** to the ordinary reader. Then they proceed to make it even murkier.

_b_ *Opaque* means   a. fascinating.   b. difficult to understand.   c. improbable.

9 **paucity**
(pô′sĭ-tē)
-noun

- The speaker's high-flown language could not conceal his **paucity** of ideas. He had nothing meaningful to say.
- Serena wanted to get away from her small town because of its **paucity** of intellectual life. It didn't even have a library or a bookstore.

_c_ *Paucity* means   a. repetition.   b. conflict.   c. lack.

10 **recapitulate**
(rē-kə-pĭch′ə-lāt′)
-verb

- "To **recapitulate** what we told you on the phone," said Ms. Brown to the baby sitter, "we'll be home at eleven o'clock, and you can reach us at the Athens Café."
- Before an exam, Professor Martin always has a review session in which she **recapitulates** some of the most important material the class has studied.

_a_ *Recapitulate* means   a. to sum up.   b. to ignore.   c. to contradict.

Matching Words with Definitions

Following are definitions of the ten words. Clearly write or print each word next to its definition. The sentences above and on the previous page will help you decide on the meaning of each word.

1. _____apocryphal_____   Of doubtful authenticity; not genuine

2. _____desultory_____   Moving from one thing to another in an unplanned way

3. _____loquacious_____   Very talkative

4. _____affable_____   Friendly; easy to get along with

5. _____irascible_____   Easily angered; irritable

6. _____opaque_____   Difficult to understand or explain; obscure; incomprehensible

7. _____recapitulate_____   To summarize or repeat briefly

8. _____obtuse_____   Slow to understand; dull

9. _____paucity_____   A scarcity; an insufficiency

10. _____garbled_____   Mixed up to such an extent as to be misleading or incomprehensible

CAUTION: Do not go any further until you are sure the above answers are correct. Then you can use the definitions to help you in the following practices. Your goal is eventually to know the words well enough so that you don't need to check the definitions at all.

➤ *Sentence Check 1*

Using the answer line, complete each item below with the correct word from the box. Use each word once.

a. **affable**	b. **apocryphal**	c. **desultory**	d. **garbled**	e. **irascible**
f. **loquacious**	g. **obtuse**	h. **opaque**	i. **paucity**	j. **recapitulate**

_____apocryphal_____ 1. Many Spanish explorers in the 1700s lost their lives searching for the ___ "fountain of youth."

_____garbled_____ 2. After a stroke, some people partially lose their ability to speak. Until they recover, their words come out ___ and unclear.

_____loquacious_____ 3. People often become ___ after they've had too much to drink. Unfortunately, not only do they talk too much, but what they say doesn't make much sense.

_____opaque_____ 4. The words of the poem sounded lovely, but their meaning was ___. In fact, they seemed to mean nothing at all.

_____affable_____ 5. Although Ms. Henderson is a(n) ___ instructor, don't let her good nature make you think that she's a pushover. She's nice and friendly, but she's also a demanding teacher.

_____irascible_____ 6. Tom always seems to have a chip on his shoulder, and he gets angry over the slightest thing. I don't know what makes him so ___.

_____desultory_____ 7. Jon's paper was a(n) ___ effort. He started late and then just threw some disconnected notes together. No wonder he got a D.

_____paucity_____ 8. "We seem to have a(n) ___ of singers this year," said the chorus director. Only three students had shown up for the auditions.

_____recapitulate_____ 9. Before I left the office, my doctor ___(e)d her advice to me: "Get extra rest, drink plenty of fluids, and don't worry."

_____obtuse_____ 10. "I've been hinting that my birthday would be a good time for Jeff to give me an engagement ring," Jan said, "but he seems completely ___. I don't think he gets the point."

NOTE: Now check your answers to these questions by turning to page 175. Going over the answers carefully will help you prepare for the next two practices, for which answers are not given.

➤ *Sentence Check 2*

Using the answer lines, complete each item below with **two** words from the box. Use each word once.

_____irascible_____
_____affable_____ 1–2. Lara had heard that the famous pianist was ___ and brusque°, but when she asked him for his autograph, he was very ___. He signed her program and gave her a charming smile.

_____desultory_____
_____recapitulate_____ 3–4. The lecture was ___, with the speaker hopping confusingly from one topic to another. At the end, when he said, "To ___ . . . ," it was hard to imagine which of his unrelated, rambling points he might choose to repeat.

_____apocryphal_____ 5–6. Stephen Hawking's study *A Brief History of Time* has become famous
_____opaque_____   as the world's most widely unread best seller. That status may be ___,
                          but the book really is ___ to people who aren't physicists.

_____loquacious_____ 7–8. When Anya's ___ husband talks too much, she tries to stop him by
_____obtuse_____   raising her eyebrows and clearing her throat, but he's often too ___ to
                          take the hint.

_____garbled_____   9–10. The weather report on the radio was ___ by static. Was the announcer
_____paucity_____   predicting a "___" of rain, meaning none, or a "possibility" of rain,
                          meaning we might get drenched?

➤ *Final Check:* A Formula for Teaching

Here is a final opportunity for you to strengthen your knowledge of the ten words. First read the following
selection carefully. Then fill in each blank with a word from the box at the top of the previous page.
(Context clues will help you figure out which word goes in which blank.) Use each word once.

There is a famous formula for communicating ideas to people: *Step 1*—Tell them what you're
going to tell them. *Step 2*—Tell them. *Step 3*—Tell them what you've told them. The formula is
said to have been invented long ago by the Army. That story may be (1)_____apocryphal_____,
but it is probably authentic. The Army had to teach many things quickly to all kinds of fledgling°
recruits, and often it had a(n) (2)_____paucity_____ of good instructors: too few teachers,
with too little training. Moreover, the instructors were also of all kinds. Some were tough and
(3)_____irascible_____, with a quick temper and no patience for a learner who seemed slow or
(4)_____obtuse_____. Others were (5)_____affable_____ and (6)_____loquacious_____,
and although these good-natured, talkative men might teach well, they could also waste time on
incidental° matters or give confusing, (7)_____garbled_____ instructions. The three-step
formula would keep all teaching focused.

The formula is simple to use, and it is effective in writing as well as teaching. In step 1, you
announce what you intend to say: how to disassemble and reassemble a rifle, how to apply for a
job—whatever it is you want to communicate. In step 2, you say it. In step 3, you say it (briefly)
again: you (8)_____recapitulate_____ it as a summary and a reminder.

No formula is foolproof, but being cognizant° of this one will definitely help you avoid
planless, (9)_____desultory_____ writing and writing that is unclear, equivocal°, vague, or
(10)_____opaque_____. What worked for the Army can work for you.

Scores Sentence Check 2 _____%	Final Check _____%

Enter your scores above and in the vocabulary performance chart on the inside back cover of the book.

CHAPTER 9

accolade	edifice
assuage	gravity
cacophony	infraction
censure	profane
diatribe	somber

Ten Words in Context

In the space provided, write the letter of the meaning closest to that of each **boldfaced** word. Use the context of the sentences to help you figure out each word's meaning.

1 accolade
(ăk′ə-lād′)
-noun

- Many people rushed out to try the new Thai restaurant on Wayne Avenue after it received an **accolade** in a newspaper review.
- Although it is more than fifty years old, *Citizen Kane* continues to earn **accolades** as one of the best movies ever made.

_a_ *Accolade* means   a. an expression of approval.   b. an apology.   c. a greeting.

2 assuage
(ə-swāj′)
-verb

- My brother's apology helped to **assuage** my anger at him.
- The grief one feels over the loss of a loved one never fully goes away, but time does **assuage** the pain.

_c_ *Assuage* means   a. to increase.   b. to explain.   c. to make less severe.

3 cacophony
(kə-kŏf′ə-nē)
-noun

- I bought my daughter headphones so I would not have to listen to the **cacophony** that she calls music.
- When we listen to the **cacophony** of orchestra members tuning their instruments, it is hard to believe that they will soon produce a beautiful melody.

_b_ *Cacophony* means   a. harmony.   b. unpleasant noise.   c. silence.

4 censure
(sĕn′shər)
-noun

- When Aaron got his ear pierced, he had to deal not only with his father's **censure**, but also with his grandfather's sarcastic remarks and icy stares.
- Jodi's parents were strongly opposed to her engagement. Unable to stand up to their **censure**, she broke off with her boyfriend.

_a_ *Censure* means   a. disapproval.   b. tolerance.   c. neglect.

5 diatribe
(dī′ə-trīb′)
-noun

- A reporter covering a preacher's sermon sat through an hour-long **diatribe** about wickedness. He later wrote, "Mr. Blank spoke on sin. He was against it."
- The art professor, normally soft-spoken, subjected the class to a loud **diatribe** when he found that someone had spilled Coca-Cola on the slide projector.

_c_ *Diatribe* means   a. a calm discussion.   b. a physical attack.   c. a verbal attack.

6 edifice
(ĕd′ə-fĭs)
-noun

- On the college's hundredth anniversary, a plaque was put up in honor of the architect who had designed its first **edifice**, now the administration building.
- The company president decided to keep our present offices. "It would be nice to build a fine new **edifice**," she said, "but I'd rather spend the money on higher salaries and a better product."

_a_ *Edifice* means   a. a structure.   b. an expense.   c. a design.

7 **gravity**
(grăv′ĭ-tē)
-noun

- "I'm not sure you understand the **gravity** of the crimes you are accused of," the lawyer told his client. "Do you realize you could go to prison for a very long time?"
- The anxious parents waited in the emergency room to learn the **gravity** of their son's condition.

_b_ *Gravity* means   a. grief.   b. seriousness.   c. usefulness.

8 **infraction**
(ĭn-frăk′shən)
-noun

- The civil-rights leader Jesse Jackson was arrested as a college student for reading a book in a library. This was an **infraction** of the rules—the library was only for whites.
- Minor traffic **infractions**, such as parking in a no-parking zone, are punished by a fine, but a major violation such as drunk driving can put you in jail.

_c_ *Infraction* means   a. an exception.   b. an explanation.   c. a violation.

9 **profane**
(prō-fān′)
-adjective

- Karen refuses to use **profane** language. She says "Oh my gosh" instead of "Oh my God."
- Movies may get an "R" rating because of violence, sexual scenes, or **profane** language.

_a_ *Profane* means   a. lacking reverence.   b. ungrammatical.   c. hard to understand.

10 **somber**
(sŏm′bər)
-adjective

- When I saw the doctor's **somber** expression, I was afraid she had bad news for me.
- The dark colors and heavy furniture in the house give it a **somber** look—I think it would hard to laugh or even smile there.

_a_ *Somber* means   a. very serious.   b. cheerful.   c. restful.

Matching Words with Definitions

Following are definitions of the ten words. Clearly write or print each word next to its definition. The sentences above and on the previous page will help you decide on the meaning of each word.

1.	*accolade*	Praise
2.	*edifice*	A building, especially of large, imposing size
3.	*infraction*	A breaking of a law or rule
4.	*diatribe*	A bitter, abusively critical speech or piece of writing
5.	*assuage*	To relieve; lessen
6.	*somber*	Solemn; sad and depressing; melancholy
7.	*censure*	Blame; a rebuke
8.	*gravity*	Severity; weighty importance
9.	*profane*	Showing disrespect or contempt for sacred things
10.	*cacophony*	Harsh, discordant sounds

CAUTION: Do not go any further until you are sure the above answers are correct. Then you can use the definitions to help you in the following practices. Your goal is eventually to know the words well enough so that you don't need to check the definitions at all.

➢ *Sentence Check 1*

Using the answer line, complete each item below with the correct word from the box. Use each word once.

| a. **accolade** | b. **assuage** | c. **cacophony** | d. **censure** | e. **diatribe** |
| f. **edifice** | g. **gravity** | h. **infraction** | i. **profane** | j. **somber** |

___*profane*___ 1. If you use ___ language around your children, don't be surprised if they repeat it—not only at home but also in public, and at the most embarrassing moment possible.

___*cacophony*___ 2. The machinery at the factory is so noisy that all employees must wear earplugs to protect themselves from the ___.

___*accolade*___ 3. Judging from the ___s the new movie has been receiving, it's sure to be nominated for several Academy Awards.

___*assuage*___ 4. The Little League team lost the championship game, but the coach ___(e)d the kids' disappointment by taking them out for banana splits.

___*gravity*___ 5. "Because of the ___ of the international situation," announced the newscaster, "we will stay on the air with constant news updates throughout the evening."

___*censure*___ 6. The doctor received a letter of ___ from the local medical association for his careless treatment of a sick homeless man.

___*edifice*___ 7. Jessie's apartment house is an ornate ___ dating from the nineteenth century.

___*infraction*___ 8. Students are sent to detention for a variety of ___s, such as fighting, talking in class, or being disrespectful to a teacher.

___*somber*___ 9. On the day of the queen's funeral, the national radio station played nothing but the most ___ music.

___*diatribe*___ 10. The nutritionist lectured passionately on the folly of eating red meat. Tired and hungry after her ___, she went out to dinner at Steak 'n' Ribs.

NOTE: Now check your answers to these questions by turning to page 176. Going over the answers carefully will help you prepare for the next two practices, for which answers are not given.

➢ *Sentence Check 2*

Using the answer lines, complete each item below with **two** words from the box. Use each word once.

___*somber*___
___*edifice*___ 1–2. The old mansion is a(n) ___-looking ___, dark and dismal. It would be a perfect setting for a horror movie.

___*profane*___
___*gravity*___ 3–4. Not so long ago, using ___ language "in the presence of ladies" was an offense of considerable ___. In some places, swearing in public was even punishable by arrest.

_____infraction_____ 5–6. True, chewing gum is an ___ of school rules, but hardly anybody thinks
_____censure_____   such a minor offense is worthy of ___.

_____cacophony_____ 7–8. The rock concert was so heavily miked that the ___ gave Jade a
_____assuage_____   pounding headache. When she got home, she put on an ice pack to ___
                                the throbbing pain.

_____diatribe_____ 9–10. The senator's hackneyed° speech was one he had given a hundred
_____accolade_____   times. After a(n) ___ against graft and corruption, he ended with a(n)
                                ___ to motherhood, the flag, and apple pie.

➤ *Final Check:* The One-Room Schoolhouse

Here is a final opportunity for you to strengthen your knowledge of the ten words. First read the following selection carefully. Then fill in each blank with a word from the box at the top of the previous page. (Context clues will help you figure out which word goes in which blank.) Use each word once.

For many years, the one-room rural schoolhouse was part of the American scene. This tiny (1)_____edifice_____ did have only one room, where all the pupils, ranging in age from five or six to their teens, sat together with one teacher—a(n) (2)_____somber_____ young man or woman newly graduated from a "normal school" (a teacher-training institute) but trying to seem as serious and dignified as possible. School was held mostly in winter, because the pupils were farm children who had to work from spring planting until the harvest was in.

If you could go back in time and enter such a schoolhouse, you would hear a clamor°—a(n) (3)_____cacophony_____ of voices as many of the pupils, grouped by grades, "said" their lessons at once. The smallest children would be memorizing the alphabet; the oldest might be reciting some famous speech from the past, perhaps an eloquent° (4)_____diatribe_____ delivered in the Roman senate, where speakers used powerful, passionate language to vilify° their opponents. All of the students would be wearing long woolen underwear and writhing° and scratching to (5)_____assuage_____ the itching. A wood-burning stove heated the room, more or less. The "big boys" would keep the woodbox filled, or a pupil might have to fetch wood as a punishment for some (6)_____infraction_____ of a rule, such as (7)_____profane_____ language, although misbehavior of such (8)_____gravity_____ was rare.

These one-room schools held a special place in the hearts of Americans. In fact, at one time in American history, any political speech was sure to draw (9)_____censure_____ if it did not include a(n) (10)_____accolade_____ in praise of the "little red schoolhouse."

_____
| **Scores**   Sentence Check 2 _____%   Final Check _____% |
_____

Enter your scores above and in the vocabulary performance chart on the inside back cover of the book.

CHAPTER

10

blasphemy	incite
enmity	languish
erroneous	peruse
garner	recluse
heretic	renounce

Ten Words in Context

In the space provided, write the letter of the meaning closest to that of each **boldfaced** word. Use the context of the sentences to help you figure out each word's meaning.

1 blasphemy
(blăs′fə-mē)
-noun

- The Smiths have lived so long in Boston and think it is such a wonderful city that they feel it's almost **blasphemy** to consider living anywhere else.
- Some of the world's greatest thinkers, such as Copernicus, have been accused of **blasphemy** because their ideas challenged the teachings of the church.

_b_ *Blasphemy* means   a. physical violence.   b. an insult to something holy.   c. daydreaming.

2 enmity
(ĕn′mĭ-tē)
-noun

- After their divorce, Harry tried not to feel **enmity** toward his ex-wife. He knew that anger and bitterness would be bad for their children.
- Lila seems to feel real **enmity** toward our boss; she criticizes everything he says or does. The rest of us can't figure it out—we think he's a pretty decent guy.

_c_ *Enmity* means   a. admiration.   b. affection.   c. hostility.

3 erroneous
(ĭ-rō′nē-əs)
-adjective

- Many first-graders have the **erroneous** idea that their teacher lives at the school.
- Because the newspaper had printed an **erroneous** date and time for the community meeting, few people showed up when it actually took place.

_b_ *Erroneous* means   a. error-free.   b. in error.   c. original.

4 garner
(gär′nər)
-verb

- Once a year, our boss sends around a questionnaire to **garner** ideas from the employees about how to improve the company.
- When the payroll clerk gives us our checks, he always says, "Are you ready to **garner** the fruits of this week's labor?"

_a_ *Garner* means   a. to gather.   b. to distribute.   c. to reject.

5 heretic
(hĕr′ĭ-tĭk)
-noun

- Martin Luther was originally a Catholic priest, but when he began to disagree with the church's teachings, he was labeled a **heretic** and left the priesthood.
- People who believed that the world was round, not flat, were once considered lunatics or **heretics**.

_b_ *Heretic* means   a. a conservative.   b. a rebel.   c. a genius.

6 incite
(ĭn-sīt′)
-verb

- The smell of blood in the water can **incite** sharks to attack.
- No one knows what **incited** the usually gentle dog to bite the mail carrier.

_b_ *Incite* means   a. to prevent.   b. to urge on.   c. to forbid.

7 languish
(lăng′gwĭsh)
-verb

• Children who **languish** in institutions, such as orphanages, often improve dramatically when they are adopted into loving homes.
• Some people **languish** in the summer heat, but others love the hot weather and feel full of energy and strength.

_c_ *Languish* means   a. to thrive.   b. to misunderstand.   c. to do poorly.

8 peruse
(pə-rōōz′)
-verb

• When the list of people killed was posted after the plane crash, the passengers' anxious relatives **perused** it fearfully.
• To **peruse** a train timetable, with its tiny type and tinier footnotes, you need good eyesight and plenty of patience.

_a_ *Peruse* means   a. to inspect.   b. to glance at.   c. to explain.

9 recluse
(rĕk′lōōs′)
-noun

• Local old-timers tell stories about Wild Man Bill, a **recluse** who lived in a cave and came into town only once a year to buy supplies.
• While she was suffering from depression, Linda became a **recluse**, rarely leaving her home and not wanting to see even her closest friends.

_a_ *Recluse* means   a. a hermit.   b. a popular person.   c. a busy person.

10 renounce
(rə-nouns′)
-verb

• Great-Uncle Abe was a member of the Communist Party when he was a young man, but he soon decided to **renounce** communism and become a Republican.
• Edward VIII was briefly king of England, but he **renounced** his throne in 1936 in order to marry Wallis Simpson, a divorced commoner.

_c_ *Renounce* means   a. to announce.   b. to remember.   c. to disown.

Matching Words with Definitions

Following are definitions of the ten words. Clearly write or print each word next to its definition. The sentences above and on the previous page will help you decide on the meaning of each word.

1. _enmity_ — Hatred
2. _peruse_ — To examine; read with great care
3. _erroneous_ — Mistaken
4. _recluse_ — A person who leads a solitary life; someone who withdraws from others
5. _blasphemy_ — Disrespect toward something sacred or important; irreverence
6. _renounce_ — To reject; give up; cast off
7. _languish_ — To lose strength; fail in health; be weak
8. _incite_ — To stir up
9. _heretic_ — A person who holds unpopular or unaccepted beliefs; dissenter; nonconformist
10. _garner_ — To collect

CAUTION: Do not go any further until you are sure the above answers are correct. Then you can use the definitions to help you in the following practices. Your goal is eventually to know the words well enough so that you don't need to check the definitions at all.

➤ *Sentence Check 1*

Using the answer line, complete each item below with the correct word from the box. Use each word once.

a. **blasphemy**	b. **enmity**	c. **erroneous**	d. **garner**	e. **heretic**
f. **incite**	g. **languish**	h. **peruse**	i. **recluse**	j. **renounce**

_____*languish*_____ 1. The poet Elizabeth Barrett ___(e)d on her couch for years, a semi-invalid, until she fell in love with Robert Browning and found the strength to elope with him.

_____*blasphemy*_____ 2. A movie which portrayed Mary, the mother of Jesus, as a homeless drug addict was attacked by many church leaders, who said it was ___.

_____*renounce*_____ 3. "I am dropping out of the race," the candidate stated after losing badly in the primary election. "I have ___(e)d all hope of becoming president."

_____*enmity*_____ 4. My girlfriend and I decided to go our separate ways without ___. We both agreed that we didn't want to spend our lives together, but we intended to remain friends.

_____*erroneous*_____ 5. Obviously, Jamie has a(n) ___ idea of where babies come from. She announced that her father and mother had bought her in a toy store.

_____*garner*_____ 6. Since I ___ so many compliments every time I wear this sweater, I must conclude that it is a very good color for me.

_____*heretic*_____ 7. Some people have no respect for anyone else's religious beliefs. According to them, if you don't believe as they do, you are a(n) ___.

_____*incite*_____ 8. The appearance of a hawk in the sky ___(e)d the other birds to attack, fearing that it was there to kill and eat their young.

_____*recluse*_____ 9. Mrs. Sheridan rarely leaves her house. She is simply a harmless old ___, but the neighborhood kids think she must be a witch or a criminal.

_____*peruse*_____ 10. Irene ___(e)d the contract slowly, reading every bit of the fine print. She didn't want to sign anything that she might regret later.

NOTE: Now check your answers to these questions by turning to page 176. Going over the answers carefully will help you prepare for the next two practices, for which answers are not given.

➤ *Sentence Check 2*

Using the answer lines, complete each item below with **two** words from the box. Use each word once.

_____*blasphemy*_____
_____*erroneous*_____
1–2. Many people think that referring to Christmas as "Xmas" is ___, but this idea is ___. In fact, the X is the Greek symbol for Christ.

_____*garner*_____
_____*peruse*_____
3–4. By "skim reading," you can ___ a lot of information, but you do not ___ every word of a book or article. Instead, you run your eye quickly over the page to find what you need.

_____ renounce _____   5–6. It's hard to see how anyone can manage to ___ the world and become
_____ recluse _____   a(n) ___. How do hermits earn a living, for instance? And what
happens when they get called for jury duty?

_____ heretic _____   7–8. A(n) ___ is likely to earn the ___ of people who hold more
_____ enmity _____   conventional beliefs and do not like to have their ideas challenged.

_____ incite _____   9–10. The young revolutionary was sent to prison for trying to ___ a riot, but
_____ languish _____   he didn't ___ there. Instead, he read widely, kept a passionate,
eloquent° diary, and emerged ready to rebel again.

➤ _Final Check:_ Galileo

Here is a final opportunity for you to strengthen your knowledge of the ten words. First read the following selection carefully. Then fill in each blank with a word from the box at the top of the previous page. (Context clues will help you figure out which word goes in which blank.) Use each word once.

The great scientist Galileo Galilei, usually known simply as "Galileo," was a brilliant man who was far ahead of his time. But instead of earning accolades°, his discoveries earned him the (1)_____ enmity _____ of the powerful Catholic Church, which tried for years to silence him. Born in 1564 in Pisa, Italy, Galileo became a student of mathematics. He invented a device for making mathematical measurements and found the first dependable way of keeping time. But his true passion was kindled° when he learned of the first telescope, which had been invented in Holland. He (2)_____ peruse _____(e)d every piece of writing he could find about the new invention, then built much stronger telescopes and began to study the sky. The information he (3)_____ garner _____(e)d led to some startling realizations. He found out that several ideas taught as facts by the universities and the Church were (4)_____ erroneous _____. For instance, the Church insisted that the moon was a perfectly smooth ball. Galileo, however, could see that the moon's surface was dotted with mountains and valleys. More important, the Church insisted that the Earth was the center of the universe. Galileo's studies showed that the Earth and other planets rotated around the sun. To the Church, this idea was (5)_____ blasphemy _____: an infraction° of its own teachings. Church officials called the scientist a(n) (6)_____ heretic _____ for saying that the universe did not rotate around the Earth. They feared that Galileo's findings would (7)_____ incite _____ people to question the Church in other ways. Therefore, they demanded that Galileo (8)_____ renounce _____ his own findings. But he ignored their reproach° and continued to write about what he knew to be true. For the last eight years of his life, Galileo (9)_____ languish _____(e)d under "house arrest," forbidden to leave his own home. Even while he was forced to live as a(n) (10)_____ recluse _____, he continued to study and to write about his discoveries. More than three hundred years after his death, Galileo was pardoned by the Church, which finally admitted that he had been right all along.

Scores	Sentence Check 2 _____%	Final Check _____%

Enter your scores above and in the vocabulary performance chart on the inside back cover of the book.

UNIT TWO: Review

The box at the right lists twenty-five words from Unit Two. Using the clues at the bottom of the page, fill in these words to complete the puzzle that follows.

affable
apocryphal
appall
assuage
cognizant
contract
diatribe
duplicity
edifice
erroneous
expedient
garner
gravity
incite
loquacious
ludicrous
opaque
peruse
recapitulate
recluse
renounce
rescind
scrutinize
untenable
vilify

ACROSS

2. To examine
6. A bitter, abusively critical speech or piece of writing
9. A large building
10. Severity; weighty importance
12. Unable to be held or defended
14. Difficult to understand or explain
18. To summarize or repeat briefly
23. Friendly
24. To relieve or lessen

DOWN

1. Laughable
3. To reduce in size
4. Self-serving; convenient
5. To make abusive statements about
7. To stir up
8. Mistaken
11. A person who leads a solitary life
13. Very talkative
15. To examine; read with great care

16. Not genuine
17. Deliberate deceit
18. To reject or give up
19. Aware
20. To horrify
21. To collect
22. To take back

UNIT TWO: Test 1

PART A
Choose the word that best completes each item and write it in the space provided.

_____recluse_____ 1. The man next door is a(n) ___. He never emerges from his house, and no one has seen him for years.

    a. recluse   b. heretic   c. edifice   d. hindrance

_____renounce_____ 2. Our family decided to ___ television for one month. We wanted to see if we could survive without watching TV.

    a. recapitulate   b. garner   c. incite   d. renounce

_____apocryphal_____ 3. The famous story of George Washington and the cherry tree is ___. There is no evidence that it ever happened at all.

    a. somber   b. affable   c. lavish   d. apocryphal

_____vilify_____ 4. Instead of addressing the issues, many politicians just badmouth and ___ their opponents.

    a. recapitulate   b. rescind   c. vilify   d. assuage

_____infraction_____ 5. Having a pet is a(n) ___ of the rules in our dorm, so Curtis keeps his turtle hidden in a box under the bed.

    a. accolade   b. clamor   c. infraction   d. cacophony

_____profane_____ 6. In earlier times, many books used asterisks instead of actually printing ___ words. For instance, a character might say: "D*** you!" or "Oh, my G**!"

    a. erroneous   b. profane   c. ludicrous   d. affable

_____equivocal_____ 7. When children ask a parent for something, they hate to get the ___ answer, "We'll see."

    a. equivocal   b. loquacious   c. lavish   d. garbled

_____somber_____ 8. The ___ expression on the surgeon's face made it plain that the operation had gone badly.

    a. ludicrous   b. stagnant   c. affable   d. somber

_____peruse_____ 9. Derek knew that his great-grandmother's grave was somewhere in the old cemetery, but to find it he had to ___ the inscriptions on more than a hundred headstones.

    a. kindle   b. peruse   c. vilify   d. rescind

_____garbled_____ 10. Todd listened in frustration to his voice mail. Something had gone wrong with his recording machine, and all the messages were hopelessly ___.

    a. irascible   b. garbled   c. cognizant   d. lavish

_____incite_____ 11. It is a crime to ___ others to riot.

    a. assuage   b. scrutinize   c. incite   d. recapitulate

(Continues on next page)

_____hindrance_____ 12. There is an old saying, "He travels fastest who travels alone." It implies that a traveling companion can be a(n) ___.

a. hindrance   b. edifice   c. heretic   d. diatribe

_____garner_____ 13. The new movie was expected to ___ praise from the reviewers. But they hated it, and it was a flop.

a. rescind   b. renounce   c. scrutinize   d. garner

PART B
Write **C** if the italicized word is used **correctly**. Write **I** if the word is used **incorrectly**.

_C_ 14. Teenagers often peer into a mirror and *scrutinize* their reflections closely. It's as if they are trying to figure out who they are.

_I_ 15. The college admissions office says that there is a *paucity* of applicants this year. More than 6,000 people have applied for the 120 places in the freshman class.

_C_ 16. For kids, a birthday is a celebration. But when middle-aged people have a birthday, their friends don't know whether to congratulate them or *commiserate* with them.

_I_ 17. The boss was in a bad mood today. He was so *affable* and grouchy that no one wanted to cross his path.

_I_ 18. Francie's husband is so *loquacious* that she says she can hardly get two words out of him. They often sit through an entire meal in complete silence.

_C_ 19. For Valentine's Day, Wendell sent his girlfriend a box of matches, with a note: "I hope these will *kindle* a flame of love in your heart."

_I_ 20. "What a miserable performance!" said Holly as she left the theater. "I've never seen such terrible acting! The entire cast deserves an *accolade*."

_C_ 21. According to the Bible, "A soft answer turneth away wrath," meaning that a gentle reply will *assuage* someone's anger.

_C_ 22. Two TV sets, three CD players, and a radio were all blaring away at once. The *cacophony* was unbearable.

_C_ 23. The candidate found it *expedient* to get votes by promising a tax cut. As soon as he took office, though, he raised taxes.

_I_ 24. The city will *contract* significantly in the coming decade. The population is expected to double, and many new developments are being built on the outskirts.

_C_ 25. The notice posted on the door of the bank seemed to suggest *duplicity* on the part of the management. It read, "To serve you better, we are closing this branch."

Score (Number correct) _____ × 4 = _____ %

Enter your score above and in the vocabulary performance chart on the inside back cover of the book.

UNIT TWO: Test 2

PART A

Complete each item with a word from the box. Use each word once.

a. **appall**	b. **blasphemy**	c. **censure**	d. **cognizant**	e. **desultory**
f. **edifice**	g. **enmity**	h. **erroneous**	i. **gravity**	j. **heretic**
k. **irascible**	l. **languish**	m. **lavish**		

lavish   1. Dorrie and Ed celebrated their first anniversary with a(n) ___ dinner at the best restaurant in town.

gravity   2. The teenagers who were caught with a stolen car treated their arrest as a joke. They didn't seem to realize the ___ of the situation.

censure   3. The Greek poet Homer observed that "praise from a friend or ___ from a foe" doesn't carry much weight. But people pay attention when our own friends criticize us or our enemies praise us!

heretic   4. In the Middle Ages, when the church was all-powerful, a(n) ___ was likely to be burnt at the stake.

edifice   5. City Hall was once the tallest ___ in town, but now it is dwarfed by the huge new skyscrapers all around it.

enmity   6. The ___ between the two nations has existed for centuries. They have gone to war against each other so often that everyone has lost count.

appall   7. Conditions in the hospital ___ the staff, the patients, and visitors. The hospital building is old-fashioned, overcrowded, run-down, and dirty.

cognizant   8. Elise is getting very deaf, but she doesn't seem to be ___ of her impairment. She says, "I would hear perfectly well if people spoke up instead of always mumbling!"

erroneous   9. Many people think that if you toss a coin and get ten heads in a row, the next toss is sure to be tails, but this idea is ___. On any toss, heads and tails are equally likely.

irascible   10. Dad is a(n) ___ man. He continually loses his temper.

languish   11. Flat-faced dogs tend to ___ in very hot weather. They suffer so much because they do not have a long enough nose to cool the air they inhale.

desultory   12. When Rita lost her wristwatch, she made only a(n) ___ effort to find it, because she had never really liked it much.

blasphemy   13. Some mild expressions, such as "gosh-darn it," "golly," and "gee," developed as a substitute for stronger words that would be taken as ___.

(Continues on next page)

PART B

Write **C** if the italicized word is used **correctly**. Write **I** if the word is used **incorrectly**.

_I_ 14. When it comes to mathematics, Mei Lin is really *obtuse*. She can do complicated calculations in her head, and she can always solve the toughest problems.

_C_ 15. In a textbook, the purpose of chapter summaries is to *recapitulate* the main points and the most important concepts.

_I_ 16. When Leni asked her father for a car, his response was a *diatribe*. He said, "Okay."

_I_ 17. Beata's wedding gown was the most beautiful I've ever seen. She looked *ludicrous*.

_I_ 18. The classroom was completely silent as Glenn walked forward to give his speech. The *clamor* made him feel even more nervous.

_I_ 19. Swollen by melting snow and spring rains, the *stagnant* brook tumbled and rushed along.

_C_ 20. To give its series of texts a *uniform* appearance, the publisher designed matching covers for all the books.

_C_ 21. Mary takes a *negligent* attitude toward her job. She arrives late and leaves early, her desk is a mess, and she is always behind in her work.

_I_ 22. The employees asked the company to *rescind* its tradition of giving a year-end bonus. They wanted to make sure the bonuses would continue in the future.

_C_ 23. Andy sent me a letter in code. It was completely *opaque* to me.

_C_ 24. Jonas is *irresolute* about whether to major in English or history. He just can't make up his mind.

_I_ 25. The candidate said she favored "clean government, better schools, and good community relations." No one could disagree with any of that, so she was in an *untenable* position.

> *Score*   (Number correct) _____ × 4 = _____ %

Enter your score above and in the vocabulary performance chart on the inside back cover of the book.

UNIT TWO: Test 3

In the space provided, write the letter of the choice that is most nearly the **same** in meaning as the **boldfaced** word.

_b_   1. **accolade**   **a)** condemnation   **b)** commendation   **c)** conspiracy   **d)** commitment

_a_   2. **apocryphal**   **a)** fictitious   **b)** proven   **c)** uninteresting   **d)** applicable

_a_   3. **appall**   **a)** to horrify   **b)** to please   **c)** to appeal to   **d)** to defend

_d_   4. **blasphemy**   **a)** silence   **b)** curiosity   **c)** piousness   **d)** contempt

_a_   5. **commiserate**   **a)** to sympathize   **b)** to confer   **c)** to exaggerate   **d)** to observe

_a_   6. **diatribe**   **a)** a denunciation   **b)** a diary   **c)** a diagram   **d)** harmony

_d_   7. **duplicity**   **a)** honesty   **b)** hardship   **c)** friendship   **d)** trickery

_b_   8. **edifice**   **a)** something educational   **b)** something constructed   **c)** an expense   **d)** a gift

_a_   9. **equivocal**   **a)** noncommittal   **b)** nonsensical   **c)** nongrammatical   **d)** nonverbal

_c_   10. **garbled**   **a)** boring   **b)** fascinating   **c)** muddled   **d)** essential

_c_   11. **gravity**   **a)** vagueness   **b)** deceptiveness   **c)** seriousness   **d)** duration

_b_   12. **heretic**   **a)** a herald   **b)** a nonconformist   **c)** an heir   **d)** a nominee

_a_   13. **incite**   **a)** to arouse   **b)** to understand   **c)** to misunderstand   **d)** to injure

_a_   14. **infraction**   **a)** an offense   **b)** an insight   **c)** a rule   **d)** an illness

_c_   15. **irascible**   **a)** irrelevant   **b)** warm-hearted   **c)** hot-tempered   **d)** stingy

_d_   16. **kindle**   **a)** to discourage   **b)** to forbid   **c)** to ignore   **d)** to ignite

_c_   17. **ludicrous**   **a)** unnoticeable   **b)** heartbreaking   **c)** absurd   **d)** terrifying

_a_   18. **peruse**   **a)** to read   **b)** to write   **c)** to say   **d)** to hear

_b_   19. **recapitulate**   **a)** to introduce   **b)** to state again   **c)** to hint   **d)** to conceal

_b_   20. **recluse**   **a)** a lawbreaker   **b)** a loner   **c)** a leader   **d)** a learner

_d_   21. **renounce**   **a)** to search for   **b)** to desire   **c)** to possess   **d)** to give up

_d_   22. **rescind**   **a)** to repeat   **b)** to recognize   **c)** to reveal   **d)** to cancel

_d_   23. **scrutinize**   **a)** to prevent   **b)** to forget   **c)** to close one's eyes to   **d)** to look at closely

_b_   24. **untenable**   **a)** unforgettable   **b)** insupportable   **c)** unforeseeable   **d)** undeniable

_b_   25. **vilify**   **a)** to admire   **b)** to malign   **c)** to trust   **d)** to help

(Continues on next page)

PART B: Antonyms

In the space provided, write the letter of the choice that is most nearly the **opposite** in meaning to the **boldfaced** word.

_c_ 26. **affable** a) affordable b) rich c) unfriendly d) unqualified

_c_ 27. **assuage** a) to assign b) to assert c) to make worse d) to make fun of

_a_ 28. **cacophony** a) harmony b) conflict c) noise d) confusion

_a_ 29. **censure** a) praise b) ridicule c) disgust d) anger

_d_ 30. **clamor** a) intensity b) stress c) conflict d) silence

_b_ 31. **cognizant** a) intelligent b) ignorant c) informed d) insightful

_a_ 32. **contract** a) to expand b) to reduce c) to watch d) to wait for

_c_ 33. **desultory** a) unfortunate b) fortunate c) purposeful d) random

_c_ 34. **enmity** a) hope b) mistrust c) friendship d) strife

_b_ 35. **erroneous** a) interesting b) correct c) incomplete d) deceptive

_b_ 36. **expedient** a) selfish b) unselfish c) planned d) accidental

_c_ 37. **garner** a) to precede b) to follow c) to lose d) to gain

_b_ 38. **hindrance** a) a burden b) a help c) a nuisance d) a mystery

_c_ 39. **irresolute** a) puzzled b) hopeful c) certain d) fearful

_c_ 40. **languish** a) to search b) to find c) to thrive d) to die

_d_ 41. **lavish** a) generous b) expensive c) permanent d) stingy

_b_ 42. **loquacious** a) enthusiastic b) silent c) insane d) sane

_a_ 43. **negligent** a) conscientious b) sloppy c) forgetful d) successful

_a_ 44. **obtuse** a) clever b) thickheaded c) obese d) obedient

_c_ 45. **opaque** a) opposite b) similar to c) clear d) murky

_c_ 46. **paucity** a) health b) absence c) abundance d) shortage

_c_ 47. **profane** a) probable b) improbable c) reverent d) outraged

_a_ 48. **somber** a) cheerful b) cheerless c) solemn d) sudden

_b_ 49. **stagnant** a) in memory b) in motion c) in view d) invisible

_b_ 50. **uniform** a) similar b) varying c) unchanging d) wordy

Score   (Number correct) _____ × 2 = _____%

Enter your score above and in the vocabulary performance chart on the inside back cover of the book.

Unit Three

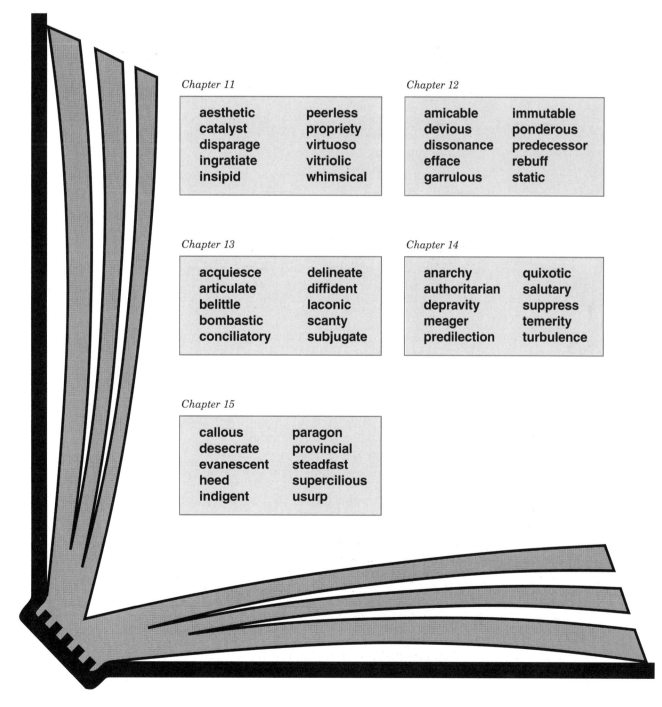

Chapter 11

aesthetic	peerless
catalyst	propriety
disparage	virtuoso
ingratiate	vitriolic
insipid	whimsical

Chapter 12

amicable	immutable
devious	ponderous
dissonance	predecessor
efface	rebuff
garrulous	static

Chapter 13

acquiesce	delineate
articulate	diffident
belittle	laconic
bombastic	scanty
conciliatory	subjugate

Chapter 14

anarchy	quixotic
authoritarian	salutary
depravity	suppress
meager	temerity
predilection	turbulence

Chapter 15

callous	paragon
desecrate	provincial
evanescent	steadfast
heed	supercilious
indigent	usurp

aesthetic	peerless
catalyst	propriety
disparage	virtuoso
ingratiate	vitriolic
insipid	whimsical

Ten Words in Context

In the space provided, write the letter of the meaning closest to that of each **boldfaced** word. Use the context of the sentences to help you figure out each word's meaning.

1 **aesthetic**
(ĕs-thĕt′ĭk)
-*adjective*

- A vegetable garden not only is practical but has **aesthetic** value, too; the shining green peppers, red tomatoes, and purple eggplants are a beautiful sight.
- Your green plaid pants and orange flowered shirt do not make a very **aesthetic** combination.

  a *Aesthetic* means   a. pleasing to the senses.   b. moral.   c. financial.

2 **catalyst**
(kăt′l-ĭst)
-*noun*

- World War II was a **catalyst** for social change. When women took factory jobs, filling in for men who were away fighting, the concept of "women's work" was permanently expanded.
- Seeing a friend die of an overdose was a **catalyst** in Herbert's decision to stop abusing drugs.

  a *Catalyst* means   a. something that   b. something that   c. something that
  or speeds up a process.   prevents a process.   is harmful.

3 **disparage**
(dĭ-spăr′ĭj)
-*verb*

- An ironclad rule of politics used to be "Never **disparage** anyone in your party." For the sake of unity, party members weren't supposed to criticize each other.
- "I hate to be the one to **disparage** your so-called best friend," Shawna told Carol, "but I happen to know she is trying to break up your marriage."

  b *Disparage* means   a. to discourage.   b. to speak ill of.   c. to ignore.

4 **ingratiate**
(ĭn-grā′shē-āt′)
-*verb*

- When he was stopped for speeding, Luke tried hard to **ingratiate** himself with the officer by complimenting the police department, but he got a ticket anyway.
- It's sickening the way Howie **ingratiates** herself with the boss by agreeing with her about every little thing and telling her how wonderful she is.

  b *Ingratiate* means   a. to argue with someone.   b. to flatter someone.   c. to make demands.

5 **insipid**
(ĭn-sĭp′ĭd)
-*adjective*

- A French novelist once said, "A story without love is like beef without mustard—an **insipid** dish."
- The cast tried hard to put some sparkle and zest into the play, but the script was so pointless and **insipid** that their efforts fell flat.

  c *Insipid* means   a. disgusting.   b. inspiring.   c. boring.

6 **peerless**
(pîr′lĭs)
-*adjective*

- "She's **peerless**," the singer's fans insisted. "No one can compete with her."
- When the beloved teacher retired, her students presented her with a plaque: "To a **peerless** professor and a matchless friend."

  a *Peerless* means   a. without an equal.   b. critical.   c. perceptive.

7 **propriety**
(prə-prī′ĭ-tē)
-noun

- Helen, a newspaper reporter, is concerned about the **propriety** of her writing stories about the town council when her husband is a member of the council.
- People questioned the **propriety** of the woman's beginning to date only two weeks after her husband had been killed.

b *Propriety* means   a. opportunity.   b. correctness.   c. cost.

8 **virtuoso**
(vûr′chōō-ō′sō)
-noun

- Woody Allen has a funny line about a woman who gave up her lifetime ambition of becoming a violin **virtuoso** when she realized she would have to study the violin.
- The pianist was disappointed by the review of his performance: "He is competent, but no **virtuoso**—that spark of genius is missing."

c *Virtuoso* means   a. a moral person.   b. a repairperson.   c. a master performer.

9 **vitriolic**
(vĭt′rē-ŏl′ĭk)
-adjective

- Some people who call in to radio talk shows make shockingly **vitriolic** remarks; they seem to be using the show as an outlet for their most bitter, vicious thoughts.
- A famous piece of advice: When you are furious at someone, write him or her a **vitriolic** letter, using the ugliest, most cutting words you can find. Read it over to make sure it's as hateful as you want. Then tear it up and throw it away.

b *Vitriolic* means   a. debatable.   b. hurtful.   c. insane.

10 **whimsical**
(wĭm′zĭ-kəl)
-adjective

- Toni and Ed's decision to marry seemed **whimsical**. They had known each other only briefly, and to tell the truth, they didn't even like each other that much.
- Some of the policies at our school seem pointless and **whimsical**. For example, students are allowed to audit courses in science but not in math, the library is closed every other Tuesday, and coffee is not served in the dining hall.

a *Whimsical* means   a. impulsive.   b. appropriate.   c. frightening.

Matching Words with Definitions

Following are definitions of the ten words. Clearly write or print each word next to its definition. The sentences above and on the previous page will help you decide on the meaning of each word.

1.	*aesthetic*	Having a sense of beauty; giving an impression of beauty
2.	*ingratiate*	To charm; win favor; make oneself agreeable
3.	*vitriolic*	Sharply critical; harsh; biting
4.	*virtuoso*	An expert, particularly in the arts
5.	*catalyst*	A person or thing that brings about change
6.	*propriety*	Appropriateness
7.	*disparage*	To criticize; put down
8.	*insipid*	Flat; tasteless; unexciting
9.	*peerless*	So superior as to be without equal; incomparable; unsurpassed
10.	*whimsical*	Fanciful; odd; arbitrary

CAUTION: Do not go any further until you are sure the above answers are correct. Then you can use the definitions to help you in the following practices. Your goal is eventually to know the words well enough so that you don't need to check the definitions at all.

➤ *Sentence Check 1*

Using the answer line, complete each item below with the correct word from the box. Use each word once.

a. **aesthetic**	b. **catalyst**	c. **disparage**	d. **ingratiate**	e. **insipid**
f. **peerless**	g. **propriety**	h. **virtuoso**	i. **vitriolic**	j. **whimsical**

_____*virtuoso*_____ 1. Mozart was considered a(n) ___ at an early age: he was performing before royalty by age six.

_____*vitriolic*_____ 2. Professor Lattimore is an unpopular teacher because his criticism is so ___. He is not only harsh about students' work but is also highly critical of students personally.

_____*insipid*_____ 3. Though I like tea, I find it ___ without lemon to liven it up.

_____*ingratiate*_____ 4. At first, Dad said we couldn't keep the little dog, but then Muffin ___(ed) herself by sitting down in front of him and politely offering her paw.

_____*disparage*_____ 5. "Don't ___ the instructor for failing you," my roommate said, "Instead, I'd suggest you stop bad-mouthing her and work harder." It was good advice.

_____*peerless*_____ 6. "Well, I see that our ___ ball club has been beaten again," Matt said sarcastically, as the baseball team lost its ninth game in a row.

_____*propriety*_____ 7. I thought my grandmother's sense of ___ would be offended by my sister's plan to be married barefoot in a meadow, but Grandma loved the idea.

_____*catalyst*_____ 8. The ___ that started World War I was the assassination of an Austrian archduke—after that, fighting broke out among many factions.

_____*aesthetic*_____ 9. I've asked Sylvia to help me redecorate my apartment, because she has the best ___ know-how of all my friends.

_____*whimsical*_____ 10. Getting a pet should not be a(n) ___, spur-of-the-moment decision. Owning a dog or cat is a long-term commitment that requires thought and planning.

NOTE: Now check your answers to these questions by turning to page 176. Going over the answers carefully will help you prepare for the next two practices, for which answers are not given.

➤ *Sentence Check 2*

Using the answer lines, complete each item below with **two** words from the box. Use each word once.

_____*disparage*_____
_____*aesthetic*_____ 1–2. "It pains me to ___ the new library," wrote the architecture critic, "but the building is needlessly ugly. All ___ considerations have been completely ignored."

_____*virtuoso*_____
_____*peerless*_____ 3–4. The composer Franz Liszt was also a piano ___, a master performer who was considered ___: no other musician of his day had such amazing technique.

_____*whimsical*_____
_____*catalyst*_____ 5–6. "Our school has too many odd, ___ rules," Reba said. "Elect me student body president, and I promise to be a(n) ___ for change. I'll work hard to rescind° these quirky regulations."

_____ingratiate_____
_____propriety_____
7–8. At work, Edgar tries to ___ himself with his supervisors by behaving with the utmost ___. He intends to win their approval by the correctness of his appearance and manners.

_____vitriolic_____
_____insipid_____
9–10. The review of the new restaurant was ___. "Most of the food is ___, and what isn't tasteless is disgusting," it read. "The waiters belong in a zoo. The decor is ludicrous°—it looks like something left over from a horror movie."

➤ *Final Check:* Isadora Duncan

Here is a final opportunity for you to strengthen your knowledge of the ten words. First read the following selection carefully. Then fill in each blank with a word from the box at the top of the previous page. (Context clues will help you figure out which word goes in which blank.) Use each word once.

Isadora Duncan was a famous dancer born in 1877. She was known for her dramatic personality as well as her revolutionary way of dancing. She rejected the strict style of ballet, considering it boring and (1)_____insipid_____. She had an affinity° for dance that was naturally (2)_____aesthetic_____, capturing the beauty of the wind, flowers, and stars. To express that idea, she danced barefoot, wearing voluminous° fluttering silk scarves. Her dancing was (3)_____whimsical_____, based on the inspiration of the moment, and was never quite the same twice. In her private life, too, Duncan cared little for most people's ideas of (4)_____propriety_____; she had two children before marrying. When she did marry, she chose a Russian poet seventeen years younger than she.

At first, audiences did not know what to make of Duncan's unusual dance style. The critics' reviews were (5)_____vitriolic_____. They (6)_____disparage_____(e)d and vilified° Duncan, calling her a joke and a fake. But her talent and charm enabled her to (7)_____ingratiate_____ herself with the public. She was eventually seen as a(n) (8)_____virtuoso_____ of her own free-spirited style.

In 1927, when Duncan was living in France, she admired a sports car driven by a guest. He offered to take her for a drive. She agreed. Wrapping one of her trademark long silk scarves around her neck, she called to the others, "Goodbye, my friends, I am off to glory!" The car started off. The end of Duncan's scarf began tangled in one of its wheels, and Duncan was strangled.

In her lifetime, Duncan was regarded as a(n) (9)_____peerless_____ dancer with an unusual style. Today she is remembered as a(n) (10)_____catalyst_____ for many of the new developments in modern dance.

**Scores**   Sentence Check 2 _____%   Final Check _____%

Enter your scores above and in the vocabulary performance chart on the inside back cover of the book.

amicable	immutable
devious	ponderous
dissonance	predecessor
efface	rebuff
garrulous	static

Ten Words in Context

In the space provided, write the letter of the meaning closest to that of each **boldfaced** word. Use the context of the sentences to help you figure out each word's meaning.

1 **amicable**
(ăm′ĭ-kə-bəl)
-adjective

- Who says that cats and dogs are enemies? Our dog and two cats live together in the most **amicable** way.
- Because the two countries had always maintained **amicable** relations, they were able to settle their border dispute through friendly talks.

b *Amicable* means   a. hostile.   b. peaceable.   c. cute.

2 **devious**
(dē′vē-əs)
-adjective

- Beware of **devious** advertising. A common trick is a sign that says in huge letters "PRICES SLASHED 75 PERCENT" and then in tiny type "on selected items only."
- Aimee's mother didn't want to ask her right out if she and her boyfriend were going to get married, so she used more **devious** wording: "Do you and Dave have any plans for the future?"

c *Devious* means   a. obvious.   b. rude.   c. sneaky.

3 **dissonance**
(dĭs′ə-nəns)
-noun

- Over time, people's ideas of **dissonance** in music change. Chords that sounded harsh and grating to previous generations now seem pleasant to us.
- Kids like to create **dissonance** on a piano by using both arms to slam down all the keys at once.

a *Dissonance* means   a. an unpleasant sound.   b. a rare sound.   c. an everyday sound.

4 **efface**
(ĭ-fās′)
-verb

- When Joanie and Gary broke up, she said, "I've thrown away all his letters and photographs. Now I wish I could **efface** my memories."
- Last Thanksgiving, the turkey slid off its platter onto the dining-room rug. We've scrubbed and rubbed, but we haven't been able to **efface** the stain completely.

b *Efface* means   a. to face up to.   b. to remove all traces of.   c. to try to preserve.

5 **garrulous**
(găr′ə-ləs)
-adjective

- I do get annoyed at **garrulous** relatives and friends who telephone during dinner and keep talking and talking while my meal gets cold.
- Some people become quiet and depressed when they drink alcohol, while others become overly lively, merry, and **garrulous**.

a *Garrulous* means   a. long-winded.   b. short-tempered.   c. open-minded.

6 **immutable**
(ĭ-myōō′tə-bəl)
-adjective

- Does Mr. Madison ever smile? The frown on his face seems **immutable**.
- For years, my aunt has followed an **immutable** schedule that includes getting up at 6:30 a.m., doing twenty minutes of exercise, and having a soft-boiled egg and toast for breakfast.

a *Immutable* means   a. changeless.   b. flawless.   c. fearless.

7 ponderous
(pŏn′dər-əs)
-*adjective*

- Ads for the circus always used to describe the elephants as "**ponderous** pachyderms."
- There used to be a theory that dinosaurs became extinct because they grew too large for their own good. They were so huge and **ponderous** that they could hardly move.

c *Ponderous* means   a. living in ponds.   b. delicate.   c. weighty.

8 predecessor
(prĕd′ĭ-sĕs′ər)
-*noun*

- It won't be easy to get used to my new boss. She seems quiet, formal, and serious, whereas her **predecessor** was easygoing and loved to laugh.
- When they moved into their new apartment, the Martins had to get rid of a lot of junk that their **predecessors** had left behind.

a *Predecessor* means   a. someone earlier.   b. someone later.   c. someone who predicts.

9 rebuff
(rĭ-bŭf′)
-*verb*

- Elyse's boss often puts his arm around her when he's talking to her. She doesn't like this, but she's afraid to **rebuff** him.
- The unfriendly cat **rebuffed** my attempts to pet him. He walked away without a backward glance.

a *Rebuff* means   a. to treat coldly.   b. to welcome warmly.   c. to reward.

10 static
(stăt′ĭk)
-*adjective*

- "This scene is too **static**," the director said to the actors. "It's dead. We've got to get some action into it."
- A still life, as the name suggests, is a **static** painting: it might show, for example, a bowl of apples. By contrast, an action painting shows a dramatic scene full of movement.

b *Static* means   a. silent.   b. stationary.   c. stressful.

Matching Words with Definitions

Following are definitions of the ten words. Clearly write or print each word next to its definition. The sentences above and on the previous page will help you decide on the meaning of each word.

1. _____ *rebuff* _____   To reject bluntly; snub
2. _____ *devious* _____   Not straightforward; tricky; shifty
3. _____ *immutable* _____   Never changing or varying
4. _____ *ponderous* _____   Heavy, labored; massive; lacking grace
5. _____ *predecessor* _____   A person who comes before another in time
6. _____ *amicable* _____   Friendly; showing goodwill
7. _____ *static* _____   Not moving or progressing; still
8. _____ *efface* _____   To wipe out; erase
9. _____ *dissonance* _____   A harsh, disagreeable combination of sounds
10. _____ *garrulous* _____   Talkative to an annoying degree

CAUTION: Do not go any further until you are sure the above answers are correct. Then you can use the definitions to help you in the following practices. Your goal is eventually to know the words well enough so that you don't need to check the definitions at all.

➤ *Sentence Check 1*

Using the answer line, complete each item below with the correct word from the box. Use each word once.

a. **amicable**	b. **devious**	c. **dissonance**	d. **efface**	e. **garrulous**
f. **immutable**	g. **ponderous**	h. **predecessor**	i. **rebuff**	j. **static**

_____*rebuff*_____   1. Zach quickly ___s anyone who calls to try to sell him something or raise funds. "I'm not interested," he says, and hangs up.

_____*devious*_____   2. Do you think surprise quizzes are a useful teaching tool? Or you you consider them ___ and unfair?

_____*efface*_____   3. The hardest of all stains to ___ is blueberry. If you drop blueberry pie on a white shirt, you'll have to throw the shirt away or dye it blue.

_____*garrulous*_____   4. Whenever I visit my ___ Uncle Hal, I tell him I have another appointment in an hour. Otherwise, I would be forced to sit and listen to him all day.

_____*ponderous*_____   5. Everyone dreads the principal's speeches. Her slow, labored way of talking and long pauses make even a short talk ___.

_____*dissonance*_____   6. As I walked through the hall of the music school, I could hear three instrumental classes in three rooms playing three different pieces all at once. My ears aching from this ___, I fled into the street.

_____*amicable*_____   7. Wanting to be on ___ terms with her new neighbors, Meg brought them a homemade pie to welcome them to the neighborhood.

_____*static*_____   8. Did you ever wonder why people in old photographs look frozen in stiff, ___ poses? It's because they could not move while the film was being exposed—a process that took a long time.

_____*predecessor*_____   9. Although the car Meg just bought is four years old, it looks like new. Whoever was her ___ in owning it took very good care of it.

_____*immutable*_____   10. The stars may look unchanging, but in fact they are not ___. Stars are born, and eventually die, over billions of years.

NOTE: Now check your answers to these questions by turning to page 176. Going over the answers carefully will help you prepare for the next two practices, for which answers are not given.

➤ *Sentence Check 2*

Using the answer lines, complete each item below with **two** words from the box. Use each word once.

_____*amicable*_____
_____*efface*_____   1–2. Marcy and Jack worked out a(n) ___ divorce. But the goodwill they put into the final settlement could not ___ the memory of the months of anger that came before it.

_____*immutable*_____
_____*static*_____   3–4. It's strange but true: one ___, constant law of nature is that nothing is ever constant or ___—everything changes all the time.

_____*devious*_____
_____*predecessor*_____   5–6. When she started her new job, Robin tried in ___ ways to find out why her ___ had left. She didn't want to ask directly if he had quit or been fired.

_____*ponderous*_____   7–8. Elaine and Jeff couldn't agree on what kind of art to put in their living
_____*rebuff*_____   room. She rejected a large piece of sculpture he had chosen, saying it was
                                    too ___, and he ___(e)d her when she suggested an abstract painting.

_____*garrulous*_____   9–10. The concert was awful. The band was too loud and badly out of tune—
_____*dissonance*_____   creating cacophony°, not music. In addition, a(n) ___ person beside me
                                    kept up an incessant° stream of conversation, adding to the general ___.

➤ *Final Check:* Miles Standish

Here is a final opportunity for you to strengthen your knowledge of the ten words. First read the following selection carefully. Then fill in each blank with a word from the box at the top of the previous page. (Context clues will help you figure out which word goes in which blank.) Use each word once.

"If you want something done right, do it yourself." Such is the message of "The Courtship of Miles Standish," a poem by one of America's most famous poets, Henry Wadsworth Longfellow.

Now, the first thing you need to know about "Miles Standish" is that the story is apocryphal°. Miles Standish was a real person, and so were John Alden and Priscilla Mullins, the other two principal characters in the poem. And John and Priscilla got married, as the poem says, and had fifteen children, which it doesn't say. But as far as we know, Miles's "courtship" was the product of Longfellow's imagination. Nevertheless, the poem tells a good story. This is how it goes:

Miles Standish, a scarred veteran of many battles, was the leader of the Puritan colony in Plymouth, Massachusetts. As the poem opens, Miles shares a secret with his young friend John Alden. Miles is in love with Priscilla. Priscilla's (1)_____*predecessor*_____ in Miles's heart was his wife, Rose, who died soon after the Pilgrims landed in the New World. Since Rose's death, Miles says, his life has been dull and (2)_____*static*_____. He asks John to do him a favor. "Go to the damsel Priscilla, the loveliest maiden of Plymouth, / Say that a blunt old Captain, a man not of words but of actions, / Offers his hand and his heart, the hand and heart of a soldier."

The problem is that unbeknownst to Miles Standish, John is also in love with Priscilla. Horrified, he tries to get out of the errand, suggesting that Miles speak to Priscilla himself. But Miles's determination is (3)_____*immutable*_____. Also, he says he is a(n) (4)_____*ponderous*_____ speaker, not graceful and eloquent° like John. He fears he would either say too little or be too (5)_____*garrulous*_____ to win her favor. And while he is a brave man in battle, he says, he fears Priscilla will (6)_____*rebuff*_____ his offer.

Out of a sense of duty and friendship, John goes to Priscilla and blurts out Miles Standish's offer of marriage. Priscilla is first amazed, then indignant. "If the great Captain of Plymouth is so very eager to wed me, / Why does he not come himself, and take the trouble to woo me?" John tries to explain that the Captain is a very busy man, but Priscilla's irritation is not assuaged°. A man who was *really* in love, she tells John, would find time to win her heart. John stumbles on, describing all the Captain's good qualities: his courage, his skill, his honor. As he talks, he seems to (7)_____*efface*_____ his own feelings and think only of his friend. To Priscilla, who has been hoping to hear John's own declaration of love, his words are (8)_____*dissonance*_____, not sweet music. Finally she boldly interrupts to say, "Why don't you speak for yourself, John?"

The rest of the poem describes how John returns to Miles and tells him the truth. Initially Standish is furious, believing that John has been (9)_____*devious*_____, going behind his back to win the girl. But he maintains his (10)_____*amicable*_____ relationship with John and Priscilla. He comes to their wedding and gives them his blessing. And perhaps he has learned that when it comes to romancing a woman, it's best to do the job yourself!

Scores	Sentence Check 2 _____%	Final Check _____%

Enter your scores above and in the vocabulary performance chart on the inside back cover of the book.

CHAPTER

13

acquiesce	delineate
articulate	diffident
belittle	laconic
bombastic	scanty
conciliatory	subjugate

Ten Words in Context

In the space provided, write the letter of the meaning closest to that of each **boldfaced** word. Use the context of the sentences to help you figure out each word's meaning.

1 **acquiesce**
(ăk′wē-ĕs′)
-verb

- When the reporter was ordered to reveal who had given her information about a gambling ring, she had to decide whether to **acquiesce** or go to jail.
- The students asked if they could use their notes during the test. They were pleased when the teacher **acquiesced**.

_a_ *Acquiesce* means   a. to consent.   b. to conquer.   c. to refuse.

2 **articulate**
(är-tĭk′yə-lĭt)
-adjective

- John Kennedy was known as one of our most **articulate** presidents. He expressed himself beautifully, whether he was giving a speech or just joking with reporters.
- Molly is unusually **articulate** for a three-year-old. She always speaks in complete sentences and uses a quite grown-up vocabulary.

_b_ *Articulate* means   a. artificial.   b. using words effectively.   c. quiet.

3 **belittle**
(bĭ-lĭt′l)
-verb

- One unpleasant little girl at the daycare center constantly **belittles** the other children, saying things like, "Can't your parents buy you nicer clothes than that?"
- It is rude to accept an invitation to dinner and then **belittle** your host's cooking.

_c_ *Belittle* means   a. to praise.   b. to emphasize.   c. to put down.

4 **bombastic**
(bŏm-băst′ĭk)
-adjective

- I don't like to invite Jerry to dinner because he is so **bombastic**. He bores everyone with his endless pretentious talk.
- "At this point in time there is little reason to think that the suspected perpetrator will soon be apprehended" is a **bombastic** way of saying, "The crook got away."

_a_ *Bombastic* means   a. pompous.   b. down-to-earth.   c. fascinating.

5 **conciliatory**
(kən-sĭl′ē-ə-tôr′ē)
-adjective

- Our new toaster broke down after one use, but when we returned it, the clerk was not **conciliatory**. He said, "You must have done something wrong to it."
- When a small child throws a temper tantrum, should a parent be **conciliatory** and try to comfort the child? Or is it better to use firm discipline?

_a_ *Conciliatory* means   a. soothing.   b. persistent.   c. proud.

6 **delineate**
(dĭ-lĭn′ē-āt′)
-verb

- The history professor carefully **delineated** the scene of the battle: where the opposing troops were, how the supply lines were set up, and where the nearby towns and roads were located.
- Prehistoric cave paintings in France and Spain **delineate** not just animals but the act of hunting—to prepare hunters for what they were about to experience.

_c_ *Delineate* means   a. to change.   b. to recall.   c. to portray.

7 diffident
(dĭf′ĭ-dənt)
-adjective

- Although Jay is outgoing with other men, he is shy and **diffident** with women and therefore finds it hard to get a date.
- Choosing a puppy out of the litter, Jeanine was drawn to a **diffident** little one who hung back timidly while the others played roughly.

_c_ *Diffident* means   a. different.   b. angry.   c. hesitant.

8 laconic
(lə-kŏn′ĭk)
-adjective

- Frieda is a woman of very few words. When she received an impassioned twenty-page letter from her boyfriend imploring her to marry him, she sent this **laconic** reply: "Sure."
- During World War II, General McAuliffe of the 101st Airborne gained fame for his **laconic** reply to a German commander who was demanding that he surrender: "Nuts."

_b_ *Laconic* means   a. sweet.   b. brief.   c. secretive.

9 scanty
(skăn′tē)
-adjective

- Our office supplies are so **scanty** that most people have to buy their own pens and note pads.
- The poor little maple tree is not doing well. Its leaves are **scanty**, and it is barely growing.

_a_ *Scanty* means   a. insufficient.   b. plentiful.   c. permanent.

10 subjugate
(sŭb′jə-gāt′)
-verb

- Judges are expected to **subjugate** their feelings during a trial. But keeping their emotions under tight control is not always easy.
- Many third world nations were **subjugated** by colonial powers in years past. In many cases, the wounds of their earlier defeat remain painful.

_b_ *Subjugate* means   a. to explore.   b. to dominate.   c. to study.

Matching Words with Definitions

Following are definitions of the ten words. Clearly write or print each word next to its definition. The sentences above and on the previous page will help you decide on the meaning of each word.

1. _____bombastic_____   Using high-sounding language without much meaning; overblown
2. _____acquiesce_____   To consent without protest; comply; assent
3. _____belittle_____   To make something seem less worthy or less important
4. _____diffident_____   Lacking self-confidence; timid
5. _____laconic_____   Using as few words as possible; terse
6. _____scanty_____   Barely sufficient; barely adequate; meager
7. _____articulate_____   Well-spoken
8. _____subjugate_____   To bring under control; enslave; conquer
9. _____delineate_____   To represent in words or pictures
10. _____conciliatory_____   Tending to win over or appease; pacifying

CAUTION: Do not go any further until you are sure the above answers are correct. Then you can use the definitions to help you in the following practices. Your goal is eventually to know the words well enough so that you don't need to check the definitions at all.

➤ *Sentence Check 1*

Using the answer line, complete each item below with the correct word from the box. Use each word once.

a. **acquiesce**	b. **articulate**	c. **belittle**	d. **bombastic**	e. **conciliatory**
f. **delineate**	g. **diffident**	h. **laconic**	i. **scanty**	j. **subjugate**

_____*articulate*_____ 1. Knowing a lot does not necessarily make people effective communicators. They need to be ___ in order to reach others with their words.

_____*belittle*_____ 2. Mr. Harrison is an unpopular teacher because of the way he ___s his students, making remarks like, "I've given up expecting good work from you."

_____*diffident*_____ 3. A(n) ___ person is not likely to do well in a sales job, where confidence and ease in talking to strangers are important qualities.

_____*laconic*_____ 4. My husband is so ___ that it's difficult to hold a conversation with him. He usually confines his remarks to "Hmm," "Oh," and "I see."

_____*acquiesce*_____ 5. When we asked the movie star for her autograph, she ___(e)d pleasantly.

_____*delineate*_____ 6. "One picture is worth a thousand words" suggests that to ___ something, a drawing is often more useful than phrases and sentences.

_____*scanty*_____ 7. It's obvious that the Hallers have not lived in their apartment very long. The furnishings are ___ — just a couch, a bed, and a kitchen table.

_____*subjugate*_____ 8. Slavery has existed in many times and places. In fact, if you go back far enough, you will find that almost every ethnic group has been ___(e)d in this way at some point in its history.

_____*conciliatory*_____ 9. When we had to work over a weekend taking inventory, the boss was ___: she told us we could dress casually, and she kept sending out for food, coffee, and sodas.

_____*bombastic*_____ 10. I've read this ___ editorial in the newspaper three times, and I'm still not sure what is being said. It's a lot of words, but what does it mean?

NOTE: Now check your answers to these questions by turning to page 176. Going over the answers carefully will help you prepare for the next two practices, for which answers are not given.

➤ *Sentence Check 2*

Using the answer lines, complete each item below with **two** words from the box. Use each word once.

_____*belittle*_____
_____*diffident*_____ 1–2. "Don't put yourself down," the self-help book urged. "If you constantly ___ yourself, you will become too timid and ___ to tackle anything important."

_____*laconic*_____
_____*articulate*_____ 3–4. When people are ___, it is sometimes because they feel they are not ___ enough. Believing that they can't express themselves well, they decide to say very little.

_____ *delineate* _____   5–6. When Jake tried to ___ the plan for his term paper to Tricia, he realized
_____ *scanty* _____   that his ideas were too ___ — he needed to do further research.

_____ *subjugate* _____   7–8. The invaders did not find it easy to ___ the town. Refusing to ___, the
_____ *acquiesce* _____   townspeople kept on fighting, building by building, street by street, for
                               many weeks.

_____ *bombastic* _____   9–10. At the dinner party, Julie was seated next to a(n) ___ man who kept
_____ *conciliatory* _____   spouting all his overblown opinions in a loud voice. She is the ___
                                   type, though, so she pretended to be interested in his diatribe°.

➤ *Final Check:* Men, Women, and Talk

Here is a final opportunity for you to strengthen your knowledge of the ten words. First read the following selection carefully. Then fill in each blank with a word from the box at the top of the previous page. (Context clues will help you figure out which word goes in which blank.) Use each word once.

Feminists, sociologists, and psychologists have been taking a long, hard look at—or listening in on—how men and women talk to each other. Their idea is that just as men (1)_____*subjugate*_____ women economically and politically—earning far more and enjoying greater power—men also (2)_____*belittle*_____ women in conversation. That is an interesting theory, but unfortunately, when these observers (3)_____*delineate*_____ their findings, their results are contradictory.

Some researchers say that men, garrulous° and long-winded, dominate conversations. They find that men are (4)_____*bombastic*_____, announcing their opinions in lofty language, laying down the law, and never allowing women to get a word in edgewise, except to (5)_____*acquiesce*_____ with a brief murmur of agreement or to be (6)_____*conciliatory*_____ if a disagreement seems to be arising. According to this theory, most women are too (7)_____*diffident*_____ to speak out; but if a woman does try, the man will ignore or rebuff° her, and if this snub doesn't shut her up, he'll interrupt her.

Other researchers find just the opposite. They say that men are (8)_____*laconic*_____, making a(n) (9)_____*scanty*_____ contribution, or none, to a conversation. The poor woman tries desperately to keep the talk going, while the man just grunts "Hmm" or "Um." Women are generally said to be more verbal and (10)_____*articulate*_____ than men, so when a man clams up, he's exploiting this trait to control the situation.

It's hard to know what to make of this equivocal° research, but the men seem to be in a no-win situation. Whether they talk or don't talk, they're accused of being domineering. It would be fascinating to hear the researchers debate this—especially if some were men and some women!

Scores   Sentence Check 2 _____ %   Final Check _____ %

Enter your scores above and in the vocabulary performance chart on the inside back cover of the book.

CHAPTER

14

anarchy	quixotic
authoritarian	salutary
depravity	suppress
meager	temerity
predilection	turbulence

Ten Words in Context

In the space provided, write the letter of the meaning closest to that of each **boldfaced** word. Use the context of the sentences to help you figure out each word's meaning.

1 anarchy
(ăn′ər-kē)
-noun

- The day after the earthquake, the city was in a state of **anarchy**, with people looting stores, stealing cars, and destroying property.
- Following the revolution, there was a period of **anarchy**, with several different groups claiming to govern the country and no one really in control.

_b_ *Anarchy* means   a. poverty.   b. disorder.   c. sorrow.

2 authoritarian
(ə-thôr′ĭ-târ′ē-ən)
-adjective

- Professor Pettigrew is easygoing outside the classroom, but when class is in session, she is a tough, **authoritarian** teacher.
- Some parents let their children argue over every decision, while others are **authoritarian** and expect to be obeyed immediately.

_b_ *Authoritarian* means   a. favoring freedom.   b. favoring firm discipline.   c. uncertain.

3 depravity
(dĭ-prăv′ĭ-tē)
-noun

- Do you think the death penalty is justified for crimes of shocking **depravity**?
- In the horror movie, the **depravity** of the villain was rendered in gory detail. I still have nightmares about it.

_c_ *Depravity* means   a. passion.   b. anger.   c. wickedness.

4 meager
(mē′gər)
-adjective

- The furniture in the apartment was **meager**, consisting of just a cot, one chair, and a small desk.
- Holly triple-spaced her paper and left very wide margins, but it still fell far short of the five pages that had been assigned. Her professor wrote on it, "This is a **meager** effort."

_b_ *Meager* means   a. inaccurate.   b. inadequate.   c. inspired.

5 predilection
(prĕd′l-ĕk′shən)
-noun

- Maddie always had a **predilection** for vegetarianism. She stopped eating meat when she was only five.
- Like most Labrador retrievers, Beau has a **predilection** for water—he will jump into any pool, pond, or river he sees.

_a_ *Predilection* means   a. a liking.   b. an avoidance.   c. a fear.

6 quixotic
(kwĭk-sŏt′ĭk)
-adjective

- Justin quit his job to protest his company's hiring policies, without considering the consequences of this **quixotic** gesture. Now he cannot support his family.
- Jim Smith's candidacy in the race for governor seems **quixotic**. He has some grand, lofty ideas, but he's an unknown with no sources of funding.

_a_ *Quixotic* means   a. noble but rash.   b. sensible but unfair.   c. sneaky.

7 salutary
(săl′yə-tĕr′ē)
-adjective

- Studies have shown that garlic has several **salutary** effects, including boosting the body's ability to fight off illness.
- The doctor recommended that Mrs. Thornton take extra calcium, which has the **salutary** effect of strengthening the bones.

a Salutary means   a. wholesome.   b. unknown.   c. dangerous.

8 suppress
(sə-prĕs′)
-verb

- Bonnie couldn't **suppress** a giggle in church when the minister, calling for prayer, said, "With eyes bowed and heads closed . . ."
- "I am opposed to censorship in any form," said the lecturer. "When free speech is **suppressed**, all other freedoms are soon crushed as well."

c Suppress means   a. to arouse.   b. to reveal.   c. to overcome.

9 temerity
(tə-mĕr′ĭ-tē)
-noun

- People who rush into marriage often regret their **temerity** later. There's an old saying: "Marry in haste; repent at leisure."
- Flagged down for a minor traffic violation, the driver had the **temerity** to try to outrace the police car. This foolhardy attempt landed him in jail.

c Temerity means   a. fear.   b. regret.   c. recklessness.

10 turbulence
(tûr′byə-ləns)
-noun

- "We may experience some **turbulence**," the pilot announced. A moment later, the plane was shaking so violently that some passengers began to scream.
- The kindergarten room was a scene of **turbulence**, with the kids racing around, throwing things, and yelling at the top of their lungs.

a Turbulence means   a. wild disorder.   b. a turning point.   c. a repeat performance.

Matching Words with Definitions

Following are definitions of the ten words. Clearly write or print each word next to its definition. The sentences above and on the previous page will help you decide on the meaning of each word.

1. _____*turbulence*_____   Violent irregularity, disturbance, or agitation, as of motion, air, or water

2. _____*meager*_____   Lacking in quality or quantity; insufficient

3. _____*quixotic*_____   Idealistic but impractical

4. _____*suppress*_____   To put down by force

5. _____*anarchy*_____   Lawlessness; lack of government; absence of authority or rules

6. _____*temerity*_____   Rash boldness

7. _____*salutary*_____   Promoting good health

8. _____*depravity*_____   Evil; moral corruption

9. _____*authoritarian*_____   Demanding or expecting total obedience

10. _____*predilection*_____   A natural preference; tendency to like something

CAUTION: Do not go any further until you are sure the above answers are correct. Then you can use the definitions to help you in the following practices. Your goal is eventually to know the words well enough so that you don't need to check the definitions at all.

➤ *Sentence Check 1*

Using the answer line, complete each item below with the correct word from the box. Use each word once.

a. **anarchy**	b. **authoritarian**	c. **depravity**	d. **meager**	e. **predilection**
f. **quixotic**	g. **salutary**	h. **suppress**	i. **temerity**	j. **turbulence**

meager   1. Kwashiorkor—a severe form of malnutrition—is caused by a(n) ___ diet, especially one that is poor in protein.

salutary   2. Mom was a great believer in the ___ effects of fresh air and sunshine, so she encouraged us children to play outside as much as possible.

anarchy   3. The famous novel *Lord of the Flies* describes young boys living alone on an island with no adult supervision, no rules, and no laws, and what happens during that period of ___.

suppress   4. People who regularly ___ anger can develop physical ailments. Rage that must stay hidden can show up as a rash, a headache, or an upset stomach.

depravity   5. Though it took place more than half a century ago, the ___ of the Nazis continues to shock and disturb us.

authoritarian   6. It's easy to see that Amanda is the oldest child in her family. Her ___ manner shows that she's accustomed to being in charge.

turbulence   7. Chaos theory seeks to describe ___ in natural systems such as whirlpools and tornadoes, in which motion is wild and unpredictable.

predilection   8. Few children have a(n) ___ for liver, broccoli, and spinach. People develop a liking for such foods later in life, if at all.

temerity   9. The foolish young man decided to try to jump across the railroad track before the train passed by. His ___ resulted in his losing a leg and nearly cost him his life.

quixotic   10. At the time, some people thought that Martin Luther King's nonviolent campaign against racial segregation was ___, but in fact his peaceful efforts had enormous results.

NOTE: Now check your answers to these questions by turning to page 176. Going over the answers carefully will help you prepare for the next two practices, for which answers are not given.

➤ *Sentence Check 2*

Using the answer lines, complete each item below with **two** words from the box. Use each word once.

authoritarian
temerity   1–2. The students were so afraid of their strict, ___ principal that if they met him in the hallway, few even had the ___ to say good morning.

quixotic
predilection   3–4. The adjective ___ comes from a famous tale of a romantic, befuddled Spanish knight who had a(n) ___ for setting forth on impossible and sometimes ludicrous° quests.

_____ turbulence _____   5–6. Water turns white with ___ when a swift current crashes against rocks. White-water canoeing is a challenge because a light, frail canoe gives only ___ protection.

_____ meager _____

_____ salutary _____   7–8. Cutting down on fats is ___, but if your diet is usually healthful, having an occasional hamburger or milkshake is not a sign of ___ —you needn't feel guilty.

_____ depravity _____

_____ suppress _____   9–10. Obedience training will not ___ your dog's natural spirit. A wolf pack does not live in a state of ___ but establishes rules of order, and dogs also need discipline.

_____ anarchy _____

➤ _Final Check:_ Is Human Nature Good or Evil?

Here is a final opportunity for you to strengthen your knowledge of the ten words. First read the following selection carefully. Then fill in each blank with a word from the box at the top of the previous page. (Context clues will help you figure out which word goes in which blank.) Use each word once.

Whether human beings are naturally good or bad is an age-old debate, and how people answer this question has influenced their ideas about government. Those who believe that a(n) (1)_____ predilection _____ toward evil is inborn tend to think that a government must be (2)_____ authoritarian _____: strong, with laws that are strict and strictly enforced. They are not misanthropes,° they insist, simply realists. Under a weak government, they argue, (3)_____ depravity _____ will result: humanity will, on the whole, behave viciously and brutally.

In contrast are those who believe that human beings are born good and would remain good if powerful governments did not (4)_____ suppress _____ their freedom. They argue that when a government crushes freedom, it also subjugates° basic human decency, and therefore all governments should be weak and their laws should be few. One extreme view actually favors (5)_____ anarchy _____: no government and no laws. Anarchists are often accused of recommending chaotic (6)_____ turbulence _____, or at best of being (7)_____ quixotic _____ idealists. They respond, though, that the effect would be (8)_____ salutary _____, a healthy society.

The debate remains unsettled. Not surprisingly, evidence favoring total absence of government is (9)_____ meager _____, since societies see it as risky and few if any have had the (10)_____ temerity _____ to try it. But the human experience with all-powerful governments— from the tyrants of centuries past to the dictatorships of our own time—has not been encouraging. As in so many disputes, we may feel that it is most sagacious° to take a middle ground.

Scores	Sentence Check 2 _____%	Final Check _____%

Enter your scores above and in the vocabulary performance chart on the inside back cover of the book.

CHAPTER

15

callous	paragon
desecrate	provincial
evanescent	steadfast
heed	supercilious
indigent	usurp

Ten Words in Context

In the space provided, write the letter of the meaning closest to that of each **boldfaced** word. Use the context of the sentences to help you figure out each word's meaning.

1 **callous**
(kăl'əs)
-adjective

- Only the most **callous** person is not touched by pictures of starving children in refugee camps.
- Doctors and nurses in emergency rooms may seem **callous**, but if they let themselves become upset by the suffering they see, they could not do their jobs.

_b_ *Callous* means   a. unfamiliar.   b. unfeeling.   c. unqualified.

2 **desecrate**
(děs'ĭ-krāt')
-verb

- My mother and her sister Belle have not been on speaking terms for years. "I wouldn't let Belle come in our door," Mother says. "Her presence would **desecrate** our home!"
- New Englanders feel that clam chowder is **desecrated** by the addition of tomatoes. There's not a speck of tomato in pure New England chowder.

_b_ *Desecrate* means   a. to adorn.   b. to dishonor.   c. to finish.

3 **evanescent**
(ěv'ə-něs'ənt)
-adjective

- My grandmother seemed to have an **evanescent** scent of vanilla about her. When I hugged her, I would sometimes catch a sweet whiff of it.
- It is a wonderful, rare thing to get a glimpse of the northern lights, which appear as **evanescent** flickers of color on the horizon.

_a_ *Evanescent* means   a. briefly present.   b. long-lasting.   c. imaginary.

4 **heed**
(hēd)
-verb

- Parents often wish that children were more willing to **heed** their advice.
- The senator was voted out of office after just one term because he refused to **heed** the voters' wishes.

_a_ *Heed* means   a. to listen to.   b. to misunderstand.   c. to ignore.

5 **indigent**
(ĭn'dĭ-jənt)
-adjective

- The nun Mother Teresa was famous for her work among the **indigent** people of India, the people she called "the poorest of the poor."
- A soup kitchen and free clothing outlet has opened on West Avenue to help the city's **indigent** population.

_c_ *Indigent* means   a. important.   b. well-behaved.   c. needy.

6 **paragon**
(păr'ə-gŏn')
-noun

- Acme Company presented itself as a **paragon** of business ethics. Therefore, the public was surprised at reports that Acme was dumping toxic wastes into streams and that its executives had fled the country with the stockholders' money.
- The New England town meeting is frequently described as a **paragon** of democracy. All citizens can participate and make their voices heard.

_c_ *Paragon* means   a. an ancestor.   b. an imitation.   c. an ideal example.

80

7 **provincial**
(prə-vĭn′shəl)
-adjective

- Just because Bill lives in the country, do not think he is **provincial**. On the contrary, he is a well-educated man who reads a great deal and keeps up with what's going on in the world.

- The local paper is too **provincial** for me. Its stories are written from a very limited point of view that doesn't consider other ways of looking at questions.

a *Provincial* means

    a. narrow-minded.   b. broad-minded.   c. calm.

8 **steadfast**
(stĕd′făst′)
-adjective

- There's an old joke about the most **steadfast** member of an orchestra: a hard-working clarinetist who comes unfailingly to every rehearsal. Then he tells the conductor that he's sorry, but he can't make it to the actual performance.

- On their golden anniversary, Dad made a touching toast to Mom, saying that she had been his "**steadfast** companion and true helpmeet for half a century."

c *Steadfast* means

    a. forgetful.   b. faithful.   c. grateful.

9 **supercilious**
(sōō′pər-sĭl′ē-əs)
-adjective

- After a conference with her son's teacher, Jane was fuming because of the teacher's **supercilious** attitude. "She treated me like dirt under her feet," Jane said bitterly.

- The **supercilious** hotel clerk lost his job when he asked a plainly-dressed foreign-looking woman in the lobby to leave. She was the hotel owner's mother.

a *Supercilious* means

    a. snobbish.   b. sensitive.   c. supportive.

10 **usurp**
(yōō-sûrp′)
-verb

- "My place has been **usurped**!" said Gordon indignantly when he found that someone had beaten him to his favorite study spot in the library.

- If you get a puppy, it is important to reassure your old dog that the newcomer won't **usurp** his place in your affections. Give the old dog plenty of extra love to show him he still comes first—the puppy won't mind.

b *Usurp* means

    a. to share.   b. to steal.   c. to support.

Matching Words with Definitions

Following are definitions of the ten words. Clearly write or print each word next to its definition. The sentences above and on the previous page will help you decide on the meaning of each word.

1. _____*desecrate*_____   To treat with extreme disrespect; to defile
2. _____*evanescent*_____   Gradually disappearing; fading away like a vapor
3. _____*paragon*_____   A model of excellence or perfection
4. _____*provincial*_____   Limited and narrow in outlook; unsophisticated
5. _____*usurp*_____   To seize power or position by force
6. _____*supercilious*_____   Proud; scornful; looking down on others
7. _____*indigent*_____   Not having enough to live on; very poor; impoverished
8. _____*steadfast*_____   Firmly and consistently loyal
9. _____*callous*_____   Hardened in mind or feelings
10. _____*heed*_____   To pay attention to

CAUTION: Do not go any further until you are sure the above answers are correct. Then you can use the definitions to help you in the following practices. Your goal is eventually to know the words well enough so that you don't need to check the definitions at all.

➤ *Sentence Check 1*

Using the answer line, complete each item below with the correct word from the box. Use each word once.

a. **callous**	b. **desecrate**	c. **evanescent**	d. **heed**	e. **indigent**
f. **paragon**	g. **provincial**	h. **steadfast**	i. **supercilious**	j. **usurp**

_____ *steadfast* _____ 1. Tyrell is the most ___ player on his soccer team. He's totally committed, and he never misses a game or a practice session.

_____ *desecrate* _____ 2. Food vendors, postcard stands, and the like are not allowed at the war memorial. Such commercial ventures would ___ this shrine to the war dead.

_____ *heed* _____ 3. The farm geese moved restlessly as the wild geese flew overhead. They were unsure whether to stay around their little pond or ___ the call of their wild cousins and fly south.

_____ *indigent* _____ 4. In the small town where I grew up, there was a simple-minded, ___ man everyone knew as Tom. The local restaurants gave him meals, and members of several churches provided him with clothes.

_____ *evanescent* _____ 5. When I woke up, I could remember little of my dream. Like many dreams, it was ___, quickly slipping away from my memory.

_____ *callous* _____ 6. Some parents fear that letting their children watch violent TV shows will make the children ___, uncaring about the suffering of others.

_____ *provincial* _____ 7. When she was a little girl, Darlene thought the pastor of her church was wise and all-knowing. But as an adult, she saw him as a narrow-minded, ___ man who saw the world in ridiculously black-and-white terms.

_____ *usurp* _____ 8. Not realizing that Dad is the only one who ever sits in the brown recliner, my date innocently sat there. "Who is this person who has ___(e)d my throne?" Dad roared at the poor boy.

_____ *supercilious* _____ 9. The elegant boutique in town must go out of its way to find ___ clerks. The last time I walked in, the woman there glanced at my shabby raincoat and said haughtily, "I doubt that we have anything in your price range."

_____ *paragon* _____ 10. Reading about our town's Woman of the Year made me so depressed that I wanted to go back to bed. This ___ not only runs her own successful business, has a happy marriage, and raises apparently perfect children, but she also makes all her own clothes from cotton she spins herself.

NOTE: Now check your answers to these questions by turning to page 176. Going over the answers carefully will help you prepare for the next two practices, for which answers are not given.

➤ *Sentence Check 2*

Using the answer lines, complete each item below with **two** words from the box. Use each word once.

_____ *supercilious* _____
_____ *heed* _____
1–2. When I took my old wind-up watch in for cleaning, the ___ clerk sneered, "No one wears those anymore." I didn't ___ him, but simply said, "Please have it ready by tomorrow."

_____ *indigent* _____
_____ *callous* _____
3–4. Father used to say, "Don't harden your heart against the poor." Having been ___ once himself, he felt strongly about teaching his progeny° never to become ___.

_____ *usurp* _____
_____ *evanescent* _____
5–6. It's common for older children to fear that a baby will ___ their place in the family. Hostility toward the newcomer is usually ___, though, if the older children are made to feel loved and wanted.

_____ *paragon* _____
_____ *steadfast* _____
7–8. The dog is often said to be a(n) ___ of ___ friendship. In fact, a traditional name for a dog, "Fido," is Latin for "I am faithful."

_____ *desecrate* _____
_____ *provincial* _____
9–10. Bettina was opposed to the exhibition of pop art, arguing that it would ___ the halls of the traditional old museum. "Don't be so ___!" her boyfriend said. "Broaden your aesthetic° horizons."

➤ *Final Check:* The Strange Case of X

Here is a final opportunity for you to strengthen your knowledge of the ten words. First read the following selection carefully. Then fill in each blank with a word from the box at the top of the previous page. (Context clues will help you figure out which word goes in which blank.) Use each word once.

X is a writer, and his case is a strange one: He still uses a typewriter—a manual typewriter. No, X is not (1)_____ *provincial* _____. He doesn't live a primitive village where computers are unheard of; he lives in a modern city. No, X is not (2)_____ *indigent* _____ either. He is not a starving artist but a successful professional who could well afford a computer. When asked about his refusal to (3)_____ *heed* _____ the call of the computer, X gives an eloquent° reply:

"My typewriter has been my loyal, (4)_____ *steadfast* _____ companion for years. How could I be so heartless, so (5)_____ *callous* _____, as to toss it aside and let a computer (6)_____ *usurp* _____ its place? Also, the manual typewriter is a(n) (7)_____ *paragon* _____ of all that is best in technology. It burns no fossil fuels. It does not pollute the atmosphere. It does not deplete the ozone layer. Why should I (8)_____ *desecrate* _____ the purity of my office with a computer?"

Also, for a long time, X predicted that computers would prove to be (9)_____ *evanescent* _____. He reasoned: Why rush out to buy something that will be just a passing fad? But he seems to have been wrong about that, and now some of his (10)_____ *supercilious* _____ friends (he calls them "computer snobs") look down on him and say he is being quixotic°.

I often think about X's case. In fact, I thought of him just yesterday when my computer announced a "disk error." I thought of him again this morning when it had a "system failure." I wonder if X and his indefatigable° typewriter might have the last laugh.

Scores	Sentence Check 2 _____%	Final Check _____%

Enter your scores above and in the vocabulary performance chart on the inside back cover of the book.

UNIT THREE: *Review*

The box at the right lists twenty-five words from Unit Three. Using the clues at the bottom of the page, fill in these words to complete the puzzle that follows.

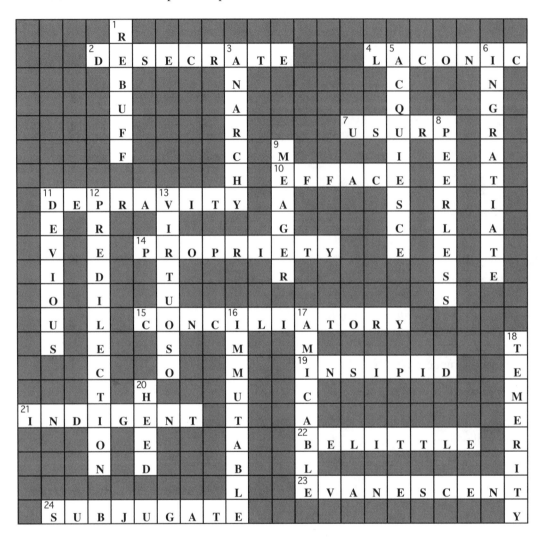

acquiesce
amicable
anarchy
belittle
conciliatory
depravity
desecrate
devious
efface
evanescent
heed
immutable
indigent
ingratiate
insipid
laconic
meager
peerless
predilection
propriety
rebuff
subjugate
temerity
usurp
virtuoso

ACROSS

2. To treat with extreme disrespect
4. Using as few words as possible
7. To seize power or position by force
10. To wipe out
11. Evil
14. Appropriateness
15. Tending to win over, soothe, or appease
19. Flat; tasteless; unexciting
21. Very poor
22. To make something seem less worthy or less important
23. Gradually disappearing
24. To bring under control; enslave

DOWN

1. To reject bluntly; snub
3. Lawlessness
5. To consent without protest
6. To charm; win favor
8. Incomparable
9. Lacking in quality or quantity
11. Not straightforward; tricky
12. A natural preference
13. An expert, particularly in the arts
16. Never changing
17. Friendly; showing goodwill
18. Rash boldness
20. To pay attention to

UNIT THREE: *Test 1*

PART A

Choose the word that best completes each item and write it in the space provided.

_____usurp_____ 1. Little Timmy was very upset when his baby sister was born. He was obviously afraid that she would ___ his place in the family.

  a. ingratiate   b. acquiesce   c. delineate   d. usurp

_____propriety_____ 2. When Meg started her new job, she wasn't quite sure what "dress-down Friday" meant there. She wondered about the ___ of wearing sneakers and blue jeans.

  a. predecessor   b. depravity   c. propriety   d. turbulence

_____temerity_____ 3. In writing a math problem on the board, the professor made an elementary mistake in multiplication, but no one in the class had the ___ to tell her.

  a. temerity   b. dissonance   c. catalyst   d. anarchy

_____immutable_____ 4. A(n) ___ law of nature is Murphy's Law: "If something can go wrong, it will."

  a. conciliatory   b. insipid   c. bombastic   d. immutable

_____scanty_____ 5. Sam tried to comb his ___ hair over his bald spot, but there wasn't enough to cover it.

  a. provincial   b. ponderous   c. immutable   d. scanty

_____diffident_____ 6. Luz felt ___ about taking a course in public speaking. She didn't think she would be brave enough to stand up and address a roomful of people.

  a. peerless   b. evanescent   c. diffident   d. amicable

_____rebuff_____ 7. Serena didn't really want to go out with Ernie, but she was too kindhearted to ___ him.

  a. delineate   b. rebuff   c. ingratiate   d. desecrate

_____whimsical_____ 8. "Our rule against eating at your desk isn't just ___," the boss explained. "Crumbs and leftover food attract mice and roaches."

  a. whimsical   b. peerless   c. steadfast   d. insipid

_____peerless_____ 9. In the 1930s, the runner Jesse Owens was ___. He was known as "the fastest man in the world."

  a. peerless   b. bombastic   c. meager   d. whimsical

_____callous_____ 10. When Acme Company downsized, it showed a(n) ___ disregard for the employees' feelings. The termination notices were issued on Christmas Eve.

  a. articulate   b. callous   c. static   d. conciliatory

(Continues on next page)

_____ *predilection* _____ 11. Isaac is majoring in math. This is not surprising, since he has always had a(n) ___ for mathematics.

a. predecessor   b. depravity   c. predilection   d. anarchy

_____ *steadfast* _____ 12. Many people think of dogs as loyal companions, but a cat can be just as faithful and ___.

a. steadfast   b. articulate   c. provincial   d. vitriolic

_____ *Authoritarian* _____ 13. ___ parents lay down the law and expect their children to obey immediately, with no questions or comments.

a. Conciliatory   b. Evanescent   c. Authoritarian   d. Indigent

PART B
Write **C** if the italicized word is used **correctly**. Write **I** if the word is used **incorrectly**.

_C_ 14. Some teachers believe they must be very strict and set many rules in order to prevent *anarchy* in the classroom.

_C_ 15. When people disagree with you, don't automatically *disparage* them and their ideas. Instead of sneering, try keeping an open mind—you may learn something.

_I_ 16. Carina and Scott constantly boast and brag about how marvelous, talented, and bright their children are. Everyone is tired of hearing them *belittle* their kids.

_I_ 17. The Nazis proclaimed that their state would be *evanescent*. They predicted that it would last a thousand years.

_C_ 18. I chose my winter coat only because it looked great, then found that it didn't keep me warm. I wish I had focused on practical rather than *aesthetic* qualities.

_I_ 19. Arthur Bryant's is a restaurant in Kansas City famous for its spicy, *insipid* barbecued spareribs.

_C_ 20. The "one-liner," as its name implies, is a *laconic* type of joke.

_C_ 21. Mozart is considered a *paragon* among composers. Many people think his music is the finest ever written.

_I_ 22. Labor-management relations at Acme Company are very *amicable*. In the past five years, there have been several walkouts, one lockout, and two long, bitter strikes.

_I_ 23. Smoking cigarettes is one of the most *salutary* habits anyone can develop.

_I_ 24. The boys' choir is famous for its sweet, harmonious sound. This *dissonance* has made it a worldwide favorite.

_C_ 25. Lynette wants a divorce. She hopes her husband will *acquiesce* and not drag her into a legal battle.

Score   (Number correct) _____ × 4 = _____ %

Enter your score above and in the vocabulary performance chart on the inside back cover of the book.

UNIT THREE: Test 2

PART A

Complete each item with a word from the box. Use each word once.

a. **catalyst**	b. **conciliatory**	c. **delineate**	d. **depravity**	e. **garrulous**
f. **heed**	g. **indigent**	h. **quixotic**	i. **provincial**	j. **subjugate**
k. **supercilious**	l. **turbulence**	m. **virtuoso**		

_____catalyst_____ 1. Sometimes a kid just seems to be a(n) ___ for trouble. Minutes after he walks into a room, sparks begin to fly and fights break out.

_____virtuoso_____ 2. The New York Philharmonic orchestra boasts that every one of its hundred musicians is a(n) ___ .

_____heed_____ 3. "Don't go out in this freezing cold without a coat," said Dick's mom; "you'll catch pneumonia!" He did not ___ her warning. He went out coatless and caught pneumonia.

_____depravity_____ 4. "The human race is sunk in ___!" thundered the street preacher. "Repent before it's too late!"

_____conciliatory_____ 5. The boss was ashamed that he had lost his temper and yelled at his secretary. As a(n) ___ gesture, he sent her a beautiful box of candy.

_____indigent_____ 6. The clothing exchange at the church was meant to benefit ___ people, but it soon became popular with bargain hunters who were far from poor.

_____supercilious_____ 7. The ___ waiter in the fancy restaurant looked down his nose at us because we didn't know how to pronounce the names of the wines.

_____delineate_____ 8. The opening chapters of the novel ___ daily life in a small Southern town.

_____subjugate_____ 9. After a siege lasting a month, the attackers were easily able to ___ the city. The inhabitants were too weak and tired to fight the conquerors off.

_____quixotic_____ 10. A rich woman in a short story, bored with life, finds a beggar sleeping on her doorstep. In a sudden ___ gesture, she gives him all her money and the key to her house.

_____turbulence_____ 11. A tornado is a condition of extreme ___: strong, violently whirling winds.

_____provincial_____ 12. Aline has a(n) ___ outlook on life. She has little interest in anything beyond her own narrow neighborhood—the rest of the world doesn't exist for her.

_____garrulous_____ 13. When my ___ cousin gets started talking on the phone, he can't seem to stop. A call from him may last an hour or two.

(Continues on next page)

PART B
Write **C** if the italicized word is used **correctly**. Write **I** if the word is used **incorrectly**.

_C_ 14. When Bryce got an A on his paper, he was unable to *suppress* his feelings. He let out a whoop of joy right in the middle of class.

_I_ 15. At Easter, several members of the congregation worked together to decorate the church with spring flowers and *desecrate* the altar with lilies.

_I_ 16. "This fine novel is beautifully written and a joy to read," the reviewer wrote. That *vitriolic* comment made the author glow with pride.

_I_ 17. Judy's severe stutter makes her especially *articulate.*

_C_ 18. Trying to *ingratiate* himself with his professor, Lorin told her, "You are the most inspiring teacher this college has ever had."

_C_ 19. Cal has trouble making ends meet on his *meager* salary. He has to watch every penny and stick to a strict budget.

_I_ 20. Everyone enjoyed the lecture because it was so *bombastic.* The speaker was down-to-earth, relaxed, casual, and plainspoken, and he used simple everyday examples.

_I_ 21. Op art—or optical art—looks *static.* Sharply slanting or curving lines and intensely bright colors are used to give these paintings a sense of pulsing, shimmering movement.

_I_ 22. The outgoing mayor was gracious as he left office. Referring to the new mayor, he said, "I wish my *predecessor* well as she takes up the leadership of our city."

_C_ 23. Sherri's father would love to know how much money she earns, but he doesn't want to ask her, so he tries to find out in *devious* ways.

_I_ 24. Greek music is so lively and *ponderous* that diners in Greek restaurants just can't keep their feet from tapping. Often, they suddenly start dancing in the aisles between the tables.

_I_ 25. To *efface* the memory of her grandparents, April had their wedding picture enlarged and framed and hung it in her living room.

Score   (Number correct) _____ × 4 = _____ %

Enter your score above and in the vocabulary performance chart on the inside back cover of the book.

UNIT THREE: Test 3

PART A: Synonyms

In the space provided, write the letter of the choice that is most nearly the **same** in meaning as the **boldfaced** word.

_b_ 1. **acquiesce**   **a)** to acquire   **b)** to agree   **c)** to become acquainted   **d)** to disagree

_a_ 2. **aesthetic**   **a)** referring to beauty   **b)** referring to science   **c)** strenuous   **d)** influential

_a_ 3. **articulate**   **a)** well-spoken   **b)** well-paid   **c)** well-meant   **d)** well-off

_d_ 4. **bombastic**   **a)** bitter   **b)** modest   **c)** explosive   **d)** pompous

_c_ 5. **catalyst**   **a)** a disaster   **b)** a catalogue   **c)** an agent of change   **d)** an analyst

_c_ 6. **delineate**   **a)** to detest   **b)** to defeat   **c)** to describe   **d)** to disgust

_a_ 7. **depravity**   **a)** immorality   **b)** immediacy   **c)** humor   **d)** charity

_c_ 8. **desecrate**   **a)** to disguise   **b)** to discourage   **c)** to dishonor   **d)** to discover

_c_ 9. **efface**   **a)** to preserve   **b)** to repair   **c)** to blot out   **d)** to use up

_a_ 10. **ingratiate**   **a)** to gain favor   **b)** to fall out of favor   **c)** to initiate   **d)** to integrate

_d_ 11. **paragon**   **a)** a part of a whole   **b)** a geometric shape   **c)** a straight line   **d)** a model

_c_ 12. **peerless**   **a)** unavoidable   **b)** unnoticed   **c)** unequaled   **d)** uncertain

_b_ 13. **predilection**   **a)** a fear   **b)** a liking   **c)** a mistake   **d)** a loss

_b_ 14. **propriety**   **a)** outrage   **b)** appropriateness   **c)** scarcity   **d)** panic

_d_ 15. **provincial**   **a)** profitable   **b)** urban   **c)** relaxed   **d)** narrow

_b_ 16. **quixotic**   **a)** having your ear to the ground   **b)** having your head in the clouds   **c)** having your tongue in your cheek   **d)** having one foot in the grave

_c_ 17. **rebuff**   **a)** to retire   **b)** to retain   **c)** to reject   **d)** to require

_a_ 18. **subjugate**   **a)** to overcome   **b)** to subsidize   **c)** to exaggerate   **d)** to surrender

_a_ 19. **supercilious**   **a)** snobby   **b)** sleepy   **c)** silly   **d)** sorry

_b_ 20. **suppress**   **a)** to supply   **b)** to defeat   **c)** to desire   **d)** to rescue

_d_ 21. **temerity**   **a)** a sense of humor   **b)** a sense of responsibility   **c)** caution   **d)** rashness

_b_ 22. **usurp**   **a)** to give up   **b)** to seize   **c)** to study   **d)** to avoid

_a_ 23. **virtuoso**   **a)** an expert   **b)** a learner   **c)** a villain   **d)** a saint

_b_ 24. **vitriolic**   **a)** sweet like sugar   **b)** stinging like acid   **c)** smooth like cream   **d)** wholesome like bread

_b_ 25. **whimsical**   **a)** without goodness   **b)** without reason   **c)** funny   **d)** serious

(Continues on next page)

PART B: Antonyms

In the space provided, write the letter of the choice that is most nearly the **opposite** in meaning to the **boldfaced** word.

_b_ 26. **amicable**   **a)** loving   **b)** hostile   **c)** gentle   **d)** old

_d_ 27. **anarchy**   **a)** odds and ends   **b)** pros and cons   **c)** wear and tear
d) law and order

_b_ 28. **authoritarian** **a)** strict   **b)** democratic   **c)** fictional   **d)** factual

_d_ 29. **belittle**   **a)** to watch   **b)** to remember   **c)** to seek   **d)** to praise

_c_ 30. **callous**   **a)** lightheaded   **b)** sure-footed   **c)** softhearted   **d)** sharp-eyed

_a_ 31. **conciliatory**   **a)** argumentative   **b)** peaceable   **c)** timid   **d)** cooperative

_b_ 32. **devious**   **a)** sly   **b)** honest   **c)** wily   **d)** sad

_d_ 33. **diffident**   **a)** different   **b)** similar   **c)** fearful   **d)** assertive

_b_ 34. **disparage**   **a)** to attack   **b)** to praise   **c)** to greet   **d)** to listen to

_a_ 35. **dissonance**   **a)** harmony   **b)** strife   **c)** noise   **d)** stress

_d_ 36. **evanescent**   **a)** eventful   **b)** uneventful   **c)** transitory   **d)** permanent

_c_ 37. **garrulous**   **a)** underhanded   **b)** evenhanded   **c)** short-spoken   **d)** long-winded

_c_ 38. **heed**   **a)** to hear   **b)** to focus on   **c)** to ignore   **d)** to study

_b_ 39. **immutable**   **a)** constant   **b)** changeable   **c)** visible   **d)** universal

_d_ 40. **indigent**   **a)** angry   **b)** faraway   **c)** nearby   **d)** rich

_b_ 41. **insipid**   **a)** bland   **b)** zesty   **c)** flavorless   **d)** dreary

_b_ 42. **laconic**   **a)** terse   **b)** wordy   **c)** traditional   **d)** new

_a_ 43. **meager**   **a)** ample   **b)** measurable   **c)** deficient   **d)** empty

_c_ 44. **ponderous**   **a)** predictable   **b)** random   **c)** light   **d)** weighty

_b_ 45. **predecessor** **a)** a predicament   **b)** a successor   **c)** an ancestor   **d)** an enemy

_b_ 46. **salutary**   **a)** useful   **b)** unhealthy   **c)** unusual   **d)** noticeable

_d_ 47. **scanty**   **a)** insufficient   **b)** incredible   **c)** logical   **d)** plentiful

_a_ 48. **static**   **a)** moving   **b)** quiet   **c)** difficult   **d)** easy

_c_ 49. **steadfast**   **a)** steady   **b)** true-blue   **c)** treacherous   **d)** trustworthy

_d_ 50. **turbulence**   **a)** uproar   **b)** upheaval   **c)** conflict   **d)** calm

Score   (Number correct) _____ × 2 = _____ %

Enter your score above and in the vocabulary performance chart on the inside back cover of the book.

Unit Four

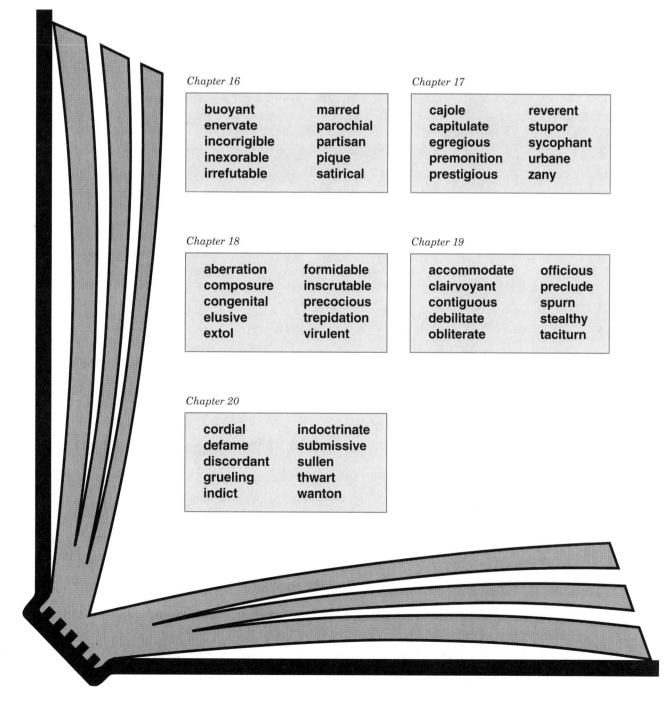

Chapter 16

buoyant	marred
enervate	parochial
incorrigible	partisan
inexorable	pique
irrefutable	satirical

Chapter 17

cajole	reverent
capitulate	stupor
egregious	sycophant
premonition	urbane
prestigious	zany

Chapter 18

aberration	formidable
composure	inscrutable
congenital	precocious
elusive	trepidation
extol	virulent

Chapter 19

accommodate	officious
clairvoyant	preclude
contiguous	spurn
debilitate	stealthy
obliterate	taciturn

Chapter 20

cordial	indoctrinate
defame	submissive
discordant	sullen
grueling	thwart
indict	wanton

buoyant	marred
enervate	parochial
incorrigible	partisan
inexorable	pique
irrefutable	satirical

Ten Words in Context

In the space provided, write the letter of the meaning closest to that of each **boldfaced** word. Use the context of the sentences to help you figure out each word's meaning.

1 buoyant
(boi′ənt)
-*adjective*

- Helium balloons are **buoyant** because the helium gas in them is lighter than air.
- To help her daughter float in the pool, Barbara bought her a swimsuit that has a **buoyant** tube attached around the waist.

_a_ *Buoyant* means   a. capable of floating.   b. tending to sink.   c. invisible.

2 enervate
(ĕn′ər-vāt′)
-*verb*

- The doctor warned me that my husband's medication might **enervate** him. "While he's taking it," she recommended, "just let him rest as much as he needs to."
- The heat wave completely **enervated** Janine. By the sixth day, she could barely drag herself out of bed.

_b_ *Enervate* means   a. to frighten.   b. to exhaust.   c. to awaken.

3 incorrigible
(ĭn-kôr′ĭ-jə-bəl)
-*adjective*

- The dog trainer shook her head in frustration. "I'll give you your money back," she told Prince's owners. "This dog is **incorrigible**. I can't teach him a thing."
- Jake has lost many friends because he is such an **incorrigible** practical joker. He hides frogs in people's beds, puts tacks on their chairs, and sprinkles "sneezing powder" on their food.

_a_ *Incorrigible* means   a. incurable.   b. intelligent.   c. influential.

4 inexorable
(ĭn-ĕk′sər-ə-bəl)
-*adjective*

- Although my grandmother is still in pretty good health, old age is taking its slow, **inexorable** toll on her.
- The Martins have an **inexorable** rule against smoking in their home—no one is allowed to do it, ever.

_b_ *Inexorable* means   a. lenient.   b. unyielding.   c. not exact.

5 irrefutable
(ĭ-rĕf′yə-tə-bəl *or*
(ĭr′-ĭ-fyoo′tə-bəl)
-*adjective*

- "It's **irrefutable**!" Mike said. "I saw it with my own eyes in the magazine at the supermarket! Elvis has definitely been seen on the moon."
- Although many people claim to have seen the Loch Ness monster, no one has ever come up with **irrefutable** proof that any such creature exists.

_c_ *Irrefutable* means   a. easy to understand.   b. unprejudiced.   c. indisputable.

6 marred
(mărd)
-*verb*

- The shore, once so peaceful and lovely, is now **marred** by a row of fast-food stands.
- Our school's reputation was **marred** when, in a single week, a dozen students were expelled for cheating and several more were arrested after a drunken brawl.

_c_ *Marred* means   a. improved.   b. disguised.   c. damaged.

7 parochial
(pə-rō′kē-əl)
-adjective

- Many young people arrive at college with little knowledge of the world, but meeting students and instructors from other places and other cultures helps them go beyond their **parochial** outlook.

- Many New Yorkers have very **parochial** ideas: they take little interest in anything happening outside their own city.

_b_ *Parochial* means   a. timid.   b. limited.   c. lacking enthusiasm.

8 partisan
(pär′tĭ-zən)
-adjective

- The League of Women Voters is not **partisan**. Rather, it remains neutral and provides information about all the candidates.

- Rachel's highly **partisan** comments sometimes annoy her friends, but her strong views might make her a real asset to a debating team.

_c_ *Partisan* means   a. uncaring.   b. objective.   c. one-sided.

9 pique
(pēk)
-noun

- When her husband told her that she talked too much, a Frenchwoman retorted, "Very well; I'll never talk again." Her **pique** lasted the rest of her life; despite the pleas of her family, she went to her grave still silent.

- Connie's boyfriend annoyed her by flirting with other women at a party. Out of **pique**, she refused to see him for a month.

_a_ *Pique* means   a. a sense of injury.   b. a sense of duty.   c. a sense of humor.

10 satirical
(sə-tĭr′ĭ-kəl)
-adjective

- *This Is Spinal Tap* is a very funny movie that takes a **satirical** look at the career of an untalented bunch of rock musicians.

- The governor was angry about a **satirical** article in the newspaper that amused readers by making fun of his many broken promises.

_b_ *Satirical* means   a. admiring.   b. criticizing through ridicule.   c. boring.

Matching Words with Definitions

Following are definitions of the ten words. Clearly write or print each word next to its definition. The sentences above and on the previous page will help you decide on the meaning of each word.

1. _____inexorable_____   Not capable of being influenced; relentless

2. _____parochial_____   Restricted to a narrow scope or outlook; narrow-minded

3. _____satirical_____   Attacking human vice or foolishness through irony or wit

4. _____enervate_____   To weaken; rob of strength or energy

5. _____irrefutable_____   Impossible to disprove

6. _____pique_____   A feeling of resentment or anger because of wounded pride

7. _____buoyant_____   Able to float or rise

8. _____partisan_____   Strongly supporting a specific party, cause, or person

9. _____marred_____   Made less perfect through injury or damage

10. _____incorrigible_____   Uncontrollable; unmanageable; not capable of being corrected or reformed

CAUTION: Do not go any further until you are sure the above answers are correct. Then you can use the definitions to help you in the following practices. Your goal is eventually to know the words well enough so that you don't need to check the definitions at all.

➤ *Sentence Check 1*

Using the answer line, complete each item below with the correct word from the box. Use each word once.

a. **buoyant**	b. **enervate**	c. **incorrigible**	d. **inexorable**	e. **irrefutable**
f. **marred**	g. **parochial**	h. **partisan**	i. **pique**	j. **satirical**

buoyant 1. Buoys are markers that float in the water to warn of dangerous spots. Their name is related to the word ___, which means "able to float."

marred 2. The mayor's spotless record has never been ___ by even a suspicion of wrongdoing.

satirical 3. Shows like *Saturday Night Live* take a(n) ___ attitude toward the famous and powerful, making fun of celebrities and government officials alike.

pique 4. When his opponent won the tennis match with a lucky shot, Nicky refused to shake hands. His ___ seemed childish to the spectators.

irrefutable 5. Lem's professor was impressed with his paper, which was a powerful combination of facts and ___ logic.

inexorable 6. The farmland in this area is slowly being swallowed up by the ___ spread of housing developments.

enervate 7. The automobile accident ___(e)d Donald for weeks, even though he had not been badly injured. His doctors said this was normal and that his energy would soon return.

incorrigible 8. "You'll have to leave now," the shop owner said to the parents and their badly behaved children. "How dare you let your ___ kids run unsupervised through the store, crashing into customers and breaking merchandise?"

partisan 9. Oliver takes a(n) ___ approach to life. He is intensely committed and sees everything as a struggle between opponents.

parochial 10. Although Uncle Don has spent his whole life in a small country town, he has never been ___: everything in the wide world interests him.

NOTE: Now check your answers to these questions by turning to page 176. Going over the answers carefully will help you prepare for the next two practices, for which answers are not given.

➤ *Sentence Check 2*

Using the answer lines, complete each item below with **two** words from the box. Use each word once.

inexorable
marred 1–2. When the ___ march of time brings wrinkles, a woman may feel that her face is hopelessly ___— but a man thinks he now looks "distinguished."

parochial
incorrigible 3–4. Margo is very ___, and her narrow-mindedness seems to be ___: no one has ever persuaded her to broaden her provincial° outlook on life.

enervate
buoyant 5–6. When summer's heat and humidity threaten to ___ me, I like to float in a pool on a(n) ___ cushion, preferably one that has a holder for a frosty drink.

_____ *satirical* _____   7–8. The students who put on the ___ show decided not to be ___: they made fun of everyone, regardless of race, creed, sexual orientation, or political affiliation.

_____ *partisan* _____

_____ *irrefutable* _____   9–10. Instead of being a good sport and admitting that his opponent's articulate°, carefully worked-out argument was ___, Perry quit the debating team in a fit of ___.

_____ *pique* _____

➤ *Final Check:* The Salem Witches

Here is a final opportunity for you to strengthen your knowledge of the ten words. First read the following selection carefully. Then fill in each blank with a word from the box at the top of the previous page. (Context clues will help you figure out which word goes in which blank.) Use each word once.

A tragic chapter in American history began with almost unbelievably trivial occurrences. The witch trials held in Salem, Massachusetts, in 1692 resulted in the execution of nineteen accused witches and the imprisonment of many others. At the height of the witchcraft frenzy, incidents between neighbors that would ordinarily cause only (1)_____ *pique* _____ resulted in accusations of involvement with the devil. A frivolous° or (2)_____ *satirical* _____ remark might be taken as serious, leading to the unfortunate speaker's trial and even death.

The witchcraft trials, which have (3)_____ *marred* _____ the reputation of Salem for more than three centuries, began when several young girls accused a slave woman named Tituba of casting spells on them. They claimed that she could read their minds and that she tormented them, causing them to fall into fits, writhe°, make animal noises, and scream at invisible enemies. Why did the girls make such claims? A possible explanation is that one girl, Abigail Williams, was angry at Tituba. Abigail was a badly behaved child whom Tituba had sometimes punished for her (4)_____ *incorrigible* _____ conduct. The girls may also have wanted to get out of work by claiming that the "spells" (5)_____ *enervate* _____(e)d them, leaving them too tired to do their chores.

Although the girls' stories seemed untenable°, even ludicrous°, they were believed. Many people in 1692 were uneducated, (6)_____ *parochial* _____, and thus intensely fearful of the unknown. Tituba was a good target for their fears: she was foreign, black, and known to be highly capable. Why did her garden yield more vegetables than other women's? Why were the animals she raised so fat and healthy? The successes she had garnered° seemed to her neighbors (7)_____ *irrefutable* _____ proof that Tituba was in league with the devil.

Once Tituba had been accused of witchcraft, a(n) (8)_____ *inexorable* _____ tide of suspicion seemed to sweep over the village, carrying away the residents' good sense. They turned on one another like savage animals, accusing friends and relatives of being witches. The trials were a mockery of justice. The judges were entirely (9)_____ *partisan* _____, convinced from the beginning that the "witches" were guilty. The accused were subject to ridiculous tests, such as being told to recite the Lord's Prayer backward. Some were thrown into water, on the theory that an innocent person would sink, while a witch was (10)_____ *buoyant* _____.

After nineteen people had been executed for witchcraft, eighteen by hanging and one by being crushed with stones, the governor of Massachusetts stopped the trials. Over a hundred people were in prison awaiting trial at the time. They were released (Tituba was among them). Later, some of the girls who had brought the original accusations admitted that they had been pretending.

Scores Sentence Check 2 _____%	Final Check _____%

Enter your scores above and in the vocabulary performance chart on the inside back cover of the book.

CHAPTER

17

cajole	reverent
capitulate	stupor
egregious	sycophant
premonition	urbane
prestigious	zany

Ten Words in Context

In the space provided, write the letter of the meaning closest to that of each **boldfaced** word. Use the context of the sentences to help you figure out each word's meaning.

1 **cajole**
(kə-jōl′)
-*verb*

- No matter how I **cajoled** him, the police officer continued to write me a ticket for speeding.
- Once my mother told us children "Absolutely not," we knew better than to **cajole** her; she would never change her mind, and begging only made her angry.

a *Cajole* means   a. to plead with.   b. to laugh at.   c. to hate.

2 **capitulate**
(kə-pĭch′ə-lāt′)
-*verb*

- Although Stacy has said she will never speak to Karen again, I expect her to **capitulate** shortly—I think she will soon miss her old friend.
- Mr. Henderson resisted the idea of his daughter going on dates, but he **capitulated** when she became a high-school senior.

c *Capitulate* means   a. to be capable.   b. to repeat.   c. to yield.

3 **egregious**
(ĭ-grē′jəs)
-*adjective*

- "You certainly made an **egregious** fool of yourself," George's wife said after the party. "Did you have to sing and dance with a lampshade on your head?"
- "It was an **egregious** mistake to paint our office hot pink," admitted the president of the accounting firm. "No one seems to take us seriously anymore."

a *Egregious* means   a. obviously bad.   b. minor.   c. easily overlooked.

4 **premonition**
(prĕ′mə-nĭsh′ən)
-*noun*

- Although I'd had a **premonition** that I shouldn't get on the airplane, nothing bad happened. It was a perfectly ordinary flight.
- "Wait!" called out the fortuneteller as Terry walked past. "I have a **premonition** about you! For only five dollars, I'll tell you your future."

b *Premonition* means   a. a memory.   b. a forewarning.   c. a plan.

5 **prestigious**
(prĕ-stē′jəs)
-*adjective*

- Are those name-brand jeans really better than less expensive ones, or are you just paying more for the **prestigious** label?
- A Rolls-Royce car, Dom Perignon champagne, a Harvard education, a Tiffany diamond—all these are regarded as the most **prestigious** items of their kinds.

b *Prestigious* means   a. common.   b. highly valued.   c. beautiful.

6 **reverent**
(rĕv′ər-ənt)
-*adjective*

- A huge, awesome natural wonder, such as the Grand Canyon or Niagara Falls, makes most visitors feel **reverent**.
- As we walked through the art museum, our teacher spoke in hushed, **reverent** tones about the masterpieces we were seeing.

c *Reverent* means   a. scornful.   b. amused.   c. worshipful.

7 **stupor**
(stoo'pər)
-*noun*

- At one time, patients who had surgery requiring general anesthesia would remain in a **stupor** for many hours afterward. But with today's improved anesthetics, they often regain full consciousness within minutes.
- A recent study reported that many truck drivers get too little sleep on long trips and often drive in a **stupor**, not aware that their senses are dulled.

_c_ *Stupor* means   a. a state of anxiety.   b. a state of grief.   c. a drowsy state.

8 **sycophant**
(sĭk'ə-fənt)
-*noun*

- "I don't expect a class full of **sycophants**," the professor told her argumentative students, "but couldn't you agree with me about something just once?"
- The manager of the restaurant where Ted works had a truly crazy idea about how to reorganize the kitchen. Ted, always the **sycophant**, told him the plan was brilliant.

_b_ *Sycophant* means   a. a chatterbox.   b. a flatterer.   c. a traitor.

9 **urbane**
(ûr-bān')
-*adjective*

- Wanting to seem **urbane** and sophisticated on her first date with Steve, Claire ordered a martini. It was so strong that she choked on it, spoiling the effect she had hoped to achieve.
- The critics loved the new movie by a director whose trademark was worldly-wise, **urbane** comedy. "As witty, clever, and artful as ever!" they wrote.

_b_ *Urbane* means   a. impulsive.   b. refined.   c. careful.

10 **zany**
(zā'nē)
-*adjective*

- The audience at the circus roared with delight at the clowns' **zany** antics.
- As kids, my brother and I couldn't get enough of *Mad* Magazine, a **zany** publication with the motto "Humor in a jugular vein."

_a_ *Zany* means   a. absurdly funny.   b. understated.   c. scary.

Matching Words with Definitions

Following are definitions of the ten words. Clearly write or print each word next to its definition. The sentences above and on the previous page will help you decide on the meaning of each word.

1. _____*capitulate*_____   To give in
2. _____*reverent*_____   Feeling or expressing respect or awe
3. _____*prestigious*_____   Having an honored name or reputation; having prestige
4. _____*stupor*_____   A state of mental numbness; a daze
5. _____*sycophant*_____   A person who tries to win favor through flattery
6. _____*zany*_____   Wildly silly or comical
7. _____*urbane*_____   Smooth in manner; elegant; polished; suave
8. _____*premonition*_____   A feeling that something bad is going to happen
9. _____*egregious*_____   Highly noticeable in a negative way; conspicuously bad
10. _____*cajole*_____   To persuade with flattery; to sweet-talk

CAUTION: Do not go any further until you are sure the above answers are correct. Then you can use the definitions to help you in the following practices. Your goal is eventually to know the words well enough so that you don't need to check the definitions at all.

➤ *Sentence Check 1*

Using the answer line, complete each item below with the correct word from the box. Use each word once.

a. **cajole**	b. **capitulate**	c. **egregious**	d. **premonition**	e. **prestigious**
f. **reverent**	g. **stupor**	h. **sycophant**	i. **urbane**	j. **zany**

_____ *capitulate* _____ 1. Stacy resisted getting an answering machine for a long time, but she finally ___(e)d when her friends complained that they could never reach her.

_____ *zany* _____ 2. Mack comes up with one ___ get-rich-quick scheme after another. He says we may find them silly now, but he'll have the last laugh: one of them will win him fame and fortune.

_____ *sycophant* _____ 3. "When my uncle is being annoying at family dinners, I wish you wouldn't be so nice to him," Amy told her husband. "He doesn't need a(n) ___ to make him think he's clever and amusing."

_____ *premonition* _____ 4. I had a(n) ___ that Lisa and Todd would not hit it off, and I was right. They were in a heated argument within five minutes of being introduced.

_____ *prestigious* _____ 5. To give himself a better chance of getting the job, the applicant faked letters of recommendation from people with ___ positions in the community.

_____ *urbane* _____ 6. The owner of the restaurant is a gracious, ___ woman, always poised and at ease greeting celebrities. And she is just as courteous and charming to all her customers.

_____ *Stupor* _____ 7. ___ is one symptom of hypothermia—very low body temperature—in the elderly. Their memory loss and dazed condition may be curable simply by turning up the heat.

_____ *cajole* _____ 8. The children managed to ___ their parents into letting them stay up long past their usual bedtime.

_____ *reverent* _____ 9. "Don't wear those torn jeans to the funeral," Maude told her son. "Put on a suit and tie so you'll seem properly ___."

_____ *egregious* _____ 10. Renata's first public performance as a pianist was a(n) ___ disaster. The piano bench collapsed under her, much to the amusement of the audience.

NOTE: Now check your answers to these questions by turning to page 176. Going over the answers carefully will help you prepare for the next two practices, for which answers are not given.

➤ *Sentence Check 2*

Using the answer lines, complete each item below with **two** words from the box. Use each word once.

_____ *egregious* _____
_____ *premonition* _____ 1–2. "What ___ idiot erased all these computer files?" the boss yelled. Monica had a(n) ___ of disaster: she had just used the computer.

_____ *urbane* _____
_____ *zany* _____ 3–4. Some people prefer ___, sophisticated comedy, such as the movies of Woody Allen. Others prefer goofy, ___ slapstick comedians like the Three Stooges.

_____prestigious_____ 5–6. When he was told he had won a(n) ___ scholarship, David was so
_____stupor_____   overwhelmed with the honor that he walked around in a dreamy ___ for
                                the rest of the day.

_____cajole_____ 7–8. When children want an expensive toy, they will usually ___ whichever
_____capitulate_____   parent they think is more likely to ___.

_____sycophant_____ 9–10. A(n) ___ is respectful, even ___, because it is expedient°. He or she is
_____reverent_____   usually buttering up the instructor or boss for some personal advantage.

➤ _Final Check:_ Fashion Show

Here is a final opportunity for you to strengthen your knowledge of the ten words. First read the following selection carefully. Then fill in each blank with a word from the box at the top of the previous page. (Context clues will help you figure out which word goes in which blank.) Use each word once.

Never again will I let anyone talk me into attending a fashion show. My sister, who lives in New York, loves to go to these shows. The last time I visited her, she (1)_____cajole_____(e)d me into going with her. "Julie, I have _no_ interest in doing this," I protested. But she kept pleading, promising me, "You'll love it. You're lucky I could even get tickets for it—Dominic is one of the most (2)_____prestigious_____ designers in the world." I hated to rebuff° her, so finally I (3)_____capitulate_____(e)d, and off we went.

When we arrived at Dominic's showroom, I saw dozens of weirdly-dressed men and women flowing in. "I have a(n) (4)_____premonition_____ that this is going to be even more awful than I feared," I said to Julie. "Suppose I go to a movie and meet you later?" But she dragged me in.

When Dominic, handsome in a dark suit, came onstage to introduce the show, I thought maybe it would be OK after all. I liked his elegant European accent and (5) _____urbane_____ manner as he told us that we were about to see the most creative, exciting clothes he had ever designed.

Colored lights flashed and loud music boomed as the models began walking down the runway. I stared in amazement. What they were wearing was as (6)_____zany_____ as any Halloween costume. One dress was made of tinfoil. Another was made of soup cans that had been flattened and fastened together with tiny chains. A third dress was printed with targets that had holes in the center. I stared at Dominic, who was standing next to the stage. He was surrounded by (7)_____sycophant_____s praising the "beauty" and "originality" of the absurd clothes. I whispered to my sister, "This is a joke, right?" She dug her elbow into my side, saying "Hush!" I looked around at the other people in the audience. They maintained a(n) (8)_____reverent_____ silence, as if they were in church.

It didn't get better. I sat in a(n) (9)_____stupor_____ of disbelief, my mouth hanging open. As the lights came up, Julie sighed happily. "Wasn't it _wonderful?_" she said to me. "Julie," I replied, "I have never in my life seen such a(n) (10)_____egregious_____ display of wasted talent and bad taste." "You just don't have enough aesthetic° sense to appreciate Dominic's work," Julie said. Her final reproach° was, "You're just too provincial°."

Maybe she's right. Maybe I'm not sophisticated. I don't think I'm going to lose any sleep over it, though.

Scores	Sentence Check 2 _____%	Final Check _____%

Enter your scores above and in the vocabulary performance chart on the inside back cover of the book.

CHAPTER

18

aberration	formidable
composure	inscrutable
congenital	precocious
elusive	trepidation
extol	virulent

Ten Words in Context

In the space provided, write the letter of the meaning closest to that of each **boldfaced** word. Use the context of the sentences to help you figure out each word's meaning.

1 **aberration**
(ăb′ə-rā′shən)
-*noun*

- Yes, we had a poor meal at Antonio's Restaurant, but that was an **aberration**. Generally the food there is excellent.
- We have seen many **aberrations** in the weather this year. For instance, it snowed in June, and it reached 70 degrees on Christmas Day.

_a_ *Aberration* means   a. something abnormal.   b. something typical.   c. something impossible.

2 **composure**
(kəm-pō′zhər)
-*noun*

- When I served as a juror, I was impressed by the foreman's **composure** as he announced our verdict. Afterward, though, he said to me, "I may have looked calm, but I was shaking inside."
- Grandma's **composure** was legendary. When her house was flooded, the Red Cross arrived to find her perched in an upstairs window, calmly knitting. "Why fuss?" she said. "I knew you'd get here sooner or later."

_b_ *Composure* means   a. understanding.   b. cool-headedness.   c. selfishness.

3 **congenital**
(kən-jĕn′ĭ-tl)
-*adjective*

- Scientists are not sure whether alcoholism is a **congenital** tendency existing from birth or a learned pattern of behavior.
- You may think that for a dog, barking is **congenital**. But sometimes puppies don't start barking on their own, and their owners must train them to do it.

_b_ *Congenital* means   a. unusual.   b. inborn.   c. insufficient.

4 **elusive**
(ĭ-lōō′sĭv)
-*adjective*

- Marta tried to follow the lecture, but the ideas seemed **elusive**. "The point escaped me," she admitted later.
- There was a faint, **elusive** scent in the air. Was it flowers? Or someone's perfume? We couldn't put a name to it.

_a_ *Elusive* means   a. difficult to capture.   b. horrible.   c. common.

5 **extol**
(ĭk-stōl′)
-*verb*

- Advertisements all **extol** the product they are selling, saying that it is the best of its type.
- The review of this movie **extols** it as one of the best films of the year.

_a_ *Extol* means   a. to glorify.   b. to combine.   c. to complete.

6 **formidable**
(fôr′mĭ-də-bəl)
-*adjective*

- The movers stood on the sidewalk, considering the **formidable** task of getting a grand piano up a long, narrow flight of stairs.
- When Joe and Maria learned they were having triplets, they wondered how they could handle such a **formidable** responsibility.

_c_ *Formidable* means   a. formless.   b. previous.   c. difficult.

100

7 **inscrutable**
(ĭn-skrōō′tə-bəl)
-*adjective*

- When the artist Vincent van Gogh cut off his ear, his motive seemed completely **inscrutable**. One possible solution to the puzzle is that he may have been poisoned by lead in his paints, leading to brain damage.

- "How can I write a paper on the meaning of this poem when I don't understand it myself?" Kiri moaned. "It's completely **inscrutable** to me."

_b_ *Inscrutable* means   a. looked at closely.   b. mysterious.   c. clear.

8 **precocious**
(prĭ-kō′shəs)
-*adjective*

- *Matilda* is an amusing book by Roald Dahl about a **precocious** little girl who reads a whole library of books before she begins first grade.

- Ms. Wolf is quite excited about one of her piano students, a **precocious** boy who not only plays very well but is already composing his own music.

_b_ *Precocious* means   a. prejudiced.   b. advanced for one's age.   c. tending to misbehave.

9 **trepidation**
(trĕp′ĭ-dā′shən)
-*noun*

- "It is with some **trepidation** that I put my plan before you," the consultant told the board of directors nervously, "since it involves moving the company to Siberia."

- "Yes," Grandpa remembered, "I experienced some **trepidation** on my wedding day. In fact, you could say I was scared to death."

_c_ *Trepidation* means   a. enthusiasm.   b. boredom.   c. anxiety.

10 **virulent**
(vîr′yə-lənt)
-*adjective*

- The mayor bitterly protested the newspaper's **virulent** attacks on her administration: "I demand an end to these attempts to poison the public's mind against me."

- Lung cancer is one of the most **virulent** forms of cancer, but though it is deadly, it is also highly preventable. Quitting smoking reduces your risk dramatically.

_c_ *Virulent* means   a. constant.   b. inconsistent.   c. destructive.

Matching Words with Definitions

Following are definitions of the ten words. Clearly write or print each word next to its definition. The sentences above and on the previous page will help you decide on the meaning of each word.

1. _____composure_____   Calmness of mind or manner; self-possession
2. _____formidable_____   Very challenging; demanding
3. _____aberration_____   An oddity
4. _____extol_____   To praise highly; exalt
5. _____elusive_____   Tending to escape; hard to catch hold of or identify
6. _____trepidation_____   Alarm or dread
7. _____virulent_____   Very injurious; lethal; deadly
8. _____precocious_____   Showing unusually early maturity or ability
9. _____inscrutable_____   Difficult to interpret or understand; puzzling
10. _____congenital_____   Existing from birth

CAUTION: Do not go any further until you are sure the above answers are correct. Then you can use the definitions to help you in the following practices. Your goal is eventually to know the words well enough so that you don't need to check the definitions at all.

➤ *Sentence Check 1*

Using the answer line, complete each item below with the correct word from the box. Use each word once.

a. **aberration**	b. **composure**	c. **congenital**	d. **elusive**	e. **extol**
f. **formidable**	g. **inscrutable**	h. **precocious**	i. **trepidation**	j. **virulent**

congenital   1. Our grandson's good nature is ___: he's been smiling since the day he was born.

extol   2. Heidi adores her new job. She ___s everything about it, from her relationship with her boss to the great coffee in the lunchroom.

composure   3. Wendy's friends vowed to maintain their ___ at her funeral, no matter how much they might break down later in private.

inscrutable   4. As the great detective peered through his magnifying glass at the fingerprint, his expression was ___. No one could tell what he might be thinking.

trepidation   5. Bob had a terrifying experience during the blackout—he was stuck in an elevator for seven hours. Now he never enters an elevator without ___.

precocious   6. One of Mrs. Thompson's first-graders is so ___ that she is reading at a high-school level and actually helps teach the other children.

virulent   7. After an hour of angry, ___ criticism from the audience, the company president stalked out of the stockholders' meeting. "I quit," he said. "Let someone else take all this abuse."

elusive   8. Jermain was trying to write a song, but the melody remained ___. Bits of it drifted into his mind but floated away before he could write them down.

formidable   9. Keeping up with housework, raising children, holding a job, and maintaining friendships is a(n) ___ task, yet many people somehow manage to do it all.

aberration   10. Chicken eggs with two yolks are a(n) ___, but although they are unusual, you do find one from time to time.

NOTE: Now check your answers to these questions by turning to page 176. Going over the answers carefully will help you prepare for the next two practices, for which answers are not given.

➤ *Sentence Check 2*

Using the answer lines, complete each item below with **two** words from the box. Use each word once.

extol
virulent   1–2. People who ___ the wonders of modern medicine are sure to mention the victory over smallpox. This ___, deadly disease has been completely wiped out.

trepidation
composure   3–4. Walking to the front of the class to give her speech, Cyndi felt such ___ that she could hardly keep her ___. She wanted to scream with terror and run away.

_____ *aberration* _____   5–6. Glenn has only one arm, and people assume that he must have lost the
_____ *congenital* _____   other in an accident. But in fact this ___ is ___: he was born that way.

_____ *formidable* _____   7–8. Parents are not always cognizant° of the fact that having a very bright
_____ *Precocious* _____   child can be a(n) ___ challenge. ___ kids need special nurturing to
                                    develop their talents.

_____ *elusive* _____   9–10. In a well-written murder mystery, the solution to the crime should be
_____ *inscrutable* _____   ___, not easy to pinpoint. At the same time, the characters mustn't be
                                     completely ___—the author should give some hints about their inner
                                     secrets and possible motives.

➤*Final Check:* Math Anxiety

Here is a final opportunity for you to strengthen your knowledge of the ten words. First read the following selection carefully. Then fill in each blank with a word from the box at the top of the previous page. (Context clues will help you figure out which word goes in which blank.) Use each word once.

No one ever talks about "history anxiety" or even "chemistry anxiety," but "math anxiety" is common and widespread. It's amazing how many otherwise intelligent, capable people will tell you that they approach mathematics with fear and trembling. As a mathematician, I'm puzzled by their (1)__*trepidation*__. But I don't think math anxiety is (2)__*congenital*__— people aren't born with a fear of math. I think it gets passed on like a(n) (3)__*virulent*__ disease: one person catches it from another.

Picture a typical scene. A kid says to Dad or Mom, "Please help me with my homework?" Dad (Mom) says "Sure" but then sees that the homework is a math problem, turns pale with terror, and loses his (her) (4)__*composure*__. "Math? Don't ask me to help with that. I can't do math. I always hated math." The kid gets the message: Mom (Dad) "can't do math," so it must be fearsome stuff. In fact, it must be a totally opaque°, (5)__*inscrutable*__ mystery. If a child happens to like math and isn't terrified by it, that's considered a(n)(6)__*aberration*__, almost freakish. What is this kid, a(n) (7)__*precocious*__ genius or something?

In fact, though, math is not all that (8)__*formidable*__: it's no harder to handle than other subjects, and it's less challenging than some. Allow me to (9)__*extol*__ the virtues of a math course. One, no labs. Two, no 500-word papers on the worst teacher you ever had. Three, no dreary hours in the library taking voluminous° notes on the Corn Laws. Four, in math—unlike history or sociology—the answers to questions are usually quite straightforward, even if they seem (10)__*elusive*__ at first. They tend to be either right or wrong. True, a math course requires brainwork, but I hope you don't consider that a hindrance°. Muster your courage and give it a try. You too can overcome math anxiety!

| *Scores* | Sentence Check 2 _____% | Final Check _____% |

Enter your scores above and in the vocabulary performance chart on the inside back cover of the book.

accommodate	officious
clairvoyant	preclude
contiguous	spurn
debilitate	stealthy
obliterate	taciturn

Ten Words in Context

In the space provided, write the letter of the meaning closest to that of each **boldfaced** word. Use the context of the sentences to help you figure out each word's meaning.

1 **accommodate**
(ə-kŏm′ə-dāt′)
-verb

- Most mini-vans can **accommodate** seven passengers.
- The hotel **accommodated** the extra children by putting cots in their parents' room.

_c_ *Accommodate* means   a. to accompany.   b. to eliminate.   c. to hold.

2 **clairvoyant**
(klâr-voi′ənt)
-adjective

- The back pages of many magazines are filled with ads for fortunetellers, palm-readers, psychics, and other supposedly **clairvoyant** people.
- "If you are really **clairvoyant**," Ben told Madam Olga, "how about coming to the track with me and telling me which horse is going to win each race?"

_a_ *Clairvoyant* means   a. seeing beyond the senses.   b. well educated.   c. well traveled.

3 **contiguous**
(kən-tĭg′yoo-əs)
-adjective

- Portugal is unusual in that it is **contiguous** to just one other country. It shares a border only with Spain.
- The shopping center in Dom's town has two **contiguous** supermarkets. No one can figure out why they were built side by side.

_c_ *Contiguous* means   a. contrasting.   b. alternating.   c. adjoining.

4 **debilitate**
(dĭ-bĭl′ĭ-tāt′)
-verb

- Influenza can seriously **debilitate** elderly patients, so older people should be sure to get a flu shot each year.
- Six of our star basketball players are graduating this year. That is likely to **debilitate** the team next season.

_b_ *Debilitate* means   a. to improve slightly.   b. to weaken.   c. to encourage.

5 **obliterate**
(ə-blĭt′ə-rāt′)
-verb

- At the ancient battlefield, the years had **obliterated** all traces of the bloody conflict. Nothing could be seen but the grass and the wildflowers.
- The commencement speaker said, "This is a proud day in your lives. I hope that time will never **obliterate** your memories of it."

_c_ *Obliterate* means   a. to preserve.   b. to add to.   c. to wipe out.

6 **officious**
(ə-fĭsh′əs)
-adjective

- Every dorm seems to have one **officious** person who takes it upon himself or herself to monitor the phones, reorganize the laundry room, and generally make everyone toe the line.
- Jayson's marriage is under a severe strain because his in-laws are too **officious**. They constantly intrude on him and his wife with suggestions, plans, and unasked-for help.

_a_ *Officious* means   a. interfering.   b. easily offended.   c. boring.

7 **preclude**
(prĭ-klōōd′)
-verb

- The sudden thunderstorm **precluded** the family picnic.
- The president of Acme Company told the employees, "Declining sales and a costly lawsuit **preclude** any pay raises this year."

<u>a</u> *Preclude* means a. to rule out. b. to include. c. to predict.

8 **spurn**
(spûrn)
-verb

- After he was **spurned** by the first girl he invited to the prom, Taylor felt too scared to ask anyone else.
- The employees **spurned** the contract their company offered them and went on strike instead.

<u>b</u> *Spurn* means a. to accept. b. to reject. c. to meet.

9 **stealthy**
(stĕl′thē)
-adjective

- The cat crept up on the bird in a slow, **stealthy** manner, keeping low to the ground and making no sound.
- All the preparations for my husband's surprise party had to be **stealthy**. I didn't want him to know what was going on, so I kept my activities hidden.

<u>a</u> *Stealthy* means a. secretive. b. stupid. c. unsteady.

10 **taciturn**
(tăs′ĭ-tûrn′)
-adjective

- Uncle Maury is a **taciturn** man. At dinner this Thanksgiving, he made only one remark: "Please pass the butter."
- Joelle listens very sympathetically to other people's troubles, but she's **taciturn** about her own. If she has a problem, you're unlikely to hear about it from her.

<u>c</u> *Taciturn* means a. opinionated. b. uninformed. c. reluctant to talk.

Matching Words with Definitions

Following are definitions of the ten words. Clearly write or print each word next to its definition. The sentences above and on the previous page will help you decide on the meaning of each word.

1. _____ *debilitate* _____ To deprive of strength or energy

2. _____ *clairvoyant* _____ Having the supposed power to see things not perceived by the normal senses

3. _____ *officious* _____ Offering unwanted advice; meddlesome

4. _____ *preclude* _____ To make impossible; prevent

5. _____ *contiguous* _____ Sharing an edge or a boundary

6. _____ *obliterate* _____ To destroy or erase completely

7. _____ *spurn* _____ To reject or refuse with scorn

8. _____ *taciturn* _____ Habitually nontalkative; uncommunicative

9. _____ *stealthy* _____ Moving or acting in a cautious, deceptive way

10. _____ *accommodate* _____ To provide with something needed; make or have room for

CAUTION: Do not go any further until you are sure the above answers are correct. Then you can use the definitions to help you in the following practices. Your goal is eventually to know the words well enough so that you don't need to check the definitions at all.

➤ *Sentence Check 1*

Using the answer line, complete each item below with the correct word from the box. Use each word once.

a. **accommodate**	b. **clairvoyant**	c. **contiguous**	d. **debilitate**	e. **obliterate**
f. **officious**	g. **preclude**	h. **spurn**	i. **stealthy**	j. **taciturn**

obliterate 1. The children's elaborate sand drawing was ___(e)d as the tide came in and a wave washed over it.

taciturn 2. If you are naturally ___, don't become a TV sportscaster. Sports announcers are expected to talk nonstop.

stealthy 3. There was nothing ___ about the bank robbery: the robbers marched in boldly in broad daylight, held everyone at gunpoint, and demanded money.

debilitate 4. My brother ran for city council, but his campaign was ___(e)d by lack of money. In the end, he had to give it up.

contiguous 5. The army base where Dad was stationed was ___ to the grounds of a mental hospital. The soldiers made a lot of jokes about who belonged where.

clairvoyant 6. "Don't ask me to order your meal," Liz pleaded with her mother at the restaurant. "I'm not ___; I don't know what you'll like or not like."

spurn 7. In the fairy tale "King Thrushbeard," a proud princess ___s a good king's offer of marriage but later learns to love and admire him.

accommodate 8. Ron's house is specially built to ___ his wheelchair. It has ramps instead of stairs, and extra-wide doors.

preclude 9. Janet decided to get married in the winter, even though the cold weather would ___ an outdoor reception.

officious 10. Grandfather's home health aide is too ___. Not content with just doing her job, she bustles in each day full of self-importance and tries to run his life.

NOTE: Now check your answers to these questions by turning to page 176. Going over the answers carefully will help you prepare for the next two practices, for which answers are not given.

➤ *Sentence Check 2*

Using the answer lines, complete each item below with **two** words from the box. Use each word once.

clairvoyant
spurn 1–2. My roommate, claiming to be ___, offered to reveal my future by reading my palm. I didn't want to rebuff° or ___ her, so I agreed, but I thought it was all nonsense.

accommodate
contiguous 3–4. The largest edifice° in Deepvale, the high school, was too small to ___ all the flood victims, so some of them were taken to a(n) ___ town for shelter.

debilitate
preclude 5–6. A migraine headache can completely ___ the victim. It may cause nausea and can be severe enough to ___ all activity: the sufferer cannot even sit up or keep his or her eyes open.

_____ *stealthy* _____   7–8. The chairman of the committee planning a surprise baby shower for our
_____ *taciturn* _____   professor promised to make all the arrangements in a(n) ___ way. But
    since he is not at all ___, we were afraid he would blurt out the secret.

_____ *officious* _____   9–10. Some ___ soul went around the dorm putting signs in the kitchens and
_____ *obliterate* _____   bathrooms: "Do not make a mess." We were annoyed, but instead of
    taking them down, we decided simply to ___ the word "not."

➤ *Final Check:* The Gypsies

Here is a final opportunity for you to strengthen your knowledge of the ten words. First read the following selection carefully. Then fill in each blank with a word from the box at the top of the previous page. (Context clues will help you figure out which word goes in which blank.) Use each word once.

    Few groups in the world today are so little understood as the people called Gypsies. It is significant that even the word "Gypsy" is based on a misunderstanding. "Gypsy" comes from "Egyptian," and Gypsies were once thought to have originated in Egypt. In fact, though, this idea was erroneous°: the Gypsy people originated in northwest India. It is more proper to call them the Roma, and the language they speak is known as Romany.

    Centuries ago, the Roma began wandering westward out of India. They became established in Hungary and in (1)___ *contiguous* ___ countries, such as Romania, Austria, and Czechoslovakia. Traditionally the Roma (2)___ *spurn* ___(e)d the notion of settling permanently in one place. Traveling in groups by horse-drawn wagons, they meandered° all across Europe. The men were known as skillful horse-trainers, blacksmiths, musicians, and carvers. Many of the women claimed to be (3)___ *clairvoyant* ___ and would tell fortunes for a fee. Then as now, the Roma inspired strong feelings in others. Their affinity° for free-spirited wandering, their colorful dress, their music and dance, and their unusual language all fascinated outsiders. But other characteristics made non-Roma suspicious of them. The Roma kept to themselves; with outsiders, they were generally (4)___ *taciturn* ___. Moving constantly, they did not consider themselves citizens of any particular country but were loyal only to their own band. Rumors followed the Roma; people claimed that they were (5)___ *stealthy* ___ bandits who stole livestock and sometimes children. They were even suspected of witchcraft. In 1721, the German emperor wanted the Roma culture (6)___ *obliterate* ___(e)d. Many Roma in Germany were tracked down and killed.

    In modern times, the Roma have not fared much better. Many countries have been unwilling to (7)___ *accommodate* ___ them or even tolerate them. It is estimated that half a million Roma were killed during the Nazi Holocaust. In parts of Europe, Roma children are often taken away for adoption or put in institutions by (8)___ *officious* ___ government agents who disapprove of the Roma culture. Skinheads and neo-Nazis have made the Roma a target of hate crimes. All these losses have (9)___ *debilitate* ___(e)d the Roma community.

    There are probably eight to ten million Roma in the world today, with perhaps one million in the United States. Most Roma no longer travel but live in settled communities. Their strong family ties and their long history of persecution (10)___ *preclude* ___ any real trust of outsiders. Thus even today, they tend to be a people apart.

Scores	Sentence Check 2 ___ %	Final Check ___ %

Enter your scores above and in the vocabulary performance chart on the inside back cover of the book.

cordial	indoctrinate
defame	submissive
discordant	sullen
grueling	thwart
indict	wanton

Ten Words in Context

In the space provided, write the letter of the meaning closest to that of each **boldfaced** word. Use the context of the sentences to help you figure out each word's meaning.

1 cordial
(kôr′jəl)
-adjective

- Moving into their new apartment, Lee and Ron received a **cordial** welcome from the family next door, who brought them flowers and a chocolate cake.
- "I hate having to act sweet and **cordial** to my in-laws," Rosa complained, "when I really don't like them very much."

_b_ *Cordial* means   a. grumpy.   b. gracious.   c. sophisticated.

2 defame
(dĭ-fām′)
-verb

- Li thought he knew who had stolen his tape deck, but he wasn't sure, and he didn't want to **defame** the person by making a false accusation. He didn't know what to do.
- After the test, the instructor quietly drew Annie aside. "I don't want to **defame** you," she said, "but I think you were cheating. Can you give me an explanation?"

_c_ *Defame* means   a. to dispute.   b. to misunderstand.   c. to slander.

3 discordant
(dĭ-skôr′dnt)
-adjective

- The colors in the living room are **discordant**. We should have realized that orange, purple, and acid green would clash.
- The performance of the marching band has improved amazingly. At the beginning of the school year it was **discordant**, but now it's in perfect tune.

_c_ *Discordant* means   a. invisible.   b. inspired.   c. inharmonious.

4 grueling
(grōō′ə-lĭng)
-adjective

- Before running the marathon, Carlene worked hard—training, eating carefully, and preparing her mind and body for the **grueling** race.
- In Japan, high-school seniors spend weeks cramming for the **grueling** exam that will determine whether or not they go to college.

_a_ *Grueling* means   a. stressful.   b. relaxing.   c. amusing.

5 indict
(ĭn-dīt′)
-verb

- You can't really **indict** a cat for killing birds; it is only doing what is natural.
- In many divorces, each person **indicts** the other as being more to blame for the marriage's breakdown.

_b_ *Indict* means   a. to advise.   b. to accuse.   c. to inform.

6 indoctrinate
(ĭn-dŏk′trə-nāt′)
-verb

- Nazi leaders **indoctrinated** their followers with the idea that there was a "master race" which deserved to rule over the rest of humanity.
- Marge has thoroughly **indoctrinated** her children about the importance of wearing seat belts—they won't go anywhere without buckling up.

_a_ *Indoctrinate* means   a. to instruct.   b. to tease.   c. to blame.

7 submissive
(səb-mĭs'ĭv)
-adjective

- Some dogs are dominant, seeking to establish power over other dogs. And some dogs are **submissive**, immediately showing that they will offer no resistance.
- Strict parents expect their children to be **submissive**. By contrast, easygoing parents focus less on being obeyed and more on developing a child's independence.

a Submissive means   a. unresisting.   b. depressed.   c. affectionate.

8 sullen
(sŭl'ən)
-adjective

- "Leave the table and go to your room!" said little Ann's father when she wouldn't stop kicking her brother. "And wipe that **sullen** look off your face, or no TV for a week."
- Cary's girlfriend has been **sullen** and silent for days. "What's wrong, sweetie?" he asks. "Nothing!" she snaps.

b Sullen means   a. frightened.   b. glum.   c. overexcited.

9 thwart
(thwôrt)
-verb

- The burglars' attempt to break into our house was **thwarted** by our dog, who barked loudly and frightened them off.
- "Lack of education will **thwart** all your ambitions," warned the guidance counselor, "so stay in school."

a Thwart means   a. to block.   b. to hide.   c. to assist.

10 wanton
(wŏn'tən)
-adjective

- As Vernon worked at his term paper at his desk near an open window, a sudden, **wanton** gust of wind scattered the pages and his notes in all directions.
- **Wanton** violence is terrifying because we can see no sense in it and therefore cannot think how to prevent or avoid it.

c Wanton means   a. disguised.   b. obvious.   c. mindless.

Matching Words with Definitions

Following are definitions of the ten words. Clearly write or print each word next to its definition. The sentences above and on the previous page will help you decide on the meaning of each word.

1. _____defame_____   To damage the good name or reputation of
2. _____grueling_____   Physically or mentally exhausting
3. _____indoctrinate_____   To teach the principles of a specific point of view
4. _____submissive_____   Giving in to the authority of others; obedient
5. _____sullen_____   Quietly resentful; bitter
6. _____thwart_____   To oppose directly; to frustrate or defeat
7. _____discordant_____   Lacking agreement; lacking harmony
8. _____indict_____   To charge with an offense; blame
9. _____cordial_____   Warm and friendly
10. _____wanton_____   Senseless

CAUTION: Do not go any further until you are sure the above answers are correct. Then you can use the definitions to help you in the following practices. Your goal is eventually to know the words well enough so that you don't need to check the definitions at all.

➤ Sentence Check 1

Using the answer line, complete each item below with the correct word from the box. Use each word once.

a. cordial	b. defame	c. discordant	d. grueling	e. indict
f. indoctrinate	g. submissive	h. sullen	i. thwart	j. wanton

discordant   1. The meal took a lot of work, but the results were ___. Pork and sauerkraut do not go very well with ice-cream cake for dessert.

indict   2. A grand jury hears evidence and then decides whether the evidence is sufficient to ___ someone for a crime.

defame   3. The prisoner's wife said he had been ___(e)d and she would clear his name.

sullen   4. The employees seemed ___ about having to work late. Hoping to improve their mood, the boss sent out for coffee and sandwiches.

grueling   5. "The movie is excellent, but watching it is a(n) ___ experience," Rafael warned his friends. "The story is so tragic that it drains you emotionally."

thwart   6. Don't let "test anxiety" ___ your efforts to earn good grades. Learn how to avoid it by being well prepared and developing a positive attitude.

indoctrinate   7. Members of racist hate groups, such as the Ku Klux Klan, ___ their children with the belief that one racial group is better than another.

wanton   8. "As flies to ___ boys, are we to the gods; they kill us for their sport." These words from Shakespeare's *King Lear* mean that fate can injure us senselessly.

submissive   9. Battered wives are often said to be too ___. This is "blaming the victim"— the real problem is the abuser's behavior, not the wife's meekness.

cordial   10. Even after their divorce, Max and Amy remained ___ to each other. "We were always good friends," Max tells people, "and we still are."

NOTE: Now check your answers to these questions by turning to page 176. Going over the answers carefully will help you prepare for the next two practices, for which answers are not given.

➤ Sentence Check 2

Using the answer lines, complete each item below with **two** words from the box. Use each word once.

cordial
defame   1–2. A false friend is one who is ___ to you to your face but then tries to ___ you behind your back.

indoctrinate
grueling   3–4. To ___ political prisoners with government propaganda, the secret police subjected them to a(n) ___ "reeducation" program and even to torture.

indict
discordant   5–6. The grand jury refused to ___ the murder suspect, because the evidence against him was meager° and did not hold together—there was too much contradictory, ___ testimony.

thwart
sullen   7–8. When small children try to do something dangerous, it is necessary to ___ them, even if being stopped makes them angry, querulous°, and ___.

_____wanton_____ 9–10. A child who is "different" will often be the object of teasing and even
_____submissive_____ ___ cruelty from other children, whether the child is ___ or fights back.

➤ _Final Check:_ The Jonestown Tragedy

Here is a final opportunity for you to strengthen your knowledge of the ten words. First read the following selection carefully. Then fill in each blank with a word from the box at the top of the previous page. (Context clues will help you figure out which word goes in which blank.) Use each word once.

Cults are religious communities which isolate their members from mainstream society. They demand extreme devotion from their members, who in turn depend on the cult for their own sense of self-worth. This isolation and loyalty can produce bizarre results. One of the most bizarre, and tragic, cult-related stories occurred in 1978 in Jonestown, a settlement in the South American country of Guyana. It involved a man named Jim Jones and an organization called the People's Temple.

By most accounts, Jones was a sincere and helpful young pastor when he founded the People's Temple in Indiana in the 1950s. He preached about racial harmony and social justice. His congregation was a mixture of black and white, mostly low-income people. In 1965, Jones and about one hundred of his followers moved to San Francisco. Now, Jones was different. He insisted that members of the temple call him "Father." In his sermons, he continued to (1)_____indict_____ American society as racist and unjust. But he also began attacking many individuals he claimed were enemies of the Temple. He predicted a nuclear war that would destroy the world, but promised that Temple members would survive if they were (2)_____submissive_____ to his will. Increasingly Jones (3)_____indoctrinate_____(e)d the members with the idea that he alone deserved their loyalty.

By 1977, things were not going well for the Temple. Some members—a(n) (4)_____discordant_____ element—had left. Jones claimed that they were trying to (5)_____defame_____ and vilify° him. When he was not preaching his hours-long diatribes°, he was often (6)_____sullen_____, refusing to speak to anyone. Finally he announced that the Temple was moving to Guyana. There, he said, no one would be able to (7)_____thwart_____ him and his mission.

After Jones and his followers left the county, former members of the Temple and relatives of those in Guyana began to fear that Temple members were being held against their will. They also said that members were being forced to keep up a(n) (8)_____grueling_____ schedule of work with little sleep. Congressman Leo Ryan, some concerned relatives, and a few journalists went to visit Jonestown. When they arrived, Jones seemed (9)_____cordial_____ enough. He encouraged them to wander through Jonestown. The people they saw seemed happy. But as Ryan and the others were leaving, two Temple families slipped notes to him. They said that they wanted to leave Jonestown, but Jones would not allow it. Ryan added the families to his party. As they started to board their plane, gunmen from the Temple opened fire. Five people, including Ryan, were killed.

As Ryan and the others were being shot, Jones gathered the community at Jonestown. He announced that the People's Temple would now commit "revolutionary suicide." Followers brought out tubs of a poisoned fruit drink. Parents fed the drink to their children, then took it themselves. By the time emergency workers reached the scene, the entire community—over nine hundred men, women, and children—had died. Jones died along with his followers.

As the news reports came out of Jonestown, people around the world were appalled° by such a (10)_____wanton_____ loss of life. Probably no one but the dead themselves could explain what drove so many to kill themselves at the request of a madman.

Scores	Sentence Check 2 _____%	Final Check _____%

Enter your scores above and in the vocabulary performance chart on the inside back cover of the book.

UNIT FOUR: Review

The box at the right lists twenty-five words from Unit Four. Using the clues at the bottom of the page, fill in these words to complete the puzzle that follows.

Word box:
- aberration
- buoyant
- cajole
- capitulate
- egregious
- elusive
- enervate
- extol
- grueling
- indoctrinate
- inexorable
- inscrutable
- irrefutable
- obliterate
- pique
- preclude
- spurn
- stealthy
- stupor
- submissive
- sullen
- taciturn
- virulent
- wanton
- zany

ACROSS

1. To give in
4. Impossible to disprove
6. Moving or acting in a cautious, deceptive way
9. To destroy or erase completely
10. Conspicuously bad
12. Hard to catch hold of or identify
13. Quietly resentful; bitter
15. To teach the principles of a specific point of view
21. Habitually nontalkative
22. Wildly silly or comical
23. Not capable of being influenced; relentless
24. To praise highly

DOWN

2. A feeling of resentment or anger due to wounded pride
3. Very injurious; deadly
5. Able to float or rise
7. To weaken; rob of strength or energy
8. To make impossible; prevent
11. To reject or refuse with scorn
14. Physically or mentally exhausting
15. Difficult to interpret or understand
16. To persuade with flattery
17. An oddity
18. Obedient
19. A state of mental numbness; daze
20. Senseless

UNIT FOUR: Test 1

PART A
Choose the word that best completes each item and write it in the space provided.

__composure__   1. When his guitar string broke during his performance, Marty did not lose his ___. He just smiled, calmly put on a new string, and continued to play.

     a. trepidation   b. composure   c. stupor   d. premonition

__enervates__   2. This hot weather ___ the polar bears at the zoo. Accustomed to cold weather, they are exhausted by the extreme heat.

     a. enervates   b. piques   c. precludes   d. cajoles

__marred__   3. The statue has been ___ by years of exposure to the rain, snow, and wind.

     a. taciturn   b. egregious   c. marred   d. submissive

__accommodate__   4. Since the Wilsons never travel anywhere without their cat and dog, they have to find hotels that are willing to ___ pets.

     a. extol   b. preclude   c. defame   d. accommodate

__taciturn__   5. "When I first met Hal, his silence made me believe he was thinking deep thoughts," admitted Rita. "He's still ___, but I now suspect that he isn't really thinking at all."

     a. stealthy   b. clairvoyant   c. satirical   d. taciturn

__cajole__   6. Somehow or other, I let my children ___ me into inviting seven of their best friends to sleep over on Friday night. What was I thinking of to say "yes" to such an idea?

     a. cajole   b. obliterate   c. extol   d. indoctrinate

__egregious__   7. The Broadway show was a(n) ___ failure—not only did it close after its first performance, but more than half of the audience walked out before the third act.

     a. egregious   b. reverent   c. zany   d. cordial

__sycophant__   8. When I shop for clothes, I need a true, honest friend to go with me, not a ___ who will say that everything I try on looks beautiful.

     a. premonition   b. sycophant   c. trepidation   c. composure

__zany__   9. The school talent show is always a lot of fun. The faculty members put on ___ costumes—last year the chair of the English department dressed as a cabbage—and make fun of themselves.

     a. urbane   b. zany   c. sullen   d. discordant

__cordial__   10. I find it hard to be ___ to my sister-in-law, knowing how she criticizes me behind my back, but so far I've managed to be polite.

     a. wanton   b. grueling   c. officious   d. cordial

(Continues on next page)

_____ _capitulated_ _____ 11. Dennis was determined not to buy the vacuum cleaner, but he ___ when the salesman threw in a combination vegetable chopper and knife sharpener.

    a. spurned   b. precluded   c. capitulated   d. obliterated

_____ _pique_ _____ 12. When a bank teller didn't recognize him and asked for some identification, the rich client was furious. In a fit of ___, he withdrew his money and took it to a different bank.

    a. pique   b. premonition   c. stupor   d. aberration

_____ _elusive_ _____ 13. A popular song of the 1960s referred to "the ___ butterfly of love," suggesting that love is difficult to find and catch hold of.

    a. elusive   b. precocious   c. formidable   d. egregious

PART B

Write **C** if the italicized word is used **correctly**. Write **I** if the word is used **incorrectly**.

_I_ 14. In order to make that plastic castle rest at the bottom of the fish tank, you'll have to weigh it down with something _buoyant_, like a stone.

_I_ 15. "I'm the world's worst poker player," Will admitted. "I'm so _clairvoyant_ that I never have a clue about what other players have in their hands."

_C_ 16. Although I have only two minutes between algebra and Spanish, that's not a problem, because the two classes meet in _contiguous_ classrooms.

_I_ 17. Since neither my friend nor I had much money, we had dinner at a _prestigious_ restaurant where we could just have a cheap hamburger.

_C_ 18. After studying all night for her exam, Greta sat in class in a red-eyed _stupor_, unable to remember anything more than her own name.

_I_ 19. The dentist keeps his radio tuned to a "smooth jazz" station, believing that patients are soothed by the quiet, _discordant_ music.

_C_ 20. Basic training in the Army is a _grueling_ experience designed to toughen the new soldiers' bodies and minds with hard work and discipline.

_I_ 21. Every kindergarten class seems to have at least one "boss," a child who is so _submissive_ that the others naturally obey him or her.

_C_ 22. Angry at having to clean her room rather than go out with her friends, Shelby stamped around the house with a _sullen_ expression on her face.

_C_ 23. Our cat and one of her kittens share an _aberration_—they each have six toes on each paw.

_I_ 24. The supervisor _extolled_ the maintenance worker for doing such a sloppy job of cleaning the floor.

_I_ 25. Whistling happily and running up the steps two at a time, Jim was clearly filled with _trepidation_.

> **_Score_** (Number correct) _____ × 4 = _____ %

UNIT FOUR: Test 2

PART A
Complete each item with a word from the box. Use each word once.

a. **debilitate**	b. **defame**	c. **formidable**	d. **indoctrinate**	e. **inscrutable**
f. **irrefutable**	g. **officious**	h. **partisan**	i. **preclude**	j. **premonition**
k. **satirical**	l. **virulent**	m. **wanton**		

_____premonition_____ 1. As soon as I heard my father's voice on the phone, I had a(n) ___ that he was about to tell me some bad news.

_____irrefutable_____ 2. We say that a theory or argument is ___ when no one can disprove it.

_____satirical_____ 3. Suzi wrote a(n) ___ essay on "The Joys of Surprise Quizzes," but the professor didn't realize that it was sarcastic. "I'm glad someone appreciates their value," he said.

_____partisan_____ 4. Don't bother trying to get Uncle Ed to vote for your candidate. He is strictly ___—he has voted for the other party's candidates since 1956.

_____debilitate_____ 5. Being trapped without food and water for two days ___(e)d the hikers, leaving them as weak as newborn kittens.

_____officious_____ 6. Elaine's coworkers are tired of her ___ attitude. They say that she should just do her own job instead of worrying about how others are doing theirs.

_____preclude_____ 7. "I'm sorry to have to cancel the party," said Mrs. Hendrix, "but Tommy's chicken pox ___s it. We shouldn't have other children at the house."

_____defame_____ 8. The angry city councilman stormed into the newspaper office, claiming that the day's editorial had ___(e)d and embarrassed him.

_____indoctrinate_____ 9. If you ___ children at an early age with the idea that they must wear a seat belt, they are unlikely ever to give up the habit.

_____wanton_____ 10. People working to aid the hungry often complain about the ___ waste by restaurants and supermarkets, which throw out enormous quantities of perfectly good food.

_____formidable_____ 11. In fairy tales, heroes and heroines are often faced with ___ tasks, such as spinning straw into gold or counting the grains of sand on a beach.

_____inscrutable_____ 12. As my instructor read my essay, her face was ___. I had no idea if she was pleased or disappointed.

_____virulent_____ 13. The flu that swept over the town was so ___ that almost every family was affected. The schools closed, and most public meetings were canceled to try to halt the spread of disease.

(Continues on next page)

PART B

Write **C** if the italicized word is used **correctly**. Write **I** if the word is used **incorrectly**.

_I_   14. From kindergarten on, Stan has always been a favorite with his teachers because he is so *incorrigible*.

_I_   15. At our annual dinner, we plan to *indict* several of the volunteers who have worked so hard to make our program a success.

_C_   16. Uncle Jake seems to take pride in being *parochial*. "I've never been outside the town I was born in, and I don't care about anything except what's right here," he says.

_I_   17. Builders, plumbers, electricians, and landscapers all worked around the clock in order to *thwart* plans to open the new supermarket on time.

_C_   18. Serafina *spurned* the job offer from a cigarette company. "I'm not going to help make something that sickens and kills people," she said.

_I_   19. The bank robbers were particularly *stealthy*, walking into the bank in broad daylight without even disguising their faces.

_I_   20. Talking loudly or laughing during a church service is considered *reverent* behavior.

_I_   21. Michelle was embarrassed by her date's *urbane* behavior at the formal dinner. He showed up in a dirty sweatshirt and put his feet on the table.

_C_   22. Romeo and Juliet are two lovers in an unfortunate situation: their families are *inexorable* enemies, sworn to hate each other for all time.

_C_   23. The invading army *obliterated* the town, burning anything that remained standing.

_I_   24. Amy's limp is *congenital*. It's due to her twisting her ankle last week.

_I_   25. Because Matthew seemed so *precocious,* his parents and teachers decided it would be best if he repeated first grade.

Score   (Number correct) _____ × 4 = _____ %

UNIT FOUR: Test 3

PART A: Synonyms

In the space provided, write the letter of the choice that is most nearly the **same** in meaning as the **boldfaced** word.

__*a*__ 1. **aberration** **a)** an oddity **b)** an expectation **c)** an absence **d)** a location

__*d*__ 2. **accommodate** **a)** to send away **b)** to reply **c)** to chase **d)** to fit in

__*b*__ 3. **cajole** **a)** to prepare **b)** to persuade **c)** to correct **d)** to torment

__*c*__ 4. **clairvoyant** **a)** intelligent **b)** cautious **c)** mind-reading **d)** strong

__*d*__ 5. **congenital** **a)** local **b)** creative **c)** borrowed **d)** inborn

__*b*__ 6. **contiguous** **a)** not matching **b)** sharing a boundary **c)** well-known **d)** surprising

__*a*__ 7. **defame** **a)** to damage the good name of **b)** to delay **c)** to offer unwanted advice to **d)** to reveal a secret

__*c*__ 8. **discordant** **a)** expensive **b)** absent **c)** lacking harmony **d)** unjust

__*c*__ 9. **egregious** **a)** very friendly **b)** silent **c)** remarkably bad **d)** tasteful

__*a*__ 10. **extol** **a)** to praise **b)** to notice **c)** to blame **d)** to insist

__*b*__ 11. **incorrigible** **a)** quiet **b)** unmanageable **c)** having leadership qualities **d)** creative

__*a*__ 12. **indoctrinate** **a)** to brainwash **b)** to soothe **c)** to try hard **d)** to imitate

__*d*__ 13. **inexorable** **a)** easily moved **b)** recent **c)** genuine **d)** inflexible

__*b*__ 14. **irrefutable** **a)** widespread **b)** undeniable **c)** washable **d)** impossible

__*a*__ 15. **marred** **a)** damaged **b)** improved **c)** made taller **d)** shrunk

__*b*__ 16. **officious** **a)** modern **b)** meddlesome **c)** well-planned **d)** licensed

__*a*__ 17. **partisan** **a)** supporting a particular side **b)** indecisive **c)** not serious **d)** hard-working

__*c*__ 18. **preclude** **a)** to separate **b)** to deceive **c)** to make impossible **d)** to surprise

__*a*__ 19. **premonition** **a)** a forewarning **b)** a rude comment **c)** an excuse **d)** a limit

__*a*__ 20. **satirical** **a)** mocking **b)** complimentary **c)** mistaken **d)** foreign

__*c*__ 21. **stupor** **a)** absence **b)** celebration **c)** daze **d)** joke

__*b*__ 22. **sycophant** **a)** a performer **b)** a flatterer **c)** an employee **d)** a wine expert

__*c*__ 23. **thwart** **a)** to allow **b)** to rehearse **c)** to defeat **d)** to complain

__*b*__ 24. **virulent** **a)** prepared **b)** injurious **c)** fake **d)** fortunate

__*b*__ 25. **wanton** **a)** lacking **b)** senseless **c)** satisfied **d)** careful

(Continues on next page)

PART B: Antonyms
In the space provided, write the letter of the choice that is most nearly the **opposite** in meaning to the **boldfaced** word.

_a_ 26. **buoyant**   **a)** sinking   **b)** laughable   **c)** needed   **d)** dangerous

_d_ 27. **capitulate**   **a)** to welcome   **b)** to ignore   **c)** to pretend   **d)** to resist

_b_ 28. **composure**   **a)** luck   **b)** panic   **c)** politeness   **d)** mercy

_a_ 29. **cordial**   **a)** rude   **b)** frightened   **c)** awkward   **d)** confused

_c_ 30. **debilitate**   **a)** to select   **b)** to purify   **c)** to strengthen   **d)** to blame

_d_ 31. **elusive**   **a)** enlarged   **b)** harsh   **c)** safe   **d)** easily found

_a_ 32. **enervate**   **a)** to energize   **b)** to give in   **c)** to annoy   **d)** to push

_b_ 33. **formidable**   **a)** not legal   **b)** not demanding   **c)** hard to find   **d)** perfect

_d_ 34. **grueling**   **a)** slow-moving   **b)** honest   **c)** expensive   **d)** easy

_a_ 35. **indict**   **a)** to praise   **b)** to search for   **c)** to explain   **d)** to hide

_d_ 36. **inscrutable**   **a)** poorly planned   **b)** calm   **c)** able to be moved   **d)** easily understood

_b_ 37. **obliterate**   **a)** to observe closely   **b)** to build   **c)** to reason with   **d)** to fasten

_a_ 38. **parochial**   **a)** sophisticated   **b)** not decorated   **c)** unhealthy   **d)** exaggerated

_b_ 39. **pique**   **a)** honesty   **b)** pleasure   **c)** annoyance   **d)** effort

_b_ 40. **precocious**   **a)** fearful   **b)** mentally slow   **c)** very shy   **d)** sweet-tasting

_d_ 41. **prestigious**   **a)** flawless   **b)** needing repairs   **c)** lazy   **d)** having a poor reputation

_a_ 42. **reverent**   **a)** disrespectful   **b)** swollen   **c)** surprised   **d)** injured

_b_ 43. **spurn**   **a)** to prevent   **b)** to accept   **c)** to instruct   **d)** to speak quietly

_d_ 44. **stealthy**   **a)** quiet and sad   **b)** slow and careful   **c)** practical   **d)** open and direct

_a_ 45. **submissive**   **a)** disobedient   **b)** humorous   **c)** careless   **d)** relaxed

_c_ 46. **sullen**   **a)** fair   **b)** stubborn   **c)** cheerful   **d)** odd

_b_ 47. **taciturn**   **a)** rebellious   **b)** talkative   **c)** without expression   **d)** cruel

_a_ 48. **trepidation**   **a)** courage   **b)** anger   **c)** noisiness   **d)** good health

_d_ 49. **urbane**   **a)** expert   **b)** talkative   **c)** sorrowful   **d)** crude

_b_ 50. **zany**   **a)** insulting   **b)** serious   **c)** educated   **d)** sorry

Score   (Number correct) _____ × 2 = _____ %

Enter your score above and in the vocabulary performance chart on the inside back cover of the book.

Unit Five

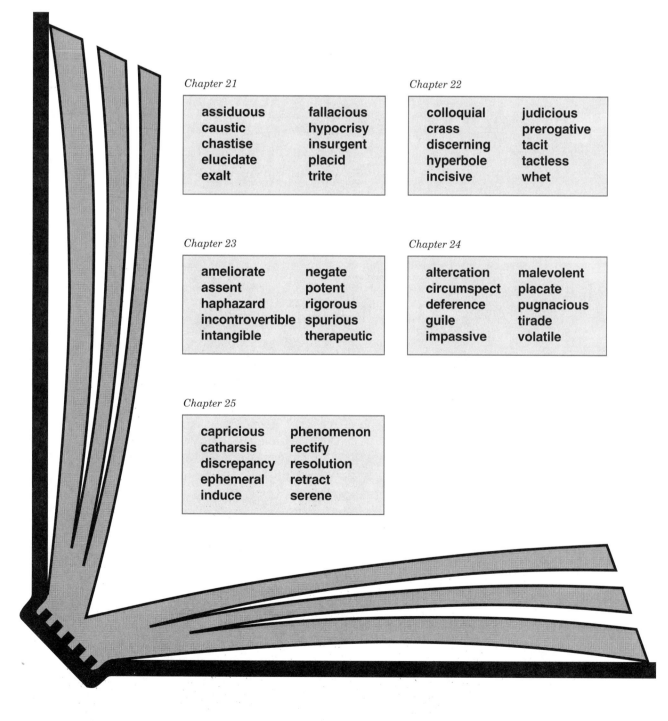

Chapter 21

assiduous	fallacious
caustic	hypocrisy
chastise	insurgent
elucidate	placid
exalt	trite

Chapter 22

colloquial	judicious
crass	prerogative
discerning	tacit
hyperbole	tactless
incisive	whet

Chapter 23

ameliorate	negate
assent	potent
haphazard	rigorous
incontrovertible	spurious
intangible	therapeutic

Chapter 24

altercation	malevolent
circumspect	placate
deference	pugnacious
guile	tirade
impassive	volatile

Chapter 25

capricious	phenomenon
catharsis	rectify
discrepancy	resolution
ephemeral	retract
induce	serene

CHAPTER

21

assiduous	**fallacious**
caustic	**hypocrisy**
chastise	**insurgent**
elucidate	**placid**
exalt	**trite**

Ten Words in Context

In the space provided, write the letter of the meaning closest to that of each **boldfaced** word. Use the context of the sentences to help you figure out each word's meaning.

1 **assiduous**
(ə-sĭj′ōō-əs)
-*adjective*

- Our dog is an **assiduous** chewer. If we give him an old leather shoe, he will spend hours gnawing at it until it is reduced to a pile of scraps.
- Because Rafael has been an **assiduous** student this term, he will probably earn all A's.

_b_ *Assiduous* means   a. uncaring.   b. hard-working.   c. peaceful.

2 **caustic**
(kô′stĭk)
-*adjective*

- The writer Dorothy Parker was famous for her **caustic** wit. When she met a woman who had recently attempted suicide, Parker said, "Better luck next time."
- Cassie must have had a bad day. When I asked her how she was, her reply was **caustic**: "Oh, I'm just *wonderful*; now, if you'll excuse me, I'm going to lie down in the middle of traffic."

_a_ *Caustic* means   a. sarcastic.   b. careful.   c. old-fashioned.

3 **chastise**
(chăs′tīz′)
-*verb*

- The officer did not give Joe a ticket, but he did **chastise** him for driving with a burned-out headlight.
- The newspaper story **chastised** several city landlords for renting out filthy, unsafe apartments to poor families.

_b_ *Chastise* means   a. to admire.   b. to criticize.   c. to fear.

4 **elucidate**
(ĭ-lōō′sĭ-dāt′)
-*verb*

- To **elucidate** the stages of decision-making, the instructor drew a helpful chart on the chalkboard.
- "Let me **elucidate** my position," the politician told the reporters. "When I said that I was in favor of raising taxes, I really meant that I am against it."

_c_ *Elucidate* means   a. to understand.   b. to remember.   c. to make clear.

5 **exalt**
(ĭg-zôlt′)
-*verb*

- Some high schools **exalt** student athletes, making it seem that winning games is the most important thing in life.
- Linda loves Siamese cats; in fact, she **exalts** them above all other pets.

_b_ *Exalt* means   a. to expect.   b. to praise.   c. to accompany.

6 **fallacious**
(fə-lā′shəs)
-*adjective*

- It would be **fallacious** to conclude that Norm and Lou are brothers just because they look alike. In fact, they're not related at all.
- Jerry's argument sounded good, but it was **fallacious**. He had based it on the wrong statistics.

_a_ *Fallacious* means   a. incorrect.   b. careful.   c. commonplace.

7 **hypocrisy**
(hĭ-pŏk'rĭ-sē)
-noun

- Many people accused the TV preacher of **hypocrisy** when he was discovered to be having an affair with a friend's wife.
- Everyone is probably guilty of **hypocrisy** from time to time—it's tempting to pretend to be better than we really are.

a *Hypocrisy* means   a. falseness.   b. honesty.   c. prejudice.

8 **insurgent**
(ĭn-sûr'jənt)
-noun

- "If I lived under a dictatorship," Mindy confessed, "I think I would just keep quiet and try to stay out of trouble. I don't have the soul of an **insurgent**."
- As a young man, Uncle Kiril joined a group of **insurgents**. When their plot against the government was discovered, he had to flee for his life, and that's how he came to America.

a *Insurgent* means   a. a rebel.   b. an elected official.   c. a candidate.

9 **placid**
(plăs'ĭd)
-adjective

- Jack and Cindy's first baby was restless and fussy, but their second baby was happy and **placid**.
- The two women who were waiting to hear if they had passed their driving test were very different. One was a bundle of nerves, while the other seemed quite **placid**.

b *Placid* means   a. tense.   b. untroubled.   c. sad.

10 **trite**
(trīt)
-adjective

- "**Trite** but true—I love you!" was the little rhyme accompanying the bouquet of roses.
- Sick and tired of the **trite** expression "Have a nice day," Barbara bought a T-shirt that said: "Don't tell me what kind of day to have."

c *Trite* means   a. misunderstood.   b. original.   c. worn-out.

Matching Words with Definitions

Following are definitions of the ten words. Clearly write or print each word next to its definition. The sentences above and on the previous page will help you decide on the meaning of each word.

1. _____*chastise*_____   To scold sharply
2. _____*elucidate*_____   To explain; clarify
3. _____*fallacious*_____   Based on error; mistaken
4. _____*assiduous*_____   Careful, hardworking, and thorough; diligent
5. _____*insurgent*_____   A person who revolts against established authority
6. _____*placid*_____   Peaceful; calm
7. _____*trite*_____   Overused and commonplace; stale
8. _____*exalt*_____   To glorify; honor
9. _____*hypocrisy*_____   A pretense of having beliefs, feelings, or virtues that one does not actually possess; insincerity
10. _____*caustic*_____   Sarcastic; biting; stinging

CAUTION: Do not go any further until you are sure the above answers are correct. Then you can use the definitions to help you in the following practices. Your goal is eventually to know the words well enough so that you don't need to check the definitions at all.

➤ *Sentence Check 1*

Using the answer line, complete each item below with the correct word from the box. Use each word once.

a. **assiduous**	b. **caustic**	c. **chastise**	d. **elucidate**	e. **exalt**
f. **fallacious**	g. **hypocrisy**	h. **insurgent**	i. **placid**	j. **trite**

_____caustic_____ 1. A good teacher can criticize her students' work without being ___; .in other words, she does not attack the students with stinging sarcasm.

_____chastise_____ 2. The police officer ___(e)d the driver for not wearing a seat belt.

_____insurgent_____ 3. Some ___s in the history class marched into the professor's office and demanded an end to surprise quizzes. She just laughed and told them to get back to the books.

_____assiduous_____ 4. The boys who washed the windows did such a(n) ___ job that they didn't leave a single speck of dust.

_____Trite_____ 5. ___ expressions weaken a paper. One expert on writing advises that if you have ever seen a phrase in print before, don't use it.

_____fallacious_____ 6. We assumed that Route 58 connects with Route 59. Unfortunately, our reasoning was ___; the two roads are nowhere near each other.

_____elucidate_____ 7. As I argued with my roommate about assisted suicide, I found it hard to ___ my opinion. I have a sense that it's wrong, but I couldn't say exactly why.

_____placid_____ 8. It took all my self-control to act ___ during the job interview. Inside I was nervous and excited.

_____hypocrisy_____ 9. Shelly's ___ bothers me. She pretends to be very fond of her roommate but makes fun of the poor girl behind her back.

_____exalt_____ 10. Because Ralph wants his daughter to go to the state university, he ___s it above all other schools whenever they discuss colleges.

NOTE: Now check your answers to these questions by turning to page 177. Going over the answers carefully will help you prepare for the next two practices, for which answers are not given.

➤ *Sentence Check 2*

Using the answer lines, complete each item below with **two** words from the box. Use each word once.

_____assiduous_____
_____trite_____
1–2. A careful writer makes ___ efforts to avoid ___, hackneyed°, overused words and phrases.

_____exalt_____
_____insurgent_____
3–4. Many people tend to admire and even ___ any rebel, believing that he or she must be a hero. But whether a(n) ___ deserves praise depends on what he or she is rebelling against.

_____fallacious_____
_____placid_____
5–6. It's ___ to assume that someone has no worries just because he or she seems ___. A calm exterior may conceal anxiety, sadness, and even rage.

_____ *elucidate* _____ 7–8. The play *Tartuffe* by Molière is about a wicked man who pretends to be
_____ *hypocrisy* _____ very righteous. When people said the play was an attack on religion, the playwright tried to ___ his point: he explained that he was attacking not true religion, but religious ___.

_____ *chastise* _____ 9–10. "I don't like to ___ anyone," the boss always says. But her brusque°
_____ *caustic* _____ remarks about anything that someone has done wrong are often so ___ and wounding that she does seem to take pleasure in scolding people.

➤ *Final Check:* Helen Keller

Here is a final opportunity for you to strengthen your knowledge of the ten words. First read the following selection carefully. Then fill in each blank with a word from the box at the top of the previous page. (Context clues will help you figure out which word goes in which blank.) Use each word once.

Most American schoolchildren know the story of Helen Keller—or at least they think they do. They know that Keller, who was born in 1880, became blind and deaf as a tiny child. They know she grew up wild and undisciplined, unable to communicate, imprisoned in her dark world. They know she was befriended by a sagacious° teacher, Anne Sullivan, who taught her to speak, read, and write. For most people, those few facts sum up the Helen Keller story. She is often (1)_____ *exalt* _____(e)d as an unfortunate child who succeeded with the help of a dedicated teacher. *The Miracle Worker,* a famous play about Keller that was also made into a movie, (2)_____ *elucidate* _____s these points.

But compared with Keller's full story, that version of her accomplishments is oversimplified and (3)_____ *trite* _____. As an adult, she led a fascinating and controversial life as one of the best-known (4)_____ *insurgent* _____s of her day. After graduating from college, she joined the American Socialist Party. She supported the communist revolution in Russia. She was a(n) (5)_____ *assiduous* _____ worker for women's rights, leading marches of women demanding the vote. Through visiting slums, sweatshops, and hospitals, she learned that most disabled people did not have the opportunities she had as a child in a well-off family. She (6)_____ *chastise* _____(e)d political leaders for supporting a system in which poor people often became blind through industrial accidents and untreated disease. Then, she herself was criticized for her attacks. One newspaper editor was particularly (7)_____ *caustic* _____: he said that Keller's thinking was (8)_____ *fallacious* _____ because of her disabilities—that she just didn't understand things very well. In her reply, Keller pointed out that she had once met this editor and suggested that he was guilty of (9)_____ *hypocrisy* _____ or duplicity°. "At the time [we met], the compliments he paid me were so generous that I blush to remember them," she wrote. "But now that I have come out for socialism he reminds me . . . that I am blind and deaf and especially liable to error. I must have shrunk in intelligence during the years since I met him." It is erroneous° to think of Keller as a(n) (10)_____ *placid* _____, sweet symbol of victory over disability. She was a fiery spokeswoman for those who were as voiceless as she had once been.

Scores Sentence Check 2 _____ % Final Check _____ %

Enter your scores above and in the vocabulary performance chart on the inside back cover of the book.

CHAPTER 22

colloquial	judicious
crass	prerogative
discerning	tacit
hyperbole	tactless
incisive	whet

Ten Words in Context

In the space provided, write the letter of the meaning closest to that of each **boldfaced** word. Use the context of the sentences to help you figure out each word's meaning.

1 colloquial
(kə-lō′kwē-əl)
-adjective

- I enjoyed the lecturer's easygoing, **colloquial** style. He made the topic more interesting than a stiff, formal speaker could have done.
- Dorian has two entirely different ways of talking: he uses **colloquial**, slangy words with his friends, but conventional, precise language at work.

_c_ Colloquial means   a. deceptive.   b. unclear.   c. informal.

2 crass
(krăs)
-adjective

- "My boss made a **crass** remark about my figure," said Annette, "but I'm not sure that's sexual harassment. He says crude things to everyone, so maybe it's just that no one ever taught him any manners."
- The candidate lost the election after making a stupid joke about his opponent's weight. We were amazed at the damage one **crass** comment can do.

_b_ Crass means   a. humorless.   b. tasteless.   c. meaningless.

3 discerning
(dĭ-sûr′nĭng)
-adjective

- "That's a very **discerning** comment," the professor said to Carmela. "Congratulations—you've been using your powers of observation."
- Mothers are the most **discerning** people on earth, as you'll agree if you've ever tried to hide anything from yours.

_a_ Discerning means   a. observant.   b. nasty.   c. bragging.

4 hyperbole
(hī-pûr′bə-lē)
-noun

- "My entire *life* will be *ruined* if you won't let me borrow your dress!" said my roommate, causing me to laugh at her **hyperbole**.
- Marcella is a very dramatic person who uses a lot of **hyperbole** to express herself: a restaurant is never just "good"—it's "the most fabulous food in the universe"; her boyfriend isn't just "good-looking"—he's "divine beyond belief."

_a_ Hyperbole means   a. overstatement.   b. compliment.   c. accuracy.

5 incisive
(ĭn-sī′sĭv)
-adjective

- Professor Martin is a great teacher whose lectures are always clear, **incisive**, and to the point.
- The actor Peter Falk played a TV detective named Columbo who acted vague and befuddled, but whose mind was actually brilliantly **incisive**.

_c_ Incisive means   a. silly.   b. hesitant.   c. keen.

6 judicious
(jōō-dĭsh′əs)
-adjective

- Merle's decisions are **judicious**: he never does anything without careful thought.
- Lilian's choice of a husband was not **judicious**. She married a man she had known for only a week, who turned out to be abusive and a heavy drinker.

_b_ Judicious means   a. predictable.   b. prudent.   c. exaggerated.

7 prerogative
(prĭ-rŏg′ə-tĭv)
-noun

- Just because you told the salesman you might buy the car doesn't mean you must buy it. You have the **prerogative** of changing your mind.
- A person suspected of a crime has the **prerogative** of refusing to answer questions unless his or her lawyer is present.

_a_ *Prerogative* means   a. a choice.   b. a duty.   c. a belief.

8 tacit
(tăs′ĭt)
-adjective

- Rosemary and her boyfriend aren't officially engaged, but they have a **tacit** understanding that they'll be getting married sooner or later.
- Most families seem to have a **tacit** agreement about who sits where at the dining table. Everyone always takes the same place, although the seating has never been discussed.

_b_ *Tacit* means   a. unusual.   b. unstated.   c. insensitive.

9 tactless
(tăkt′lĭs)
-adjective

- "If you don't want to eat the spinach quiche," Richard told his kids, "just say, 'No, thanks.' It's **tactless** to say, 'No, it's yucky.'"
- There's an old joke about a guest who gets a rotten egg at breakfast. Not wanting to be **tactless**, he assures his host, "Parts of it are excellent."

_b_ *Tactless* means   a. long-winded.   b. insensitive.   c. intelligent.

10 whet
(wĕt)
-verb

- The opening scene of a play or movie must capture the spectators' attention immediately, to **whet** their interest in the story that is about to unfold.
- At newspaper stands in New York, the headlines are usually hidden from view. In London, however, headlines are boldly displayed. I wonder which system **whets** people's curiosity more.

_a_ *Whet* means   a. to arouse.   b. to account for.   c. to distract.

Matching Words with Definitions

Following are definitions of the ten words. Clearly write or print each word next to its definition. The sentences above and on the previous page will help you decide on the meaning of each word.

1. _discerning_ — Having keen insight; perceptive; clear-eyed
2. _incisive_ — Penetrating; clear and sharp; pointed
3. _crass_ — Coarse; vulgar
4. _colloquial_ — Related to informal speech or writing; conversational
5. _judicious_ — Showing good judgment; wise and careful
6. _tactless_ — Lacking skill or sensitivity in dealing with others
7. _tacit_ — Understood although not spoken
8. _whet_ — To excite or stimulate (the mind or appetite)
9. _prerogative_ — A special right or privilege
10. _hyperbole_ — Obvious exaggeration, usually for effect or emphasis

CAUTION: Do not go any further until you are sure the above answers are correct. Then you can use the definitions to help you in the following practices. Your goal is eventually to know the words well enough so that you don't need to check the definitions at all.

➤ *Sentence Check 1*

Using the answer line, complete each item below with the correct word from the box. Use each word once.

a. **colloquial**	b. **crass**	c. **discerning**	d. **hyperbole**	e. **incisive**
f. **judicious**	g. **prerogative**	h. **tacit**	i. **tactless**	j. **whet**

_____*whet*_____ 1. I can spend a long time reading the dictionary. Looking up one word ___s my curiosity about another, and the time passes without my noticing.

_____*colloquial*_____ 2. The play seemed very realistic: the stage set looked just like an ordinary apartment, and the dialogue was ___—the characters used ordinary, commonplace words and phrases.

_____*hyperbole*_____ 3. True, Aunt Myra can be irritating, but to call her "the most annoying person in the solar system" is ___.

_____*incisive*_____ 4. The TV journalist is famous for her ___ questioning. Her sharp, pointed questions quickly reveal her subjects' real thoughts and feelings.

_____*discerning*_____ 5. Before Uncle Trevor came to visit, we brought down from the attic the hideous painting he had given us and hung it up again. He's a(n) ___ man and would have noticed immediately if it was missing.

_____*crass*_____ 6. Lon took his parents to a nightclub for their anniversary, but they didn't like the comedian's ___ routine, with its four-letter words and off-color jokes.

_____*tacit*_____ 7. The salesclerk seemed to make a(n) ___ assumption that I had a lot of money to spend on a coat. She lost interest when I said that I was on a tight budget.

_____*tactless*_____ 8. It was rather ___ of Jon to brag about his great new job in front of Stan, who had just lost his.

_____*prerogative*_____ 9. Schools used to hold "Sadie Hawkins Day" dances, to which girls had the ___ of inviting boys. But these days, girls don't need a special day to exercise that right.

_____*judicious*_____ 10. Dropping out of school is seldom a(n) ___ decision, but many young people drop out anyway.

NOTE: Now check your answers to these questions by turning to page 177. Going over the answers carefully will help you prepare for the next two practices, for which answers are not given.

➤ *Sentence Check 2*

Using the answer lines, complete each item below with **two** words from the box. Use each word once.

_____*discerning*_____
_____*hyperbole*_____ 1–2. Lidia is not a very ___ woman. She never noticed when her own husband shaved off his beard, or when her son lost fifty pounds—and that's fact, not ___!

_____*incisive*_____
_____*prerogative*_____ 3–4. Our instructor's comments on our papers are so ___ that they're nearly sharp enough to draw blood. It's his ___ to criticize, but I wish he would do it more gently.

_____ *judicious* _____   5–6. In writing a paper, it is ___ to avoid ___ language. Although these
_____ *colloquial* _____   casual phrases are fine for everyday conversation, they are often
                                                          considered out of place in a student essay.

_____ *whet* _____   7–8. The speaker intended to ___ his audience's interest by opening with a
_____ *crass* _____   deliberately ___ remark. But his egregious° vulgarity shocked and
                                                     angered his listeners.

_____ *tacit* _____   9–10. There was a(n) ___ agreement in the office never to mention the boss's
_____ *tactless* _____   speech impediment. But one day a(n) ___ visitor blurted out, "What a
                                                        terrible stutter!"

➤ *Final Check:* Figures of Speech

Here is a final opportunity for you to strengthen your knowledge of the ten words. First read the following
selection carefully. Then fill in each blank with a word from the box at the top of the previous page.
(Context clues will help you figure out which word goes in which blank.) Use each word once.

Authors often use figures of speech, and a(n) (1)_____ *discerning* _____ reader should be able to

perceive and analyze these expressions. But figurative language is not the (2)_____ *prerogative* _____

of only professional writers; fledgling° student writers are entitled to use it too. Here are a few

examples.

(3)_____ *Hyperbole* _____, or exaggeration, is a common figure of speech, as in "The lecturer

never used a word with fewer than ten syllables." Meiosis, or understatement, is its opposite—as

when you get an A+ on a paper and say, "Not too bad." Simile and metaphor are very well-known.

In a simile, you state a comparison: "Jane is as thin as a toothpick." In a metaphor, however, the

comparison is not stated but (4)_____ *tacit* _____: "Jane is a toothpick."

We all use euphemism to avoid sounding (5)_____ *tactless* _____ or unfeeling: "Jane had a

nervous breakdown" seems more sympathetic than "Jane went nuts." Dysphemism is the opposite

of euphemism: it means being harsher than necessary, often for a humorous effect, as when you

call a child "the little monster." Dysphemism appears in many (6)_____ *colloquial* _____ and

slang expressions, such as "bad" (meaning *good*) and "crazy" (meaning *wonderful*). Another type

of dysphemism is deliberately using a vulgar, (7)_____ *crass* _____ expression—such as an

obscenity in a formal setting—to jolt and shock the audience.

Thoughtful, (8)_____ *judicious* _____ use of figures of speech can improve your writing. But

don't pepper your papers with them, and don't expect them to work miracles: they won't turn a

flabby, desultory° paper into a sharp, (9)_____ *incisive* _____ one, and they won't make a dull,

plodding paper effervescent°. There are many other figurative expressions. If this brief review

(10)_____ *whet* _____s your appetite for more, try looking up *oxymoron, onomatopoeia,* and

paronomasia.

Scores   Sentence Check 2 _____ %   Final Check _____ %

Enter your scores above and in the vocabulary performance chart on the inside back cover of the book.

ameliorate	negate
assent	potent
haphazard	rigorous
incontrovertible	spurious
intangible	therapeutic

Ten Words in Context

In the space provided, write the letter of the meaning closest to that of each **boldfaced** word. Use the context of the sentences to help you figure out each word's meaning.

1 **ameliorate**
(ə-mēl′yə-rāt′)
-*verb*

- The precinct Outreach Committee was established to **ameliorate** police-community relations.
- Communication between parents and kids can often be **ameliorated** by just a few meetings with a family therapist.

_a_ *Ameliorate* means   a. to improve.   b. to make worse.   c. to end.

2 **assent**
(ə-sĕnt′)
-*verb*

- A doctor wrote a book advising parents to let their kids live on candy if that's what the kids wanted. Most parents would not **assent** to this proposal, though.
- When a motion is voted on in a formal meeting, the "ayes" or "yes" votes are those who **assent**. The "nays" or "no" votes are those who disagree.

_a_ *Assent* means   a. to have the same opinion.   b. to have a different opinion.   c. not to care.

3 **haphazard**
(hăp-hăz′ərd)
-*adjective*

- I never make a shopping list; I just wander through the grocery store, picking up items in a **haphazard** manner.
- Dan did a **haphazard** job of proofreading his term paper. Consequently, he caught some errors but missed many others.

_c_ *Haphazard* means   a. happy.   b. carefully planned.   c. unplanned.

4 **incontrovertible**
(ĭn-kŏn′trə-vûr′tə-bəl)
-*adjective*

- It's **incontrovertible** that Jeffrey is Paul's son; he looks exactly like his dad.
- Even in mathematics, there is not always one **incontrovertible** answer to a problem—sometimes two or more answers can be defended.

_c_ *Incontrovertible* means   a. unknown.   b. mistaken.   c. unquestionable.

5 **intangible**
(ĭn-tăn′jə-bəl)
-*adjective*

- Although Grandpa died with little money, he left us an **intangible** legacy: his strength, his warmth, and his honesty.
- As a child, I thought of Christmas in terms of the gifts I'd get. Now I focus on its **intangible** aspects—family closeness and sharing.

_c_ *Intangible* means   a. not permanent.   b. not important.   c. not touchable.

6 **negate**
(nĭ-gāt′)
-*verb*

- The jury awarded a million dollars to the accident victim, but the judge later **negated** that award, reducing it to only a few thousand.
- The board of elections had to **negate** the results of the mayoral race when it was discovered that more than half of the voting machines were malfunctioning.

_a_ *Negate* means   a. to make invalid.   b. to demonstrate.   c. to confirm.

7 potent
(pōt′nt)
-adjective

- A child can easily overdose on pills meant to reduce pain and fever—they are **potent** medicines that need to be given carefully and in the right dosage.
- Alcohol is **potent** stuff—just as with drugs, one can die from an overdose.

 b *Potent* means   a. pure.   b. strong.   c. expensive.

8 rigorous
(rĭg′ər-əs)
-adjective

- There are several hiking trails in this area, ranging from easy ones for beginners to **rigorous** ones for experts.
- Erin is going through **rigorous** fitness training to get ready to run a marathon next month.

 b *Rigorous* means   a. easy.   b. difficult.   c. unfair.

9 spurious
(spyŏor′ē-əs)
-adjective

- "I asked for real cream for my coffee," said the customer in the restaurant, "not some **spurious**, tasteless substitute made of chemicals."
- When a supposed new work by Beethoven was discovered, music experts came from all over the world to decide if it was real or **spurious**.

 a *Spurious* means   a. false.   b. improved.   c. left over.

10 therapeutic
(thĕr′ə-pyōo′tĭk)
-adjective

- Melina had always heard that the "milk" in milkweed gets rid of warts, so she wrote to the Board of Health about it. The reply stated: "Its **therapeutic** properties, if any, are not proved."
- Diego's insurance company would not pay for his surgery. The company ruled that the operation was experimental, not **therapeutic**.

 c *Therapeutic* means   a. dangerous.   b. magical.   c. healing.

Matching Words with Definitions

Following are definitions of the ten words. Clearly write or print each word next to its definition. The sentences above and on the previous page will help you decide on the meaning of each word.

1. *ameliorate*   To make better
2. *potent*   Powerful
3. *spurious*   Fake; counterfeit
4. *haphazard*   Careless; lacking a plan; lacking order
5. *negate*   To make ineffective; void; invalidate
6. *rigorous*   Challenging
7. *therapeutic*   Serving to cure or heal
8. *intangible*   Not material; not perceivable by touch; not concrete
9. *assent*   To agree to
10. *incontrovertible*   Undeniable

CAUTION: Do not go any further until you are sure the above answers are correct. Then you can use the definitions to help you in the following practices. Your goal is eventually to know the words well enough so that you don't need to check the definitions at all.

➤ *Sentence Check 1*

Using the answer line, complete each item below with the correct word from the box. Use each word once.

a. **ameliorate**	b. **assent**	c. **haphazard**	d. **incontrovertible**	e. **intangible**
f. **negate**	g. **potent**	h. **rigorous**	i. **spurious**	j. **therapeutic**

haphazard   1. "You did a really ___ job of mowing the lawn," Mr. Dixon told his son. "Look—you left strips of tall grass all over the yard."

intangible   2. Exercise not only improves your health and fitness, but it also has a(n) ___ advantage: it raises your spirits.

potent   3. Good study skills are a(n) ___ tool for any college student.

rigorous   4. Sandra wasn't sure she would make it through the ___ computer programming class, but when it was over, she felt very proud of herself.

spurious   5. When he was caught with the stolen jewels, the man made up a(n) ___ story about having found them in an alley.

assent   6. Jerry was nervous about asking Zoe to live with him, not sure if she would ___ to the suggestion.

incontrovertible   7. The evidence against the accused man is ___. Even his lawyers admit that he'll be found guilty.

negate   8. "I said I'd let you have the car next weekend," Tom's mother said, "but I'll ___ that agreement if your behavior doesn't improve between now and then."

therapeutic   9. "This procedure is diagnostic, not ___," the doctor explained. "That is, it's used just to find out what's wrong with you, not to treat you."

ameliorate   10. "Settlement houses" such as the famous Hull House in Chicago were established to ___ conditions in the slums by providing social services.

NOTE: Now check your answers to these questions by turning to page 177. Going over the answers carefully will help you prepare for the next two practices, for which answers are not given.

➤ *Sentence Check 2*

Using the answer lines, complete each item below with **two** words from the box. Use each word once.

intangible
potent   1–2. Ghost stories grip our imagination partly because the spooks are ___ but nevertheless ___: how can creatures that are just thin air be so powerful?

rigorous
haphazard   3–4. To do well on a difficult, ___ exam, you need to plan and organize your studying. An unplanned, ___ approach will not get you a good grade.

incontrovertible
negate   5–6. The evidence against the defendant seemed ___—beyond dispute—but his lawyer intended to call a surprise witness whose testimony would ___ the prosecution's supposedly irrefutable° case.

_____ *therapeutic* _____   7–8. "Snake oil," worthless stuff with no ___ effects, was sold in traveling medicine shows as a cure-all. Now the term "snake oil" refers to any kind of phony, ___ claim.

_____ *spurious* _____

_____ *assent* _____   9–10. "I can't ___ to your proposal to cut tuition in half," the college president told the protesting students. "It might ___ your finances, but it would wreck the school's budget."

_____ *ameliorate* _____

➤ *Final Check:* When Is a Treatment Therapy?

Here is a final opportunity for you to strengthen your knowledge of the ten words. First read the following selection carefully. Then fill in each blank with a word from the box at the top of the previous page. (Context clues will help you figure out which word goes in which blank.) Use each word once.

When a news item appears about a health insurer's refusal to pay for "experimental" medical treatment, people often wonder exactly what this means. The answer is that an experimental procedure is being contrasted with a(n) (1)_____ *therapeutic* _____ treatment, which offers a good chance of recovery or improvement: it will cure patients or (2)_____ *ameliorate* _____ their condition. In addition, to be considered a therapy, a treatment must be safe. For instance, a(n) (3)_____ *potent* _____ medicine may have equally strong, but unwanted, side effects that can lessen or even (4)_____ *negate* _____ its benefits.

How does a new treatment become established as therapy? This is not a(n) (5)_____ *haphazard* _____ process: it does not happen by chance but involves a lengthy period of (6)_____ *rigorous* _____ research. The research is usually done first with animals and then with large numbers of people. The humans, of course, must (7)_____ *assent* _____ to being experimental subjects: this is the meaning of the well-known term "informed consent." The scientists who test a treatment must be objective and dispassionate°. They disregard (8)_____ *intangible* _____ effects such as "giving the patient hope." Instead, they look for solid, (9)_____ *incontrovertible* _____ evidence of physical results, and they are not swayed by (10)_____ *spurious* _____, untenable° claims of nonexistent cures.

Only a treatment that performs well on this formidable° test has real promise, so insurers that are wary of "experiments" are not necessarily being unreasonable or whimsical°.

Scores   Sentence Check 2 _____ %   Final Check _____ %

altercation	malevolent
circumspect	placate
deference	pugnacious
guile	tirade
impassive	volatile

Ten Words in Context

In the space provided, write the letter of the meaning closest to that of each **boldfaced** word. Use the context of the sentences to help you figure out each word's meaning.

1 altercation
(ôl′tər-kā′shən)
-*noun*

- The **altercation** between the store clerk and customer began when the customer accused the clerk of shortchanging him.
- The party guests were embarrassed when they heard their host and hostess having a bitter **altercation** in the kitchen.

c *Altercation* means   a. an embrace.   b. a task.   c. a quarrel.

2 circumspect
(sûr′kəm-spĕkt′)
-*adjective*

- Tory's two roommates are feuding. Tory has wisely decided to be **circumspect** and consider every aspect of the situation before becoming involved.
- Someone was stealing money from the cash register, but the boss chose to be **circumspect** and not act for a while. He didn't want to make an accusation without weighing all the possible consequences.

a *Circumspect* means   a. careful.   b. honest.   c. aggressive.

3 deference
(dĕf′ər-əns)
-*noun*

- A few generations ago, a young person was expected to stand up when an older person entered the room. That kind of **deference** is rare nowadays.
- In **deference** to his parents' wishes, Alan agreed not to get his eyebrow pierced until he was over twenty-one.

b *Deference* means   a. defiance.   b. a respectful giving in.   c. a difference of opinion.

4 guile
(gīl)
-*noun*

- The older boy used **guile** to decide who would get the last piece of pie. He told his little brother, "We'll flip a coin for it. Heads, I win; tails, you lose."
- Psalm 24 in the Bible says: "Keep thy tongue from evil, and thy lips from speaking **guile**."

a *Guile* means   a. deceit.   b. nonsense.   c. truthfulness.

5 impassive
(ĭm-păs′ĭv)
-*adjective*

- No one could tell what the judges were thinking during the competition—they had trained themselves to remain **impassive**.
- How could you remain **impassive** during that heartbreaking movie? I cried so much I used up a box of tissues.

c *Impassive* means   a. expressing horror.   b. expressing love.   c. expressing no feelings.

6 malevolent
(mə-lĕv′ə-lənt)
-*adjective*

- The ancient Egyptian tomb of Tutankhamen was said to be haunted by a **malevolent** spirit—a curse would fall on anyone who entered it.
- Early religions typically believed in many gods. Some gods were good and helpful, but others were **malevolent** and would cause harm if they were displeased.

c *Malevolent* means   a. friendly.   b. visible.   c. evil.

7 placate
(plā′kāt′)
-verb

- José had not finished his homework, but he was able to **placate** his teacher by offering to do it at lunchtime.
- In ancient times, people tried to keep volcanoes from erupting by offering food and gifts to **placate** the "volcano god."

_b_ *Placate* means   a. to anger.   b. to calm.   c. to fight.

8 pugnacious
(pŭg-nā′shəs)
-adjective

- There are two **pugnacious** children in the class who constantly start fights on the playground.
- Although Max is a professional boxer, he is not **pugnacious** in his private life. In fact, he is kind and gentle.

_a_ *Pugnacious* means   a. quarrelsome.   b. curious.   c. funny.

9 tirade
(tī′rād′)
-noun

- The meeting of the school board was interrupted by a long **tirade** from a parent who had come to express his fury about the amount of homework his son had to do.
- The history instructor, whose lectures were usually scholarly and calm, startled the class one day with a heated **tirade** about the Vietnam war.

_b_ *Tirade* means   a. a dialogue.   b. an angry speech.   c. a theory.

10 volatile
(vŏl′ə-tl)
-adjective

- Manic-depressives have a psychiatric disorder that makes them extremely **volatile**. They have episodes of excitement and giddy cheerfulness but then fall into deep gloom.
- Jean is a difficult roommate because her moods are so **volatile**. One day she's on top of the world; the next day she's in the depths of despair.

_c_ *Volatile* means   a. insensitive.   b. indirect.   c. changeable.

Matching Words with Definitions

Following are definitions of the ten words. Clearly write or print each word next to its definition. The sentences above and on the previous page will help you decide on the meaning of each word.

1.   *altercation*   A heated argument
2.   *circumspect*   Considering all the circumstances relevant to an action or a decision; prudent; cautious
3.   *placate*   To soothe or pacify, especially by making concessions
4.   *tirade*   A long, passionate, critical speech
5.   *guile*   Slyness and cunning; trickery
6.   *volatile*   Tending to change often; unstable
7.   *deference*   A courteous yielding to another's wishes
8.   *malevolent*   Having or showing ill will; malicious; spiteful
9.   *pugnacious*   Eager and ready to fight
10.   *impassive*   Showing no emotion

CAUTION: Do not go any further until you are sure the above answers are correct. Then you can use the definitions to help you in the following practices. Your goal is eventually to know the words well enough so that you don't need to check the definitions at all.

➤ *Sentence Check 1*

Using the answer line, complete each item below with the correct word from the box. Use each word once.

a. **altercation**	b. **circumspect**	c. **deference**	d. **guile**	e. **impassive**
f. **malevolent**	g. **placate**	h. **pugnacious**	i. **tirade**	j. **volatile**

circumspect   1. Steve is not being at all ___ about his affair. He meets the "other woman" in public places where his wife frequently goes, as if he hasn't considered the consequences of getting caught.

guile   2. The newspaper story warned of a band of thieves who used ___ to charm and befriend elderly people, get into their homes, and then rob them.

impassive   3. Jerry will never be a good poker player, because he can't keep his face ___. If he gets a good hand, he looks delighted; if the hand is bad, he frowns and shakes his head.

altercation   4. The two children were friendly with each other until they both wanted to play with the toy truck. Then there was a fierce ___ over who would get it.

pugnacious   5. I never speak to my neighbor if I can avoid it. He is so ___ that he can take offense and start a fight over the most innocent remark.

deference   6. Alana and Len postponed their wedding in ___ to his parents, who were about to leave on a world cruise they'd been planning for years.

volatile   7. The French have a saying about their ___ climate: "If you don't like our weather, wait ten minutes." And the weather in France often does seem to change that quickly!

tirade   8. Invited to present a talk about the work his drug rehabilitation center was doing, the director instead gave a harsh ___ about cuts in state funding.

placate   9. After Cindy was served a slice of meat with a piece of glass in it, the restaurant manager tried to ___ her by giving her several gift certificates for free meals.

malevolent   10. Ferocious animals are not ___. They act out of instinct, not from any spiteful desire to hurt.

NOTE: Now check your answers to these questions by turning to page 177. Going over the answers carefully will help you prepare for the next two practices, for which answers are not given.

➤ *Sentence Check 2*

Using the answer lines, complete each item below with **two** words from the box. Use each word once.

impassive
tirade   1–2. June tried to remain stoic° and ___ during her father's angry ___, but finally she could no longer hide her feelings and burst into tears.

volatile
pugnacious   3–4. The crowd at the game seemed ___. There was a lot of rough kidding, and though some of it was good-natured, the fans looked as if they might turn mean and ___ at any moment.

malevolent   5–6. The poisoner in the movie was ___ but also ___. She concealed her
circumspect   warped, evil plans by posing as a prim, proper librarian.

deference   7–8. "In ___ to our neighbors," said a sign at the sidewalk café, "let's not
placate   make too much noise." Nearby residents had complained, and the
   owner wanted to ___ them.

altercation   9–10. To end a long, grueling° ___ with his roommate, Adam resorted to ___.
guile   "I guess you're right," he said, not meaning a word of it.

➤ _Final Check:_ Hawks and Doves

Here is a final opportunity for you to strengthen your knowledge of the ten words. First read the following selection carefully. Then fill in each blank with a word from the box at the top of the previous page. (Context clues will help you figure out which word goes in which blank.) Use each word once.

Are you a hawk or a dove? According to some scientists who study behavior, a "hawk" is a fighter, a(n) (1)_____ _pugnacious_ _____ individual who meets every issue head-on. Hawks are not necessarily (2)_____ _malevolent_ _____: they don't wish evil on other people. But they are (3)_____ _volatile_ _____: in a conflict, they tend to react angrily—to "explode"—and they are not likely to back down. They may use words, in an abusive (4)_____ _tirade_ _____, or they may use physical violence, or both.

A "dove" is cautious and (5)_____ _circumspect_ _____. Doves want to avoid trouble. If a(n) (6)_____ _altercation_ _____ arises, they will try to stop it or at least keep the quarrel from getting any worse. They'll try to (7)_____ _placate_ _____ their opponents by being soothing, soft-spoken, and submissive°, and by listening with polite (8)_____ _deference_ _____. Doves aren't necessarily angels: they sometimes use (9)_____ _guile_ _____ and duplicity° to obtain their own ends; and their unemotional, (10)_____ _impassive_ _____ reaction may be part of a plan of deceit. Usually, though, they are sincere about being peaceable and about their willingness to acquiesce° in another's wishes or capitulate° to another's demands.

Of course, people cannot be divided neatly into these two categories, and most of us probably show some dovish traits as well as some hawkish traits. But the question above is a fair one. Think about yourself and about people you know: On the whole, are you peace-loving, conciliatory° doves or warlike, irascible° hawks?

Scores	Sentence Check 2 _____%	Final Check _____%

Enter your scores above and in the vocabulary performance chart on the inside back cover of the book.

CHAPTER
25

capricious	phenomenon
catharsis	rectify
discrepancy	resolution
ephemeral	retract
induce	serene

Ten Words in Context

In the space provided, write the letter of the meaning closest to that of each **boldfaced** word. Use the context of the sentences to help you figure out each word's meaning.

1 **capricious**
(kə-prĭsh′əs)
-adjective

- It's understandable when a child says "I want to be a firefighter" one day and "I want to be a doctor" the next, but it's strange for an adult to be so **capricious**.
- The actress is so spoiled and **capricious** that she'll order an entire new wardrobe, then decide she doesn't like any of it and throw all the clothes away.

_a_ *Capricious* means   a. impulsive.   b. wicked.   c. intelligent.

2 **catharsis**
(kĕ-thär′sĭs)
-noun

- Some therapists advise their clients to punch and kick pillows. The idea is that the patients can experience **catharsis** by releasing their anger that way.
- People in some families never raise their voices, while others seem to need to achieve **catharsis** by yelling at each other occasionally.

_b_ *Catharsis* means   a. confusion.   b. letting out feelings.   c. love.

3 **discrepancy**
(dĭ-skrĕp′ən-sē)
-noun

- After a **discrepancy** was found in the accounts, an investigation revealed that one of the bookkeepers had been stealing.
- The police solved the homicide case by asking all the suspects to account for their movements on the night of the killing. There was a **discrepancy** in one person's story—half an hour was missing—and he turned out to be the killer.

_c_ *Discrepancy* means   a. a reduction.   b. an increase.   c. a difference.

4 **ephemeral**
(ĭ-fĕm′ər-əl)
-adjective

- "Cooking is an **ephemeral** art," said Mom. "You create something beautiful, people gobble it up, and in minutes it's gone."
- One theory about fireworks is that they fascinate us because they are so **ephemeral**: they burst and fade away almost immediately.

_c_ *Ephemeral* means   a. worthless.   b. impossible to explain.   c. brief.

5 **induce**
(ĭn-do͞os′)
-verb

- The hypnotist claimed to be able to **induce** a trance in any volunteer.
- Whatever **induced** you to do your Bugs Bunny imitation at that very formal dinner?

_a_ *Induce* means   a. to cause.   b. to prevent.   c. to predict.

6 **phenomenon**
(fĭ-nŏm′ə-nŏn′)
-noun

- "Déja vu" is a **phenomenon** almost everyone has experienced. It is the sensation, while hearing or seeing something for the first time, that one has heard or seen it before.
- A comet was a terrifying **phenomenon** in earlier centuries. No one knew what comets were, so when one appeared in the sky, people saw it as a sign of disaster.

_a_ *Phenomenon* means   a. an observable event.   b. something imaginary.   c. a failure.

7 rectify
(rĕk′tə-fī′)
-verb

• According to an old story, when Abraham Lincoln was a store clerk, he short-changed a customer by a nickel, then walked miles to her house to **rectify** the situation.

• I put a cup of salt instead of a cup of sugar into the cake batter. There's no way to **rectify** the mistake; I'll have to throw the whole mess out.

_c_ *Rectify* means   a. to repeat.   b. to discuss.   c. to correct.

8 resolution
(rĕz′ə-lōō′shən)
-noun

• By increasing the police force, installing better street lights, and encouraging neighborhood watch programs, the new mayor demonstrated her **resolution** to make the city a safer place to live.

• When Jane's brother made a nasty remark about her husband, Jane forgot her **resolution** not to lose her temper.

_b_ *Resolution* means   a. a question.   b. a vow.   c. a repetition.

9 retract
(rĭ-trăkt′)
-verb

• Jane says she will never speak to her brother again unless he will **retract** his insult to her husband.

• No one can trust Harry's promises: he **retracts** them as soon as he makes them.

_a_ *Retract* means   a. to withdraw.   b. to strengthen.   c. to remember.

10 serene
(sə-rēn′)
-adjective

• On a day like this, when the ocean is so smooth and **serene**, it is hard to imagine that it can be rough and stormy.

• Shaking and upset after her accident, Jolene sat very still and had a cup of tea to try to make herself feel **serene** again.

_a_ *Serene* means   a. quiet and at peace.   b. anxious.   c. angry.

Matching Words with Definitions

Following are definitions of the ten words. Clearly write or print each word next to its definition. The sentences above and on the previous page will help you decide on the meaning of each word.

1. ___*phenomenon*___   A fact or event that can be observed
2. ___*induce*___   To bring on
3. ___*capricious*___   Changeable; acting on impulses; unpredictable
4. ___*rectify*___   To remedy; make right
5. ___*discrepancy*___   A lack of agreement, as between facts; an inconsistency
6. ___*catharsis*___   Emotional release
7. ___*serene*___   Peaceful; calm
8. ___*ephemeral*___   Lasting for only a short time; fleeting
9. ___*retract*___   To take back
10. ___*resolution*___   Determination

CAUTION: Do not go any further until you are sure the above answers are correct. Then you can use the definitions to help you in the following practices. Your goal is eventually to know the words well enough so that you don't need to check the definitions at all.

➤ Sentence Check 1

Using the answer line, complete each item below with the correct word from the box. Use each word once.

a. **capricious**	b. **catharsis**	c. **discrepancy**	d. **ephemeral**	e. **induce**
f. **phenomenon**	g. **rectify**	h. **resolution**	i. **retract**	j. **serene**

_____ *induce* _____ 1. When a pregnant woman has gone past her due date, her doctors sometimes give her medication to ___ labor—in other words, to cause the baby to be born.

_____ *rectify* _____ 2. "I feel bad about what happened, and I'd like to ___ it," said our neighbor. "How much will it cost to fix the window my kids broke with their baseball?"

_____ *serene* _____ 3. After a rough day at work, what makes you feel ___ again? For some people, the answer is a brisk walk; others prefer a hot bath or a brief nap.

_____ *discrepancy* _____ 4. When Leonard gets his monthly bank statement, there is usually a(n) ___ between it and his own records. The gap isn't large—just five or ten dollars—but it's almost always there.

_____ *catharsis* _____ 5. After years of holding back her anger at her father, Mimi achieved ___ by writing him a long, furious letter—and then burning it.

_____ *ephemeral* _____ 6. An old French song describes the joys of love as ___, but the sorrows of love as lasting a lifetime.

_____ *retract* _____ 7. "I said I would marry you," Marie told Hank. "But now that I know how you've lied to me, I ___ that promise."

_____ *phenomenon* _____ 8. Superstitions are a puzzling ___. What is it that makes otherwise well-informed and sensible people step aside to avoid walking under a ladder?

_____ *resolution* _____ 9. Having decided that TV was taking up too much of her life, Angie made a(n) ___ not to watch it for a week.

_____ *capricious* _____ 10. Tina seems to take pleasure in being ___. One day she says she loves school; the next day she says she hates it. On Tuesday she decides that she likes being single; on Wednesday she's upset that she's not married.

NOTE: Now check your answers to these questions by turning to page 177. Going over the answers carefully will help you prepare for the next two practices, for which answers are not given.

➤ Sentence Check 2

Using the answer lines, complete each item below with **two** words from the box. Use each word once.

_____ *serene* _____ 1–2. To escape the stress and turbulence° of city life, my parents retired to a
_____ *induce* _____ quiet, ___ small town. Now they say nothing would ___ them to leave that placid° spot.

_____ *phenomenon* _____ 3–4. Her next-door neighbor's cold, unfriendly attitude was a puzzling ___
_____ *resolution* _____ to Lucy. She made a(n) ___ to ask him directly if she had somehow offended him.

_____ *capricious* _____   5–6. The heat in our apartment building is ___: we're either too hot or too

_____ *rectify* _____   cold. The owner is afraid that only an expensive new boiler can ___ the situation.

_____ *catharsis* _____   7–8. People who have a "near-death" experience often describe it as a(n)

_____ *ephemeral* _____   ___ that leaves them feeling purified. But the effect can be ___: it soon fades, and they return to their old ways of life.

_____ *retract* _____   9–10. I hated to ___ my promise to buy the kids new bicycles, but there was a

_____ *discrepancy* _____   large ___ between what the bikes cost and what I could afford to pay.

➤ *Final Check:* New Year's Resolutions

Here is a final opportunity for you to strengthen your knowledge of the ten words. First read the following selection carefully. Then fill in each blank with a word from the box at the top of the previous page. (Context clues will help you figure out which word goes in which blank.) Use each word once.

Breathes there the man, with soul so dead (to quote Sir Walter Scott), who never to himself has said, *This year I resolve to . . .* ? Probably not. Every year, everyone seems to make at least one New Year's (1)_____ *resolution* _____. It's a recurring (2)_____ *phenomenon* _____: no matter how little success we've had in quitting smoking or getting more exercise in the months just past, we still believe we'll do it now. We have a touching faith that expressing our determination will somehow (3)_____ *induce* _____ us to be better, will lead us to (4)_____ *rectify* _____ whatever is wrong with our lives. And perhaps making these promises also serves as a(n) (5)_____ *catharsis* _____: we feel cleaner and purer, (6)_____ *serene* _____ and at peace with the world.

However, we seem to overlook a few incontrovertible° facts. For one thing, most New Year's vows prove to be (7)_____ *ephemeral* _____. It's amazing how soon we forget them and return to our former depravity°. This may be because so many of them are (8)_____ *capricious* _____: we make a whimsical° or quixotic° promise on the spur of the moment without thinking, "Can I really do this?" or even "Do I really want to do this?" Thus (if we consider the matter at all), we will usually see a huge (9)_____ *discrepancy* _____ between our goals and what we actually achieve. Interestingly, though, no one ever seems to (10)_____ *retract* _____ a resolution. You've probably never said, "No, I take it back. I won't lose ten pounds this year." And although time after time, our New Year's goals turn out to be elusive°, we keep on setting them.

This year, I resolve to read some Scott, instead of just quoting him.

Scores	Sentence Check 2 _____ %	Final Check _____ %

Enter your scores above and in the vocabulary performance chart on the inside back cover of the book.

UNIT FIVE: *Review*

The box at the right lists twenty-five words from Unit Five. Using the clues at the bottom of the page, fill in these words to complete the puzzle that follows.

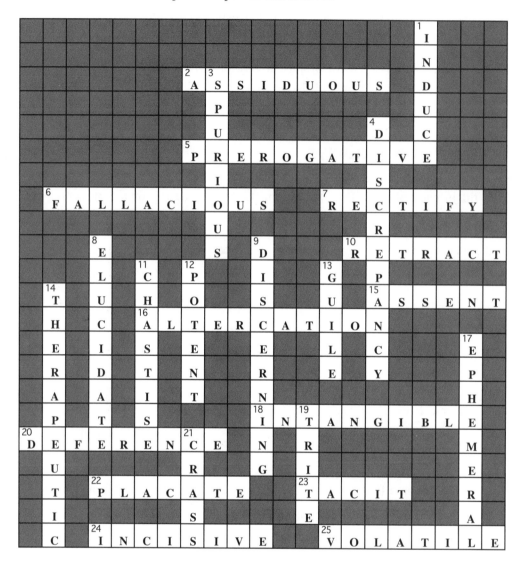

altercation
assent
assiduous
chastise
crass
deference
discerning
discrepancy
elucidate
ephemeral
fallacious
guile
incisive
induce
intangible
placate
potent
prerogative
rectify
retract
spurious
tacit
therapeutic
trite
volatile

ACROSS

2. Careful, hardworking, and thorough
5. A special right or privilege
6. Based on error; mistaken
7. To correct; make right
10. To take back
15. To agree to
16. A heated argument
18. Not material
20. A courteous yielding to another's wishes
22. To soothe or pacify
23. Understood although not spoken
24. Penetrating; pointed
25. Tending to change often; unstable

DOWN

1. To bring on
3. Fake
4. A lack of agreement, as between facts; inconsistency
8. To explain; clarify
9. Having keen insight; clear-eyed
11. To scold sharply
12. Powerful
13. Slyness and cunning
14. Serving to cure or heal
17. Lasting for only a short time; fleeting
19. Overused and commonplace
21. Coarse; vulgar

UNIT FIVE: Test 1

PART A
Choose the word that best completes each item and write it in the space provided.

discrepancy   1. To his horror, the bank teller realized that there was a $4,000 ___ between the money in his drawer and what his records showed he should have.

     a. phenomenon   b. deference   c. discrepancy   d. catharsis

exalted   2. The job applicant's letters of recommendation were very impressive. They ___ her as a model employee whom any company would be lucky to hire.

     a. exalted   b. induced   c. assented   d. placated

placid   3. The peaceable old hound lay quietly on the porch, gazing ahead with a sweet, ___ expression.

     a. capricious   b. crass   c. placid   d. malevolent

negate   4. The movie about a kindly man who murders in a moment of panic poses an interesting question: does one horrible act ___ a lifetime of good works?

     a. negate   b. elucidate   c. whet   d. rectify

haphazard   5. The boys certainly did a(n) ___ job of shoveling the sidewalk. A few places are cleared, but others are still covered with snow and ice.

     a. serene   b. haphazard   c. ephemeral   d. discerning

therapeutic   6. Old-time doctors used to recommend that their patients visit the seashore, believing that salty sea breezes were ___.

     a. spurious   b. insurgent   c. impassive   d. therapeutic

guile   7. _Gaslight_ is a chilling movie about an evil man who uses ___ to convince his wife that she is insane.

     a. tirade   b. phenomenon   c. guile   d. hyperbole

potent   8. The town council is a(n) ___ force in our city. Its members are effective leaders who get things done.

     a. potent   b. tactless   c. impassive   d. volatile

hypocrisy   9. When Rena fell into debt, her husband criticized her for careless spending. Later, when she learned he was even more in debt, she was angry at his ___.

     a. phenomenon   b. prerogative   c. hypocrisy   d. resolution

rectify   10. It took me only half an hour to put my daughter's new toy together wrong, but it took me three hours to ___ my error.

     a. chastise   b. exalt   c. rectify   d. induce

pugnacious   11. Why is Chuck such a bully? No one else in his family is the least bit ___, but he is constantly looking for a fight.

     a. pugnacious   b. serene   c. assiduous   d. colloquial

(Continues on next page)

_____malevolent_____ 12. The "bad guy" in many Disney movies is actually a(n) ___ female. *Snow White* has a wicked queen; *Sleeping Beauty* has an evil fairy, Maleficent; and *The Little Mermaid* has Ursula the Sea Witch.

      a. judicious   b. ephemeral   c. malevolent   d. intangible

_____whetted_____ 13. An article on the history of birth control in the United States ___ my interest in learning about Margaret Sanger, a pioneering nurse who went to jail for distributing "obscene" material about family planning.

      a. ameliorated   b. chastised   c. negated   d. whetted

PART B

Write **C** if the italicized word is used **correctly**. Write **I** if the word is used **incorrectly**.

_I_ 14. For the first time in years, our whole family was together for Thanksgiving. It was a wonderful *altercation*, with everyone laughing and talking and telling old family stories.

_I_ 15. The neighbor *assented* angrily when the children asked if they could retrieve their baseball from his yard, saying, "Don't even think of stepping on my property!"

_C_ 16. My husband and I have a *tacit* understanding that whoever doesn't make dinner washes the dishes. We've never discussed it; we just started it when we got married, and we've continued that way.

_C_ 17. Beware of workmen who come to your door and offer to pave your driveway with materials they have "left over from another job." The story is probably *spurious,* and you'll end up paying money for nothing.

_I_ 18. "I'm too embarrassed to tell Kathleen I lost the ring she lent me," Cindy said to Kathleen's husband. "Could you tell her? You're so *tactless*—you'll make her understand and forgive me."

_I_ 19. It was strange to finally meet my pen pal. After all those years of imagining what she'd be like, suddenly there she was, solid and *intangible*.

_I_ 20. With so many bills waiting to be paid, it was *judicious* of Kenneth to spend his entire paycheck on a new leather jacket.

_C_ 21. Although Susan is usually very gentle with her children, she *chastises* them sharply if they do something that could endanger themselves or others.

_I_ 22. Don't ever put butter on a burn. Although butter was once believed to relieve the pain, it could actually *ameliorate* the injury.

_C_ 23. No matter how many times I see a rainbow, I still find it a fascinating *phenomenon*. What a wonderful display of light and color!

_C_ 24. It's hard to know how upset Lee really is about her fight with Bob. She says, "This is the worst thing that ever happened to me," but since she always uses *hyperbole*, I'm not sure how serious she is.

_I_ 25. Finding Rebekah nervously pacing the floor at 3 a.m., her housemate asked worriedly, "Why are you so *serene*? What's the matter?"

Score   (Number correct) _____ × 4 = _____ %

Enter your score above and in the vocabulary performance chart on the inside back cover of the book.

UNIT FIVE: Test 2

PART A

Complete each item with a word from the box. Use each word once.

a. **assiduous**	b. **capricious**	c. **catharsis**	d. **caustic**	e. **circumspect**
f. **colloquial**	g. **elucidate**	h. **fallacious**	i. **incontrovertible**	j. **insurgent**
k. **prerogative**	l. **tirade**	m. **trite**		

incontrovertible 1. The link between cigarette smoking and lung cancer is not merely suspected—it is a(n) ___ fact.

caustic 2. When I struck out at the company softball game, everyone was polite about it except the office sourpuss. "Nice work, loser," he said in a(n) ___ tone of voice.

capricious 3. Spring is often a(n) ___ season, with the weather changing hour to hour from summery heat to autumn chill.

trite 4. When someone asks you "How are you?" do you usually give the expected but ___ answer—"Fine"—or do you describe how you really are?

fallacious 5. I had to rewrite my entire paper after I realized that my reasoning was ___ —I had drawn the wrong conclusions from some of my facts.

insurgent 6. The revolution was begun by a few ___s who had come to believe that the king was evil and corrupt and had to be overthrown.

tirade 7. No one in the office had ever heard Howard raise his voice, so everyone was astonished when he delivered an angry ___ to a client who was being rude and abusive to the receptionist.

colloquial 8. Will Rogers, a famous humorist in the 1920s and 1930s, was beloved for his informal, ___ style. He had been a cowboy, and he talked in plain language that everyone could understand and enjoy.

catharsis 9. The congregation was so moved by the powerful preacher that many of them wept and prayed aloud. Afterward, churchgoers seemed exhausted by the ___ they had experienced.

assiduous 10. It's not "luck" that makes Juan a success at his job. It's old-fashioned effort—he's a very ___ worker.

circumspect 11. Because Angie's approach is so ___, her friends often ask her for advice. She listens carefully and considers every detail before making a suggestion.

prerogative 12. Don't cut the birthday cake! It is the ___ of the guest of honor to cut the first slice.

elucidate 13. I couldn't figure out what my daughter's drawing was supposed to be, so I said "Tell me about it," hoping that she would ___ the meaning of the brown squiggles and purple stripes.

(Continues on next page)

PART B
Write **C** if the italicized word is used **correctly**. Write **I** if the word is used **incorrectly**.

_I_   14. My grandmother is the most *volatile* person I know. Nothing seems to affect her mood, which is always calm and peaceful.

_I_   15. The Martins are so *crass* that their home is always open to anyone who needs a place to stay and some friendly assistance for a few days.

_C_   16. In Japan, students are expected to show their teacher a good deal of *deference,* accepting his or her wishes and never arguing back.

_I_   17. When I play "Monopoly" with my little daughter. I give her too much of my money so that she can win and the game can finally end. She's so *discerning* that she never notices.

_C_   18. The doctor's *impassive* face as she sat down to tell me my test results told me nothing—the news could have been either good or tragic.

_C_   19. Becoming a restaurant chef may sound like fun, but it's not easy. The courses at most restaurant schools are *rigorous*—many people drop out without completing the work.

_I_   20. Realizing that the clerk had not heard her request, Dinah *retracted* her question again, more loudly.

_I_   21. I groaned when I saw that Dr. Latham was teaching my American history class. His lectures are so *incisive* that I have to struggle to stay awake.

_C_   22. In order to *placate* the neighbors after our dog dug up their garden, we spent a Saturday repairing the damage and even bought them some new garden tools.

_I_   23. The movie was not only terrible but also *ephemeral,* lasting for nearly three long, boring hours.

_C_   24. Dorrie has made up her mind to stay in school until she graduates. "Nothing would *induce* me to leave without my diploma," she declares.

_I_   25. Matt has too much *resolution* to decide what he wants to do next. He keeps waffling among ideas: College? The military? Vocational school? A job?

> *Score*   (Number correct) _____ × 4 = _____ %

Enter your score above and in the vocabulary performance chart on the inside back cover of the book.

UNIT FIVE: Test 3

PART A: Synonyms
In the space provided, write the letter of the choice that is most nearly the **same** in meaning as the **boldfaced** word.

  _d_ 1. **altercation**   a) a bruise   b) a widely-known fact   c) a luxury   d) a fight

  _a_ 2. **assiduous**   a) hard-working   b) doubtful   c) sly   d) messy

  _c_ 3. **catharsis**   a) a medical procedure   b) a journey   c) an emotional release
d) a period of solitude

  _c_ 4. **circumspect**   a) busy   b) tolerant   c) prudent   d) lazy

  _d_ 5. **deference**   a) self-righteousness   b) confusion   c) dislike   d) respect

  _d_ 6. **discerning**   a) argumentative   b) undersized   c) dishonest   d) perceptive

  _c_ 7. **discrepancy**   a) an announcement   b) an observation   c) an inconsistency
d) an explanation

  _a_ 8. **hypocrisy**   a) insincerity   b) cleanliness   c) bad temper   d) generosity

  _c_ 9. **incisive**   a) legal   b) boring   c) penetrating   d) swift

  _b_ 10. **incontrovertible** a) sad   b) undeniable   c) blameless   d) never tiring

  _d_ 11. **induce**   a) accuse   b) leave alone   c) set free   d) bring about

  _b_ 12. **insurgent**   a) an instructor   b) a rebel   c) an assistant   d) an annoyance

  _d_ 13. **intangible**   a) flawless   b) from another country   c) rare; nearly extinct
d) not able to be touched

  _b_ 14. **negate**   a) to make strong b) to make ineffective c) to make fun of d) to make larger

  _d_ 15. **phenomenon**   a) a tradition   b) a religious belief   c) a story with a moral   d) an event

  _d_ 16. **potent**   a) lengthy   b) humble   c) bitter   d) strong

  _a_ 17. **prerogative**   a) a special privilege   b) a way of life   c) a habit   d) an absence

  _c_ 18. **rectify**   a) to collapse   b) to carry   c) to correct   d) to connect

  _d_ 19. **resolution**   a) supplies   b) self-importance   c) wastefulness   d) determination

  _a_ 20. **retract**   a) to take back   b) to be careful   c) to take for granted   d) to worry

  _c_ 21. **serene**   a) talkative   b) lonely   c) peaceful   d) greedy

  _c_ 22. **tacit**   a) sarcastic   b) rapid   c) implied   d) polite

  _c_ 23. **therapeutic**   a) unknown   b) loosely connected   c) curative   d) modern

  _d_ 24. **tirade**   a) a refusal to speak   b) a plea   c) an exclamation   d) an angry speech

  _b_ 25. **whet**   a) to disgust   b) to stimulate   c) to bore   d) to listen

(Continues on next page)

PART B: Antonyms
In the space provided, write the letter of the choice that is most nearly the **opposite** in meaning to the **boldfaced** word.

_b_ 26. **ameliorate**   a) to remove   b) to worsen   c) to repeat   d) to steal

_a_ 27. **assent**   a) to refuse   b) to pretend   c) to insist   d) to construct

_a_ 28. **capricious**   a) steady   b) worried   c) strong   d) famous

_d_ 29. **caustic**   a) calm   b) unusual   c) boring   d) kindly

_d_ 30. **chastise**   a) to give directions to   b) to confuse   c) to grasp   d) to praise

_b_ 31. **colloquial**   a) spoken by one person   b) formal   c) lengthy   d) humorous

_a_ 32. **crass**   a) tasteful   b) enlarged   c) noisy   d) absurd

_b_ 33. **elucidate**   a) to forget   b) to make confusing   c) to add to   d) to lose

_a_ 34. **ephemeral**   a) permanent   b) vicious   c) honest   d) friendly

_b_ 35. **exalt**   a) to waste time   b) to ridicule   c) to search for   d) to trick

_c_ 36. **fallacious**   a) far away   b) harmless   c) truthful   d) graceful

_a_ 37. **guile**   a) honesty   b) stubbornness   c) ability   d) action

_c_ 38. **haphazard**   a) talkative   b) highly educated   c) carefully planned   d) lonely

_a_ 39. **hyperbole**   a) understatement   b) translation   c) excuse   d) betrayal

_d_ 40. **impassive**   a) forgiving   b) pushy   c) musical   d) emotional

_b_ 41. **judicious**   a) colorful   b) foolish   c) talented   d) abnormal

_b_ 42. **malevolent**   a) foreign-born   b) well-meaning   c) complicated   d) smooth

_a_ 43. **placate**   a) to irritate   b) to befriend   c) to allow   d) to destroy

_a_ 44. **placid**   a) excited   b) loyal   c) stubborn   d) careless

_b_ 45. **pugnacious**   a) wise   b) peaceful   c) mentally slow   d) useful

_d_ 46. **rigorous**   a) amusing   b) based on false information   c) unstable   d) easy

_a_ 47. **spurious**   a) genuine   b) common   c) generous   d) insulting

_b_ 48. **tactless**   a) recent   b) sensitive   c) unfair   d) positive

_b_ 49. **trite**   a) bad-smelling   b) original   c) lengthy   d) graceful

_d_ 50. **volatile**   a) wealthy   b) proud   c) numerous   d) stable

---

Score   (Number correct) _____ × 2 = _____ %

Enter your score above and in the vocabulary performance chart on the inside back cover of the book.

Unit Six

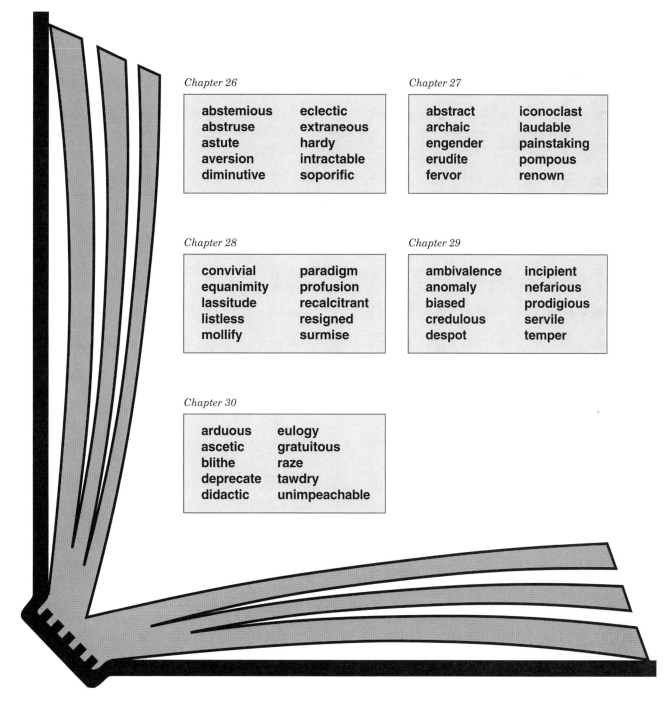

Chapter 26

abstemious	eclectic
abstruse	extraneous
astute	hardy
aversion	intractable
diminutive	soporific

Chapter 27

abstract	iconoclast
archaic	laudable
engender	painstaking
erudite	pompous
fervor	renown

Chapter 28

convivial	paradigm
equanimity	profusion
lassitude	recalcitrant
listless	resigned
mollify	surmise

Chapter 29

ambivalence	incipient
anomaly	nefarious
biased	prodigious
credulous	servile
despot	temper

Chapter 30

arduous	eulogy
ascetic	gratuitous
blithe	raze
deprecate	tawdry
didactic	unimpeachable

abstemious	eclectic
abstruse	extraneous
astute	hardy
aversion	intractable
diminutive	soporific

Ten Words in Context

In the space provided, write the letter of the meaning closest to that of each **boldfaced** word. Use the context of the sentences to help you figure out each word's meaning.

1 **abstemious**
(ăb-stē′mē-əs)
-*adjective*

- Although I may enjoy eating a pint of cookie-dough ice cream, I know I look and feel better when I am more **abstemious**.
- We say that an **abstemious** person who eats very little "eats like a bird," but in fact birds eat almost all the time.

 _b_ *Abstemious* means   a. self-indulgent.   b. moderate in eating and drinking.   c. sophisticated.

2 **abstruse**
(ăb-strōos′)
-*adjective*

- The scholarship winner is so bright that as a high school freshman, she was already taking university-level courses in **abstruse** subjects.
- The Swedish art film was too **abstruse** for me—it was full of symbols and references that I couldn't understand.

 _a_ *Abstruse* means   a. hard to comprehend.   b. absurd.   c. elementary.

3 **astute**
(ə-stōot′)
-*adjective*

- How kind of you to give me a sweater, and how **astute** of you to have noticed that sea-green is my favorite color!
- If you were a little more **astute**, you would have noticed that Betsy and Dave are not getting along well—they didn't say a word to each other all during dinner.

 _b_ *Astute* means   a. surprised.   b. shrewdly observant.   c. courageous.

4 **aversion**
(ə-vûr′zhən)
-*noun*

- Dad has such an **aversion** to answering machines that he hangs up as soon as he hears a recorded message.
- Denise has an **aversion** to dresses and skirts. She wears only pants.

 _a_ *Aversion to* means   a. a strong distaste for.   b. a strong preference for.   c. a knowledge of.

5 **diminutive**
(dĭ-mĭn′yə-tĭv)
-*adjective*

- Tory's income last year seemed so **diminutive** that he assumed he wouldn't have to pay taxes. He was wrong.
- When I saw a display of eighteenth-century costumes at the museum, I was surprised at their small size. Our ancestors must have been **diminutive** people!

 _c_ *Diminutive* means   a. impossible to measure.   b. sizable.   c. little.

6 **eclectic**
(ĭ-klĕk′tĭk)
-*adjective*

- "We're having an **eclectic** dinner tonight," Kris announced; "first wonton soup, then Swedish meatballs, and then Pennsylvania Dutch shoofly pie for dessert!"
- The concert program was **eclectic**: the songs came from America, Germany, Italy, Spain, and Japan; and they included musical comedy, grand opera, and children's songs.

 _b_ *Eclectic* means   a. lacking in diversity.   b. varied.   c. lengthy.

7 **extraneous**
(ĭk-strā′nē-əs)
-*adjective*

- If you want to tell a joke well, do not include a lot of **extraneous** remarks, such as, "OK, here comes the funny part," or "Wait, I didn't tell that part right."
- On the old TV show *Dragnet,* the detective, Sergeant Joe Friday, was constantly saying, "Just the facts, ma'am," to prevent witnesses from wasting his time with **extraneous** comments and ideas.

a *Extraneous* means   a. unrelated.   b. excellent.   c. important.

8 **hardy**
(här′dē)
-*adjective*

- Although they are small, Shetland ponies are **hardy**, able to survive the long cold winters of their native Shetland Islands.
- Farm children had to be **hardy**; they were expected to work long hours in the fields.

a *Hardy* means   a. healthy and sturdy.   b. delicate.   c. hardhearted.

9 **intractable**
(ĭn-trăk′tə-bəl)
-*adjective*

- Doria came home from her job at the day-care center looking worn out. "The kids were really **intractable** today," she said. "We just couldn't get them to calm down and behave."
- Mules are notoriously **intractable**. You've probably heard the expression, "As stubborn as a mule."

b *Intractable* means   a. unclassifiable.   b. uncontrollable.   c. unrecognizable.

10 **soporific**
(sŏp′ə-rĭf′ĭk)
-*adjective*

- If you're having trouble sleeping, try a glass of warm milk, which is supposed to have a **soporific** effect.
- Jill plays tapes of soft, dreamy music in her baby's room at nap time. She hopes it will have a **soporific** effect.

c *Soporific* means   a. causing anger.   b. causing excitement.   c. causing drowsiness.

Matching Words with Definitions

Following are definitions of the ten words. Clearly write or print each word next to its definition. The sentences above and on the previous page will help you decide on the meaning of each word.

1. _____*abstruse*_____   Difficult to understand; deep

2. _____*aversion*_____   An intense dislike

3. _____*eclectic*_____   Coming from many sources

4. _____*extraneous*_____   Not essential; irrelevant

5. _____*astute*_____   Clever; perceptive

6. _____*soporific*_____   Causing sleep

7. _____*hardy*_____   Tough; strong

8. _____*abstemious*_____   Self-denying

9. _____*intractable*_____   Difficult to manage; hard to control; unruly

10. _____*diminutive*_____   Much smaller than the average

CAUTION: Do not go any further until you are sure the above answers are correct. Then you can use the definitions to help you in the following practices. Your goal is eventually to know the words well enough so that you don't need to check the definitions at all.

➤ Sentence Check 1

Using the answer line, complete each item below with the correct word from the box. Use each word once.

a. **abstemious**	b. **abstruse**	c. **astute**	d. **aversion**	e. **diminutive**
f. **eclectic**	g. **extraneous**	h. **hardy**	i. **intractable**	j. **soporific**

_____ *hardy* _____ 1. Many birds fly south in the winter, but some ___ species, such as cardinals and chickadees, stay to add color and life to the cold northern landscape.

_____ *intractable* _____ 2. At first, our puppy seemed ___; we couldn't teach him to obey. But a professional trainer showed us how to control him using praise and rewards.

_____ *aversion* _____ 3. Rosa used to love olives, but once she ate so many of them that she got sick. Since then, she has had a real ___ to them—she can't even stand to look at one.

_____ *astute* _____ 4. When there's a death in the family, don't try to hide it from the children. Even very young children can be ___ enough to see that something is wrong.

_____ *diminutive* _____ 5. Grandmother was a(n) ___ woman, not even five feet tall, but she had the strength of a much larger person.

_____ *soporific* _____ 6. I feel sorry for our pastor; he wants his sermons to inspire people, but they are so long and boring that they have a(n) ___ effect instead.

_____ *extraneous* _____ 7. "You need to edit your report," Professor Hawkins told the student. "You've got some good, useful information here, but it's buried under paragraphs of ___ data."

_____ *abstemious* _____ 8. Please be ___ in your use of Scotch tape—we've got only one roll to wrap all these presents.

_____ *abstruse* _____ 9. Trying to impress his intelligent new girlfriend, Al pretended to be reading books on ___ subjects such as quantum physics and chaos theory.

_____ *eclectic* _____ 10. Joel is a great dinner guest because his interests are so ___; no matter what the topic is, he can talk about it intelligently and amusingly.

NOTE: Now check your answers to these questions by turning to page 177. Going over the answers carefully will help you prepare for the next two practices, for which answers are not given.

➤ Sentence Check 2

Using the answer lines, complete each item below with **two** words from the box. Use each word once.

_____ *abstemious* _____
_____ *aversion* _____ 1–2. Vaughn is a(n) ___ man who has a(n) ___ to any kind of excess: he doesn't smoke or drink, he never overeats, and he limits his spending.

_____ *abstruse* _____
_____ *soporific* _____ 3–4. The ___ chapter in the chemistry text had a(n) ___ effect on Yasmine. As she tried to peruse° the difficult material, she had to struggle to stay awake.

_____ *hardy* _____
_____ *intractable* _____ 5–6. Mildew is a very ___ form of life. In damp weather, this fungus can start to grow on shower curtains and walls and soon becomes ___: it's almost impossible to control.

_____ *diminutive* _____ 7–8. A bonsai is a(n) ___ tree that is made tiny by special cultivation. When
_____ *astute* _____ her parents got one, three-year-old Lani was ___ enough to see where it
belonged: she put it by the front porch of her dollhouse.

_____ *eclectic* _____ 9–10. The readings in the course were ___: old and new, from many cultures,
_____ *extraneous* _____ by women and men. But they were all on one theme—growing up—
with no peripheral° or ___ topics.

➤ *Final Check:* Weird Facts

Here is a final opportunity for you to strengthen your knowledge of the ten words. First read the following
selection carefully. Then fill in each blank with a word from the box at the top of the previous page.
(Context clues will help you figure out which word goes in which blank.) Use each word once.

"The world is so full of a number of things, I'm sure we should all be as happy as kings."
These lines were written by the poet Robert Louis Stevenson more than a hundred years ago. The
world *is* full of a number of things, many of them strange, some of them wonderful, some funny,
some nearly unbelievable. Some are basic to everyone's education; others are (1)___*extraneous*___
but still fun to know. Here is a(n) (2)___*eclectic*___ collection of facts, taken from fields
including science, psychology, and just plain silliness:

• Albert Einstein was known as one of the most discerning°, (3)___*astute*___ thinkers of
all time. He had a remarkable understanding of such (4)___*abstruse*___ topics as time
and space. Yet when Einstein was nine years old, he still couldn't speak fluently. His parents
thought he might be retarded.
• If you're going into an area where there are lots of mosquitoes, be (5)___*abstemious*___
about eating bananas. Assiduous° research has found that mosquitoes are attracted to people
who have recently eaten this fruit.
• You probably know already that the penguin must be a(n) (6)___*hardy*___ bird to survive
in the fierce cold of Antarctica. Did you know, though, that a penguin can jump six feet in the air?
• Donald Duck comics were banned in Finland because Donald doesn't wear pants.
• In the movie *E.T.: The Extraterrestrial,* the sound of E.T. walking was made by a woman
squishing her hands in Jello.
• The famous psychiatrist Sigmund Freud had such an (7)___*aversion*___ to ferns that he
could not stay in the same room with a fern.
• There are more plastic flamingos in America than real ones.
• When opossums "play possum," they are not actually playing. Oddly enough, terror has a(n)
(8)___*soporific*___ effect on possums. Fright makes them go to sleep.
• A duck's quack does not echo. No one knows why.
• Mosquitoes have teeth. Since mosquitoes are so tiny, imagine how (9)___*diminutive*___
their teeth must be!
• Snakes are occasionally born with two heads. Such a two-headed snake is extremely
(10)___*intractable*___. Not only is it pugnacious° with other animals, but its two heads
fight each other for food.
• Thomas Edison was afraid of the dark. (Do you suppose that's why he invented the light bulb?)

Scores   Sentence Check 2 _____%   Final Check _____%

Enter your scores above and in the vocabulary performance chart on the inside back cover of the book.

27

abstract	iconoclast
archaic	laudable
engender	painstaking
erudite	pompous
fervor	renown

Ten Words in Context

In the space provided, write the letter of the meaning closest to that of each **boldfaced** word. Use the context of the sentences to help you figure out each word's meaning.

1 abstract
(ăb′străkt′)
-*adjective*

- For a person who has been blind since birth, color is just an **abstract** idea.
- A couple may believe in the **abstract** idea of "commitment," but they find out what true commitment is only when they face difficult experiences together.

_a_ *Abstract* means   a. vague.   b. absurd.   c. temporary.

2 archaic
(är-kā′ĭk)
-*adjective*

- Computers are changing so rapidly that a system bought just two years ago is already **archaic**.
- Marriage vows used to include the bride's promise to obey her husband. Today many couples consider this **archaic** and leave it out of the ceremony.

_a_ *Archaic* means   a. old-fashioned.   b. necessary.   c. permanent.

3 engender
(ĕn-jĕn′dər)
-*verb*

- An introductory music course in college can **engender** a lifelong love of music.
- Ken's rivalry with his cousin was **engendered** long ago, when they were in the same kindergarten class and competed to see who would learn the alphabet first.

_c_ *Engender* means   a. to endanger.   b. to complete.   c. to begin.

4 erudite
(ĕr′yə-dīt′)
-*adjective*

- Abby has earned several graduate degrees, although no one else in her family went to college. Her parents are proud of their **erudite** daughter.
- You don't have to be **erudite** to enjoy action movies—they are designed to entertain you, not make you think.

_b_ *Erudite* means   a. unskilled.   b. learned.   c. kindhearted.

5 fervor
(fûr′vər)
-*noun*

- Before the game, the coach talked to her players with great **fervor**, making them feel excited and determined to win.
- You can tell that Christy really loves the piano by the **fervor** with which she practices.

_c_ *Fervor* means   a. fear.   b. humor.   c. passion.

6 iconoclast
(ī-kŏn′ə-klăst′)
-*noun*

- Most politicians glorify the flag, apple pie, and motherhood; but our mayor is an **iconoclast** who says the flag is just a piece of cloth, apple pie is full of saturated fat, and mothers should be replaced by cloning.
- It's always risky to get Grandma and Jerry in the same room. Grandma is a very traditional Italian Catholic, while Jerry is an **iconoclast** who makes jokes about the pope and questions the teachings of Catholicism.

_b_ *Iconoclast* means   a. a conservative.   b. a rebel.   c. a criminal.

7 **laudable**
(lô′də-bəl)
-*adjective*

- The work of the Prom Committee was really **laudable**. As people entered the ballroom and saw the magnificent decorations, many burst into applause.
- The congresswoman has demonstrated a **laudable** concern for the voters, who have shown their appreciation by reelecting her twice.

_a_ *Laudable* means   a. admirable.   b. insufficient.   c. undesirable.

8 **painstaking**
(pānz′tā′kĭng)
-*adjective*

- The **painstaking** effort that went into the century-old patchwork quilt is hard to imagine. There are thousands of tiny patches, each stitched patiently by hand.
- Providing footnotes and a bibliography for a paper is **painstaking** work. Don't leave this to the last minute, but give it careful thought from the beginning.

_b_ *Painstaking* means   a. painful.   b. careful.   c. enjoyable.

9 **pompous**
(pŏm′pəs)
-*adjective*

- The ship's captain was so **pompous** that he would not eat at the same table with his officers. Instead, he sat in solitary splendor at a special table set with the ship's best china.
- "Do you expect me to stand in line with all these people to buy a concert ticket?" the man asked in a **pompous** voice. "Don't you realize who I am and how valuable my time is?"

_a_ *Pompous* means   a. self-important.   b. modest.   c. cruel.

10 **renown**
(rĭ-noun′)
-*noun*

- The artist Vincent van Gogh was unknown in his lifetime, but after his death his **renown** grew enormously.
- Throughout our neighborhood, Mrs. Lewis has won **renown** for her fabulous chocolate-chip cookies.

_c_ *Renown* means   a. criticism.   b. reality.   c. reputation.

Matching Words with Definitions

Following are definitions of the ten words. Clearly write or print each word next to its definition. The sentences above and on the previous page will help you decide on the meaning of each word.

1. ____erudite____   Having or showing wide knowledge
2. ____fervor____   Great warmth or intensity of emotion
3. ____engender____   To cause or produce; bring into existence
4. ____laudable____   Worthy of praise
5. ____painstaking____   Showing much care, effort, and hard work; diligent
6. ____pompous____   Having an inflated idea of one's own importance; arrogant
7. ____renown____   Fame
8. ____iconoclast____   Someone who attacks traditional ideas; someone who considers nothing sacred
9. ____archaic____   No longer current; out-of-date
10. ____abstract____   Theoretical; not applied; not practical

CAUTION: Do not go any further until you are sure the above answers are correct. Then you can use the definitions to help you in the following practices. Your goal is eventually to know the words well enough so that you don't need to check the definitions at all.

➤ *Sentence Check 1*

Using the answer line, complete each item below with the correct word from the box. Use each word once.

| a. **abstract** | b. **archaic** | c. **engender** | d. **erudite** | e. **fervor** |
| f. **iconoclast** | g. **laudable** | h. **painstaking** | i. **pompous** | j. **renown** |

archaic   1. My children have been brought up with modern cordless phones. To them, their grandmother's old-fashioned rotary dial telephone looks positively ___.

erudite   2. We are lucky to have such a(n) ___ speaker with us today. Dr. Volkmer holds three doctoral degrees and has taught at some of the world's greatest universities.

iconoclast   3. Year after year, the town pageant was very traditional until its new director—a real ___—decided to wrap the actors in aluminum foil and have them speak their lines in rap style.

fervor   4. I knew that Ron would feel strongly about our change of plans, but I didn't expect him to respond with such ___— he ranted and raved for half an hour.

abstract   5. Dan and his brother Barry are very different. Dan is down-to-earth and practical, while Barry loves to discuss ___ concepts like infinity and time.

engender   6. Little things can often ___ long-standing hostility. My aunts were on bad terms for years because one of them turned down a dinner invitation from the other.

painstaking   7. The new biography of Emily Dickinson won high praise. "The author's ___ research has revealed many details about the poet that were not previously known," one reviewer wrote.

pompous   8. After winning a small part in a Broadway show, the actor became so ___ that he wouldn't speak to his old friends. "I don't have time for little people," he said.

renown   9. That restaurant enjoys such ___ that it's almost impossible to get a reservation there—the tables are booked months in advance.

laudable   10. "It's ___ to go out and help clean up the neighborhood streets," Mother told us, "but it would also be praiseworthy for you to clean up your rooms."

NOTE: Now check your answers to these questions by turning to page 177. Going over the answers carefully will help you prepare for the next two practices, for which answers are not given.

➤ *Sentence Check 2*

Using the answer lines, complete each item below with **two** words from the box. Use each word once.

laudable
engender   1–2. Do you think it is ___ for a parent to give children everything they want? I don't think it's praiseworthy at all; it will just ___ in the children a sense that the world owes them a living.

erudite

abstract

3–4. The lecturer was certainly ___, but despite her vast knowledge, she was hard to follow because her talk was too ___. She just talked about theories and principles without ever giving concrete, specific examples.

renown

iconoclast

5–6. Marya gained ___ as a(n) ___ in third grade, when she drew a moustache and an eye patch on Washington's picture in the auditorium. Today she's still known as a rebel and a heretic°.

pompous

fervor

7–8. In the movie, the stiff, formal, ___ young businessman suddenly falls in love, and he sweeps the heroine off her feet with his passionate, eloquent° ___.

painstaking

archaic

9–10. Completing the crossword puzzle took hours of ___ work because many of the answers were ___ words—terms so old they weren't in my dictionary.

➤ Final Check: The Scholar

Here is a final opportunity for you to strengthen your knowledge of the ten words. First read the following selection carefully. Then fill in each blank with a word from the box at the top of the previous page. (Context clues will help you figure out which word goes in which blank.) Use each word once.

New students at a university are usually cognizant° of an important fact about the faculty—that these people are scholars. But some students have formed a mistaken notion of scholarship: they think of a scholar as stuffy and (1)_____pompous_____, as having only impractical, (2)_____abstract_____ ideas and being out of touch with reality. They dismiss scholarship as (3)_____archaic_____, something left over from the distant past. The truth is quite different, though.

Scholarship has three aspects, each (4)_____laudable_____ and admirable. First, there is learning. Scholars are (5)_____erudite_____: they know all about their own field, and often a great deal else. Second is teaching. Scholars are expected to pass their knowledge along to the next generation. They also hope to convey their own (6)_____fervor_____ for the subject—to (7)_____engender_____ in some of their students a similar passion and commitment. Third, scholars are expected to make a contribution to their subject, to add to the body of knowledge. This involves rigorous°, (8)_____painstaking_____, often lengthy research and writing.

Scholars may win (9)_____renown_____ for their knowledge, for inspired teaching, for exemplary° writing, or for all three. Occasionally, such fame is a source of controversy: a scholar whose approach is highly original may become known as a(n) (10)_____iconoclast_____ and may set off an intellectual revolution. Look around you—is there such a rebel on your campus?

| Scores | Sentence Check 2 _____% | Final Check _____% |

Enter your scores above and in the vocabulary performance chart on the inside back cover of the book.

28

convivial	paradigm
equanimity	profusion
lassitude	recalcitrant
listless	resigned
mollify	surmise

Ten Words in Context

In the space provided, write the letter of the meaning closest to that of each **boldfaced** word. Use the context of the sentences to help you figure out each word's meaning.

1 convivial
(kən-vĭv′ē-əl)
-adjective

- Dawn and Freddy's date at the candlelit restaurant was not as romantic as they hoped. They had to shout at each other to be heard over the loud laughter and singing of the **convivial** group at the next table.

- The emcee at my cousin's wedding was too **convivial**. He kissed all the women and dragged couples onto the dance floor instead of letting them sit and talk.

_c_ *Convivial* means   a. dull.   b. argumentative.   c. sociable.

2 equanimity
(ĕ′kwə-nĭm′ĭ-tē)
-noun

- We can usually react to misfortune with **equanimity** when it happens to someone else. When it happens to us, we tend to be much more distressed.

- My sister-in-law gave a birthday party for her four-year-old son and ten of his little friends without losing her **equanimity**. However, she spent the next day in bed, weakly sipping tea.

_b_ *Equanimity* means   a. equality.   b. calmness.   c. grief.

3 lassitude
(lăs′ĭ-tood′)
-noun

- **Lassitude**, a strange drowsiness or lack of vigor, is one symptom of spring fever.

- It used to be thought that people in southern climates were naturally lazy. In fact, their apparent **lassitude** was caused by a widespread disease, malaria.

_b_ *Lassitude* means   a. illness.   b. tiredness.   c. resistance.

4 listless
(lĭst′lĭs)
-adjective

- Children who seem **listless** on school mornings, complaining of pains or nausea, may actually have "school phobia." They're not really sick; they're afraid.

- Depression often goes undiagnosed in the elderly because people assume—mistakenly—that being **listless** and weary is just part of being old.

_a_ *Listless* means   a. without energy.   b. lonely.   c. refusing to obey.

5 mollify
(mŏl′ə-fī′)
-verb

- My roommate is furious when anyone disagrees with him. We've learned to **mollify** him by saying, "You're right. We were just tossing ideas around."

- When Ruben forgot to show up for their date, Jillian was enraged. But she was **mollified** when he sent her candy and flowers and begged her to forgive him.

_b_ *Mollify* means   a. to mislead.   b. to calm down.   c. to reject.

6 paradigm
(păr′ə-dīm′)
-noun

- The Constitution of the United States became a **paradigm** for several emerging democracies, which based their own governments on it.

- The "disease model" of mental disturbance—seeing it as comparable to physical illness—has been a **paradigm** for other conditions, such as addiction.

_a_ *Paradigm* means   a. a form to follow.   b. a puzzle to solve.   c. a descendant.

7 **profusion**
(prə-fyo͞o′zhən)
-*noun*

- If you're hungry, get off the highway at the next exit. You'll find a **profusion** of fast-food restaurants there.
- When Tim returned from his summer vacation, he found his yard overgrown with a **profusion** of weeds.

a *Profusion* means   a. a great quantity.   b. a shortage.   c. a probability.

8 **recalcitrant**
(rĭ-kăl′sĭ-trənt)
-*adjective*

- As other shoppers watched with amusement, a father tried to persuade his child to climb out of the dress rack she was hiding in, while the **recalcitrant** child cried, "No—you climb in."
- A truly **recalcitrant** person would not do well in the army—soldiers must be willing to follow orders.

a *Recalcitrant* means   a. disobedient.   b. disappointed.   c. dishonest.

9 **resigned**
(rĭ-zīnd′)
-*adjective*

- Scott had become **resigned** to being the shortest boy in his class, but over the summer he grew four inches!
- Although Rita has never learned to like spinach, she has become **resigned** to eating it once in a while.

b *Resigned to* means   a. refusing to believe in.   b. consenting to without protest.   c. eager about.

10 **surmise**
(sər-mīz′)
-*verb*

- Archaeologists in the year 2998, digging up the ruins of a twentieth-century baseball stadium, find a hand-lettered banner: KILL THE UMPIRE! They write: "We **surmise** that this place was used for human sacrifices."
- Arriving for dinner on December 25, Uncle Jake looked at the tree with its ornaments, the holly, and the brightly wrapped gifts. "I **surmise**," he said thoughtfully, "that it is Christmas."

c *Surmise* means   a. to express surprise.   b. to deny.   c. to suppose.

Matching Words with Definitions

Following are definitions of the ten words. Clearly write or print each word next to its definition. The sentences above and on the previous page will help you decide on the meaning of each word.

1. _____ *lassitude* _____   Lack of energy; weariness; fatigue
2. _____ *mollify* _____   To soothe the temper of
3. _____ *profusion* _____   An abundance; a rich supply
4. _____ *recalcitrant* _____   Stubbornly refusing to obey
5. _____ *surmise* _____   To infer something; guess
6. _____ *resigned* _____   Unresisting; passively accepting; accepting as inevitable
7. _____ *paradigm* _____   An example that serves as a model for others
8. _____ *equanimity* _____   The quality of staying calm and even-tempered
9. _____ *convivial* _____   Fond of social pleasures; merry
10. _____ *listless* _____   Lacking enthusiasm; sluggish

CAUTION: Do not go any further until you are sure the above answers are correct. Then you can use the definitions to help you in the following practices. Your goal is eventually to know the words well enough so that you don't need to check the definitions at all.

➤ *Sentence Check 1*

Using the answer line, complete each item below with the correct word from the box. Use each word once.

| a. **convivial** | b. **equanimity** | c. **lassitude** | d. **listless** | e. **mollify** |
| f. **paradigm** | g. **profusion** | h. **recalcitrant** | i. **resigned** | j. **surmise** |

equanimity   1. The professor's ___ was tested when, during a single class, the slide projector broke, his chair collapsed, and a pregnant student went into labor. But he proceeded calmly and even finished his lecture.

listless   2. For months after his father's death, Kareem felt ___: he was uninterested in his usual activities and seemed incapable of exerting any effort.

profusion   3. Each spring the meadow is filled with a(n) ___ of wildflowers.

convivial   4. Johanna's ___ neighbor gives a party every weekend.

recalcitrant   5. Ray has trouble keeping a job because he tends to be ___. He doesn't understand that a worker has to do what the boss orders.

resigned   6. The rebel leader never grew ___ to being in jail. Every day, all day, he thought about how to escape.

paradigm   7. "I'm handing out a sample research paper," said the instructor. "You can use its footnotes and references as a(n) ___ for your own."

lassitude   8. There is actually a good reason why we feel so sleepy after Thanksgiving dinner. Turkey contains a chemical that produces ___ in many people.

mollify   9. The Hoof 'n' Claw Restaurant advertised a special lobster dinner and then ran out of lobster. The manager tried to ___ the angry customers by offering them free steaks.

surmise   10. As no one answers the phone at my neighbor's house and the newspapers are piling up on his porch, I ___ that he is on vacation.

NOTE: Now check your answers to these questions by turning to page 177. Going over the answers carefully will help you prepare for the next two practices, for which answers are not given.

➤ *Sentence Check 2*

Using the answer lines, complete each item below with **two** words from the box. Use each word once.

lassitude
listless   1–2. Most people experience ___ during a heat wave—they have little energy. But for me, cold weather, rather than hot weather, has that effect: I feel ___ and enervated° when it's freezing out.

profusion
paradigm   3–4. To avoid a(n) ___ of different methods for teaching gifted children, the board of education developed one model program that would serve as a(n) ___ for all schools statewide.

equanimity
resigned   5–6. When his girlfriend broke off their engagement, Jonas reacted with stoic° ___. "I've seen this coming for months," he said calmly, "and I'm ___ to it."

convivial   7–8. The ___ people in the upstairs apartment do a lot of entertaining. but to
mollify   ___ their neighbors, they try to keep the noise to a minimum.

surmise   9–10. Bill keeps getting into trouble in the navy by refusing to obey orders. I
recalcitrant   ___ that he must also have been ___ as a child.

➤ *Final Check:* **A Case of Depression**

Here is a final opportunity for you to strengthen your knowledge of the ten words. First read the following selection carefully. Then fill in each blank with a word from the box at the top of the previous page. (Context clues will help you figure out which word goes in which blank.) Use each word once.

Gina is known to her friends as an outgoing, (1)_____*convivial*_____ person who responds with exuberance° to any invitation: "Sounds like fun! Let's go!" So when Gina stopped accompanying the gang to parties, movies, and nights out last year, it seemed strange. "You go," she would tell her friends. "I'm tired. I just don't feel like it."

"She's just a little blue," her friends told one another. "She'll snap out of it." But she didn't. Weeks turned into months, and Gina's (2)_____*listless*_____ attitude persisted. She had no appetite, and she told her friends that she couldn't sleep. They were concerned, but Gina didn't appear to have enough energy to worry. She seemed (3)_____*resigned*_____ to the idea that she would go through life as a morose°, tired loner. Luckily, her friends kept insisting that she see a doctor. To (4)_____*mollify*_____ them, she agreed. Despite her (5)_____*lassitude*_____, she made an appointment and dragged herself to it. Her doctor quickly confirmed what her friends had (6)_____*surmise*_____(e)d: Gina was suffering from serious depression. He suggested that she try an antidepressant medication. At first Gina was (7)_____*recalcitrant*_____—she stubbornly insisted that she should be able to "tough it out" on her own. Her doctor listened, then said something that made sense to her. "Nobody goes through life in a state of total (8)_____*equanimity*_____," he said. "Ups and downs are perfectly normal. But the kind of depression that you're experiencing is not normal. It's an aberration°, and it's not something you can control. It's a sign that something's gone wrong with the chemistry of your brain. The (9)_____*paradigm*_____ I like to use is diabetes: If you were diabetic, it would be erroneous° to think you should 'tough it out' without insulin."

There is a(n) (10)_____*profusion*_____ of antidepressant medications available these days, and it took a few tries to find the one that worked well for Gina. But a few weeks into her treatment, she realized that the dark cloud of depression had lifted. She was once again eagerly looking forward to all life had to offer. Today she continues to take her medication, knowing that it is something her body needs. "I had a disease called depression," she tells anyone who asks. "But it didn't have me."

| *Scores* | Sentence Check 2 _____% | Final Check _____% |

Enter your scores above and in the vocabulary performance chart on the inside back cover of the book.

CHAPTER

29

ambivalence	incipient
anomaly	nefarious
biased	prodigious
credulous	servile
despot	temper

Ten Words in Context

In the space provided, write the letter of the meaning closest to that of each **boldfaced** word. Use the context of the sentences to help you figure out each word's meaning.

1 ambivalence
(ăm-bĭv′ə-ləns)
-noun

- Rita and Phil have broken their engagement three times now. If they feel such **ambivalence** about getting married, why do you think they stay together?
- Many people approach a job change with **ambivalence**. They want a new job to provide them with new challenges and rewards, but they dislike giving up the security of the old job.

_a_ *Ambivalence* means   a. conflicting attitudes.   b. ambition.   c. ignorance.

2 anomaly
(ə-nŏm′ə-lē)
-noun

- Elaine's poor score on the math test was an **anomaly**; she usually does very well in math.
- A colored diamond is an **anomaly**; most diamonds are colorless or bluish-white.

_c_ *Anomaly* means   a. an annoyance.   b. a source of anxiety.   c. an abnormality.

3 biased
(bī′əst)
-adjective

- Studies show that names influence how we react to other people. For instance, a group of teenaged boys expected that any girl named "Michelle" would be attractive, while they were **biased** against anyone named "Hulga."
- Every human group seems to be **biased** against some other group. For example, the French tell jokes about the Belgians, and people in Quebec make fun of people from Newfoundland.

_b_ *Biased* means   a. thinking well of.   b. having a preconceived opinion.   c. having no opinion.

4 credulous
(krĕj′ə-ləs)
-adjective

- Marya reads her horoscope every day but insists that she's not **credulous**. "It's just for fun," she says. "I never take it seriously."
- **Credulous** Dave believed his girlfriend when she told him she was an actress. In fact, the only part she ever had was in a health play in third grade, as a radish.

_a_ *Credulous* means   a. too trustful.   b. too skeptical.   c. not paying attention.

5 despot
(dĕs′pət)
-noun

- During the American Revolution, the English king, George III, was seen as an unjust **despot**, but history has dealt more kindly with him in recent years.
- Some parents are harsh **despots** who make their children obey their every command, while others are lenient and easygoing.

_b_ *Despot* means   a. an elected official.   b. an oppressive ruler.   c. a revolutionary.

6 incipient
(ĭn-sĭp′ē-ənt)
-adjective

- Are Bill and Lisa just friends, or is there an **incipient** romance developing?
- "Precancerous" cells are an **incipient** tumor—a cancer that may be starting to develop.

_b_ *Incipient* means   a. coming to an end.   b. coming into existence.   c. fully grown.

160

7 nefarious
(nə-fâr′ē-əs)
-adjective

- The name of Jack the Ripper, whose **nefarious** murders shocked nineteenth-century England, has become almost a synonym for a brutal killer.
- The movie, about a **nefarious** plot by terrorists to kidnap a bus full of school-children, had us on the edge of our seats.

c *Nefarious* means   a. praiseworthy.   b. amusing.   c. evil.

8 prodigious
(prə-dĭj′əs)
-adjective

- This week the lottery prize is a **prodigious** amount of money—almost a hundred million dollars.
- It takes a **prodigious** supply of patience to put together a 5,000-piece jigsaw puzzle.

a *Prodigious* means   a. huge.   b. unknown.   c. small.

9 servile
(sûr′vīl *or*
(sûr′vəl)
-adjective

- In the play, George portrayed a fawning, **servile** hotel clerk who would do anything to please the hotel's clients.
- The spoiled celebrity likes to surround herself with **servile** people who do whatever she wants and constantly tell her how fabulous she is.

b *Servile* means   a. bossy.   b. acting like a slave.   c. powerful.

10 temper
(tĕm′pĕr)
-verb

- "**Temper** justice with mercy"—a phrase from Milton's *Paradise Lost*—suggests that we need to combine being just with being merciful.
- There is a saying, "God **tempers** the wind to the shorn lamb," which suggests that God does not send the weak more than they can bear.

b *Temper* means   a. to reinforce.   b. to tone down.   c. to continue.

Matching Words with Definitions

Following are definitions of the ten words. Clearly write or print each word next to its definition. The sentences above and on the previous page will help you decide on the meaning of each word.

1.   *biased*   Prejudiced

2.   *ambivalence*   Mixed feelings; uncertainty; indecisiveness

3.   *incipient*   Beginning; early

4.   *servile*   Humbly obedient

5.   *temper*   To reduce in intensity, especially by mixing in some other quality; moderate; soften

6.   *despot*   A tyrant

7.   *prodigious*   Enormous

8.   *nefarious*   Very wicked; villainous

9.   *credulous*   Tending to believe too readily; easily convinced

10.   *anomaly*   Something different, odd, or peculiar

CAUTION: Do not go any further until you are sure the above answers are correct. Then you can use the definitions to help you in the following practices. Your goal is eventually to know the words well enough so that you don't need to check the definitions at all.

➤ *Sentence Check 1*

Using the answer line, complete each item below with the correct word from the box. Use each word once.

a. **ambivalence**	b. **anomaly**	c. **biased**	d. **credulous**	e. **despot**
f. **incipient**	g. **nefarious**	h. **prodigious**	i. **servile**	j. **temper**

temper   1. Sandra is very funny, but she needs to ___ her humor with kindness—sometimes her jokes can hurt others.

ambivalence   2. Amy feels some ___ about spending the holidays alone in her new apartment. On the one hand, she thinks celebrating there will make her new place feel more like home. On the other hand, she will miss her family.

servile   3. There are two kinds of waiters I dislike: the one who jokes with me and the one who is overly humble and ___.

anomaly   4. On our campus, almost everyone drives a battered second-hand car. Cecil's shiny new sports car is a real ___.

incipient   5. Jen takes an aspirin at the first sign of a(n) ___ headache. Marsha, by contrast, resists taking medicine even when she's really sick.

biased   6. It's silly to be ___ against all red-haired people just because you had one bad date with a redhead.

nefarious   7. The thriller was the kind of book you can't put down—it traced a(n) ___ plan by a mad scientist to turn his neighbors into zombies.

credulous   8. "Sorry," said Professor Chiu. "I am not ___ enough to believe that aliens from a flying saucer flew away with your term paper."

despot   9. Shelley's famous poem "Ozymandias" is about a cruel ___ whose kingdom has vanished in the desert sands.

prodigious   10. Thomas Jefferson was a man of ___ talent. Not only was he president of the United States, but he was also an inventor, a writer, and an architect.

NOTE: Now check your answers to these questions by turning to page 177. Going over the answers carefully will help you prepare for the next two practices, for which answers are not given.

➤ *Sentence Check 2*

Using the answer lines, complete each item below with **two** words from the box. Use each word once.

despot
ambivalence   1–2. The people's attitude toward the ___ who ruled them was one of ___. They hated him for his cruelty but admired him for making the nation rich and powerful.

nefarious
servile   3–4. Uriah Heep is a famous character created by the novelist Charles Dickens. The evil Heep conceals his ___ plans by acting very ___: he constantly describes himself as "humble."

_____ *biased* _____   5–6. The report was ___: the authors included only the evidence supporting their theory and left out the contrary evidence. But although it was spurious°, ___ people simply accepted it without examining the facts.

_____ *credulous* _____

_____ *anomaly* _____   7–8. The term "child prodigy" describes a(n) ___: a rare instance of ___ knowledge, talent, or skill in someone who is still very young.

_____ *prodigious* _____

_____ *temper* _____   9–10. People are always looking for ways to ___ the effects of a(n) ___ cold. Some swear by certain vitamins and herbs to keep the cold from getting worse.

_____ *incipient* _____

➤ *Final Check:* Scientific Discoveries

Here is a final opportunity for you to strengthen your knowledge of the ten words. First read the following selection carefully. Then fill in each blank with a word from the box at the top of the previous page. (Context clues will help you figure out which word goes in which blank.) Use each word once.

Students in a biology class were arguing about some recent developments in science and what they might mean to the world.

"I love science, so I am (1)_____ *biased* _____ in favor of scientific discoveries. I tend to think they are laudable° and wonderful," said Ms. Kirschfeld, the teacher. "But even I feel some (2)_____ *ambivalence* _____ about certain discoveries and how they might be used. For instance, cloning. Scientists have been able to clone animals that are exact copies of other animals. There is a(n) (3)_____ *prodigious* _____ amount of research going on in related fields. What are some results that such developments could engender°?"

"Cloning scares me," said Eileen. "Imagine some evil (4)_____ *despot* _____ who wants a country full of people who will do exactly what he wants. He could clone a population of (5)_____ *servile* _____ citizens who obeyed his every command."

"But cloning is just one part of a field that is full of wonderful discoveries," said Todd. "Every day, scientists are learning more about how they can eliminate certain diseases and disorders, like Down syndrome or sickle-cell anemia, which are caused by a(n) (6)_____ *anomaly* _____ in the genes. And other (7)_____ *incipient* _____ breakthroughs are on the way. Imagine a person who is badly burned and needs a skin graft, or someone who needs a heart transplant. Someday, scientists might be able to grow skin or a heart from the person's own genetic material."

"Don't be so (8)_____ *credulous* _____," Brad said. "You have too much faith that any discovery will be put only to good use. Evil people often have (9)_____ *nefarious* _____ plans for new discoveries. As Eileen said, some nut could decide to produce an army of submissive° people who would do anything he wanted."

"Clearly, these discoveries have good and bad possibilities," said Ms. Kirschfeld. "Let's hope that scientists will (10)_____ *temper* _____ their fervor° about what they are learning with caution about what use will be made of it."

Scores	Sentence Check 2 _____%	Final Check _____%

Enter your scores above and in the vocabulary performance chart on the inside back cover of the book.

CHAPTER

30

arduous	eulogy
ascetic	gratuitous
blithe	raze
deprecate	tawdry
didactic	unimpeachable

Ten Words in Context

In the space provided, write the letter of the meaning closest to that of each **boldfaced** word. Use the context of the sentences to help you figure out each word's meaning.

1 arduous
(är′jōō-əs)
-*adjective*
- According to an ancient story, the hero Hercules had to perform twelve **arduous** tasks, including killing a serpent with nine heads.
- By the time she finished the fifth bridesmaid's gown, Martha wished she had not taken on the **arduous** task of making all the dresses for her daughter's wedding.

_b_ *Arduous* means   a. effortless.   b. demanding great effort.   c. useless.

2 ascetic
(ə-sĕt′ĭk)
-*adjective*
- Monks live a very **ascetic** life. Their rooms, for example, have nothing more than plain white walls, a single bed, and one hard-backed chair.
- Many religious people believe in being **ascetic**. They feel that too many luxuries and possessions get in the way of their relationship with God.

_a_ *Ascetic* means   a. self-denying.   b. selfish.   c. lazy.

3 blithe
(blīth)
-*adjective*
- In the play ***Blithe Spirit***, a lighthearted ghost haunts her former husband.
- The students were in a **blithe** mood after their teacher canceled the midterm exam.

_c_ *Blithe* means   a. bitter.   b. tragic.   c. joyful.

4 deprecate
(dĕp′rĭ-kăt′)
-*verb*
- Many writers **deprecate** television as a harmful influence, describing it as a "vast wasteland" and a "plug-in drug." But people keep watching!
- The Italian chef on television **deprecated** store-bought pasta. "Make your own fresh pasta!" she urged. I started to feel guilty about buying packaged spaghetti but then reminded myself that it always tastes great.

_a_ *Deprecate* means   a. to look down on.   b. to appreciate.   c. to describe.

5 didactic
(dī-dăk′tĭk)
-*adjective*
- Students are sometimes in college for reasons that have little to do with its **didactic** function: they care less about learning than about pleasing their parents, finding a husband or wife, "making contacts," and so on.
- Tests and examinations are not given just to annoy students. They have a **didactic** purpose as part of the learning process.

_b_ *Didactic* means   a. twofold.   b. educational.   c. secret.

6 eulogy
(yōō′lə-jē)
-*noun*
- In Shakespeare's play *Julius Caesar,* the famous **eulogy** for Caesar begins like this: "Friends, Romans, countrymen: lend me your ears . . ."
- In a touching children's book called *The Tenth Good Thing About Barney,* a little boy creates a **eulogy** for his dead cat, listing ten things he loved about the cat.

_a_ *Eulogy* means   a. a statement of praise.   b. an attack.   c. a plan.

7 gratuitous
(grə-tōo′ĭ-təs)
-adjective

- In some very good movies, violence is an important part of the story, but many other movies include **gratuitous** violence just to sell tickets.
- Mark makes a lot of **gratuitous** comments about how much money he has. He wants to be sure that the other students realize he is richer than they are.

_b_ *Gratuitous* means   a. showing gratitude.   b. unnecessary.   c. unclear.

8 raze
(rāz)
-verb

- More than a dozen homes were **razed** to make way for the new shopping mall.
- The children spent hours building houses out of popsicle sticks, **razing** them with a toy bulldozer, then building them again.

_c_ *Raze* means   a. to build.   b. to repair.   c. to wreck.

9 tawdry
(tô′drē)
-adjective

- Katia has no taste in clothes and always chooses something **tawdry**. Her gold prom dress was trimmed with red and purple feathers and covered with silver spangles.
- The restaurant looked **tawdry**: the pink velvet curtains were grimy; the deep-shag white rug was stained; the crystal chandelier—actually plastic—was covered with dust.

_b_ *Tawdry* means   a. old-fashioned.   b. sleazy.   c. elegant.

10 unimpeachable
(ŭn′ĭm-pē′chə-bəl)
-adjective

- Janos said, "My mother's parenting has been **unimpeachable**. You can tell she was an excellent parent simply by the fact that I have turned out perfect."
- "I expect your conduct on the playing field to be **unimpeachable**," the coach told the team. "Your every action should bring credit and honor to the school."

_a_ *Unimpeachable* means   a. without fault.   b. difficult to judge.   c. inadequate.

Matching Words with Definitions

Following are definitions of the ten words. Clearly write or print each word next to its definition. The sentences above and on the previous page will help you decide on the meaning of each word.

1. _____blithe_____   Cheerful and lighthearted

2. _____arduous_____   Difficult to do; strenuous

3. _____didactic_____   Designed to teach

4. _____gratuitous_____   Uncalled for; without any good reason

5. _____ascetic_____   Practicing self-denial; austere

6. _____raze_____   To tear down completely; demolish

7. _____tawdry_____   Tastelessly showy; cheap and gaudy; vulgar

8. _____eulogy_____   A spoken or written tribute, especially to someone who has died

9. _____unimpeachable_____   Blameless; beyond reproach; beyond criticism

10. _____deprecate_____   To express disapproval of

CAUTION: Do not go any further until you are sure the above answers are correct. Then you can use the definitions to help you in the following practices. Your goal is eventually to know the words well enough so that you don't need to check the definitions at all.

➤ *Sentence Check 1*

Using the answer line, complete each item below with the correct word from the box. Use each word once.

| a. **arduous** | b. **ascetic** | c. **blithe** | d. **deprecate** | e. **didactic** |
| f. **eulogy** | g. **gratuitous** | h. **raze** | i. **tawdry** | j. **unimpeachable** |

blithe — 1. Although the older children were upset about moving, their four-year-old sister was her usual ___ self. She said, "This will be fun!"

didactic — 2. Student teachers take some classes in specific subjects, such as math, and some in ___ methods, such as "Teaching the Elementary-School Child."

gratuitous — 3. Readers are beginning to object to the newspaper's ___ use of photographs of bloody crime scenes. Several times a week, the paper unnecessarily splashes some gruesome photo across the front page.

arduous — 4. Before the invention of the modern printing press, publishing books was a(n) ___ task—it required copying every word by hand.

unimpeachable — 5. The work of the Widget Department has been ___. In the latest shipment of 633,521 widgets, there was not a single defect.

eulogy — 6. At the music teacher's funeral, one student spoke the ___, and then several others offered a musical tribute, singing some of her favorite choruses.

tawdry — 7. For his wedding, Bert wore a powder-blue tuxedo with fake leopard lapels. "It may be ___," he said, "but it's more fun than quiet good taste."

raze — 8. A big crowd gathered to watch the demolition crew ___ the old department store. It was strange to see the huge building crumble like a house of cards.

ascetic — 9. The Martins have adopted a(n) ___ lifestyle in order to remember the many people in the world who are hungry. They often have only a little rice and some beans for dinner.

deprecate — 10. Dr. Krankheit ___s prescribing antibiotics for every case of the sniffles. "Let nature take its course," he says.

NOTE: Now check your answers to these questions by turning to page 177. Going over the answers carefully will help you prepare for the next two practices, for which answers are not given.

➤ *Sentence Check 2*

Using the answer lines, complete each item below with **two** words from the box. Use each word once.

deprecate
raze — 1–2. I don't ___ the town council's decision to ___ the old theater— sometimes old buildings must come down. But I wish we could preserve more landmarks from our past.

gratuitous
didactic — 3–4. A lecturer may make "asides"—comments that seem to be off the main point. Don't assume that these are ___ and can be ignored: they may have a(n) ___ purpose.

_____eulogy_____   5–6. Eleanor's brother delivered an eloquent° ___ at her funeral. He said she
_____blithe_____   had been a(n) ___ spirit, and her joyfulness would always remain with
                             her family and friends.

_____arduous_____   7–8. "Your performance on this ___ assignment has been ___," the instructor
____unimpeachable____   told the research group. "You achieved perfection on a formidable° task."

_____tawdry_____   9–10. Cognizant° of her own affinity° for ___, cheap-looking furnishings,
_____ascetic_____   Lorna hired a decorator for her new apartment. But his taste was so ___
                              that she now thinks the place looks stark and bare.

➤ _Final Check:_ Saint Francis of Assisi

Here is a final opportunity for you to strengthen your knowledge of the ten words. First read the following
selection carefully. Then fill in each blank with a word from the box at the top of the previous page.
(Context clues will help you figure out which word goes in which blank.) Use each word once.

Saints are generally thought of as, well, saintly. It's easy to surmise° that anyone who became
a saint must have been born that way. But this is not true of the man who became known as Saint
Francis of Assisi.

Francis was born into a wealthy family in Assisi, Italy, in the year 1182. A convivial°, fun-
loving young man, he was known as the life of the party. He neglected his studies, enjoyed
practical jokes, and ran around with a fast crowd. Serving as a soldier at the age of twenty, he was
captured and held as a prisoner of war. After he was released, he was seriously ill for many
months. When he recovered, Francis had changed. He (1)_____deprecate_____(e)d his former
frivolous° life and renounced° its meaningless, (2)_____gratuitous_____ pleasures. He began to
be more concerned about doing good, and so he decided to rebuild an old church that had been
(3)_____raze_____(e)d. When Francis's father learned of this, he objected. In turn, Francis
gave up any claim to his father's wealth. He sold his property, even gave away his shoes, and
began the (4)_____ascetic_____ life of a barefoot monk. He wandered through Italy, caring
for the poor. He spoke with all he met, telling them that money and possessions were
(5)_____tawdry_____, and extolling° the blessings of the spirit. Throughout his travels, he
impressed people with his joyous spirit. His (6)_____blithe_____ personality attracted many
followers, and eventually he founded the Franciscan order of monks and the Poor Clares, an order
of nuns. Francis preached to thousands in his lifetime, teaching them to love and care for the poor,
but while his talks were (7)_____didactic_____, they were never dull. He was a natural
teacher, preaching even to the birds, whom he called "my little sisters," and reminding them
always to praise God. According to legend, Francis was so kind to animals that wild rabbits ran to
him for protection.

Francis's faith in God was so strong that he once undertook a(n) (8)_____arduous_____
forty-day fast on a mountain, where he prayed and meditated. Such acts made him widely known
as a man of (9)_____unimpeachable_____ goodness, simplicity, and love. He died at the age of 45 and
was declared a saint by the Catholic Church two years later. After Francis's death the artist Giotto
painted a famous picture of the joyful saint preaching to the birds—a tribute more fitting than any
spoken (10)_____eulogy_____ for the modest man who called himself "little brother Francis."

Scores	Sentence Check 2 _____%	Final Check _____%

Enter your scores above and in the vocabulary performance chart on the inside back cover of the book.

UNIT SIX: *Review*

The box at the right lists twenty-five words from Unit Six. Using the clues at the bottom of the page, fill in these words to complete the puzzle that follows.

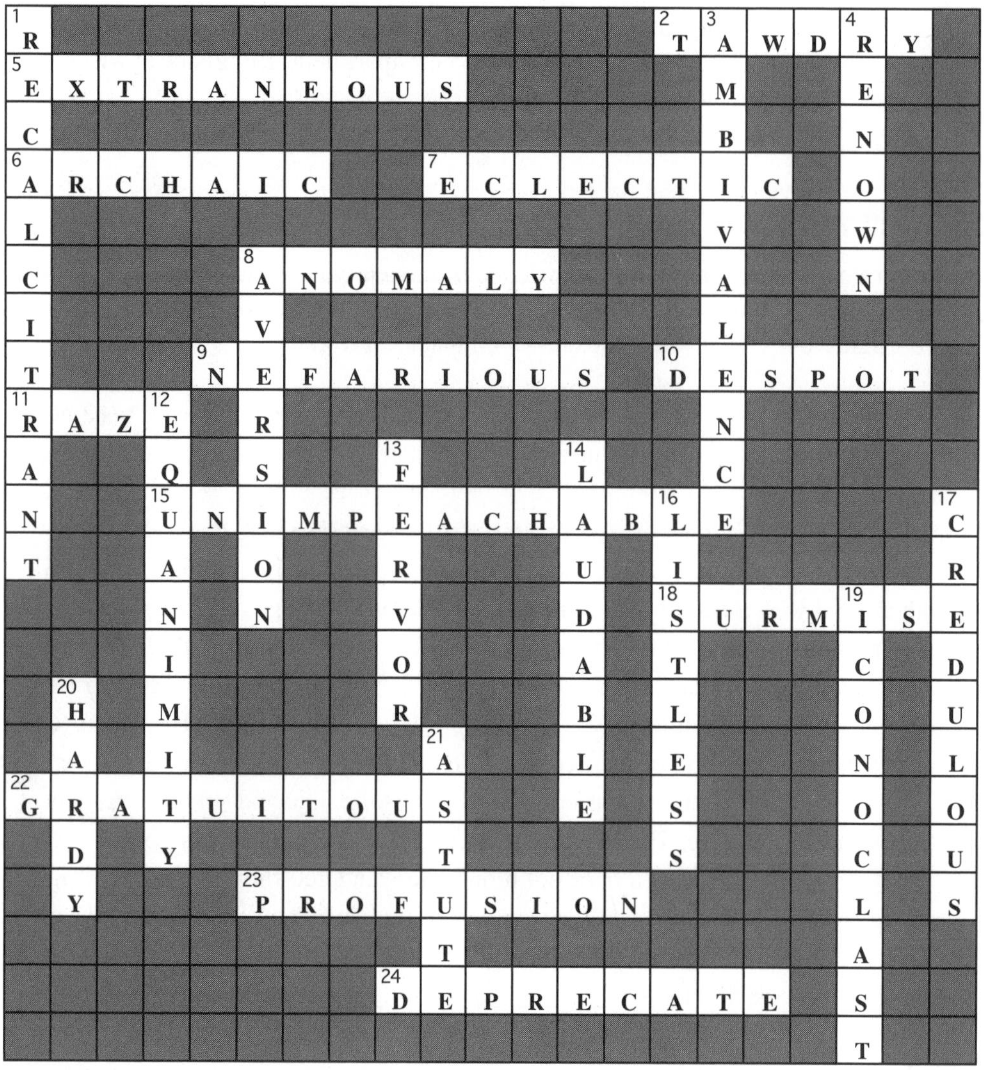

Word list:

- ambivalence
- anomaly
- archaic
- astute
- aversion
- credulous
- deprecate
- despot
- eclectic
- equanimity
- extraneous
- fervor
- gratuitous
- hardy
- iconoclast
- laudable
- listless
- nefarious
- profusion
- raze
- recalcitrant
- renown
- surmise
- tawdry
- unimpeachable

The crossword grid (filled answers):

- 1 Down: RECALCITRANT
- 2 Across: TAWDRY
- 3 Down: AMBIVALENCE
- 4 Down: RENOWN
- 5 Across: EXTRANEOUS
- 6 Across: ARCHAIC
- 7 Across: ECLECTIC
- 8 Across: ANOMALY
- 8 Down: AVERSION
- 9 Across: NEFARIOUS
- 10 Across: DESPOT
- 11 Across: RAZE
- 12 Down: EQUANIMITY
- 13 Down: FERVOR
- 14 Down: LAUDABLE
- 15 Across: UNIMPEACHABLE
- 16 Down: LISTLESS
- 17 Down: CREDULOUS
- 18 Across: SURMISE
- 19 Down: ICONOCLAST
- 20 Down: HARDY
- 21 Down: ASTUTE
- 22 Across: GRATUITOUS
- 23 Across: PROFUSION
- 24 Across: DEPRECATE

ACROSS

2. Cheap and gaudy
5. Not essential; irrelevant
6. No longer current; out-of-date
7. Coming from many sources
8. Something different or odd
9. Very wicked
10. A tyrant
11. To tear down completely
15. Blameless
18. To infer; guess
22. Uncalled for; without good reason
23. An abundance; rich supply
24. To express disapproval of

DOWN

1. Stubbornly refusing to obey
3. Mixed feelings
4. Fame
8. An intense dislike
12. The quality of staying calm
13. Great warmth or intensity of emotion
14. Worthy of praise
16. Lacking enthusiasm; sluggish
17. Easily convinced
19. Someone who attacks traditional ideas
20. Tough; strong
21. Clever; perceptive

UNIT SIX: *Test 1*

PART A
Choose the word that best completes each item and write it in the space provided.

diminutive   1. Although our new boss is ___ and young-looking, he is every bit as in control as our previous employer, who was six foot four and middle-aged.

       a. tawdry   b. diminutive   c. extraneous   d. eclectic

soporific   2. "This book," wrote the critic, "could be sold as a sleeping aid—it is that ___."

       a. soporific   b. unimpeachable   c. recalcitrant   d. credulous

eulogy   3. Instead of having the preacher deliver the usual ___, friends of the woman who had died took turns speaking about her and her wonderful qualities.

       a. eulogy   b. paradigm   c. profusion   d. despot

profusion   4. Spring came suddenly this year. One week, it seemed, the earth was dead and dull, but the next there was a(n) ___ of wildflowers .

       a. paradigm   b. iconoclast   c. eulogy   d. profusion

extraneous   5. When you write a paper, stick to your point. Don't introduce any ___ topics.

       a. extraneous   b. nefarious   c. didactic   d. diminutive

erudite   6. Hoping to sound ___ to his date, Stan spent the afternoon reading the *Wall Street Journal,* the *New York Times,* and some articles in the encyclopedia.

       a. hardy   b. credulous   c. erudite   d. incipient

archaic   7. "Dost thou take this woman to be thy lawfully wedded wife?" the preacher asked. Amused by the ___ language, the couple couldn't help giggling.

       a. recalcitrant   b. soporific   c. archaic   d. resigned

servile   8. "Are you comfortable? Can I get you something to eat? You're looking awfully pretty today. Would you like a pillow for your head?" my brother asked me, making me very suspicious. Why was he being so ___?

       a. resigned   b. incipient   c. listless   d. servile

pompous   9. To me, geese always look ___, strutting around with their chests puffed out and their heads held high in the air.

       a. servile   b. credulous   c. gratuitous   d. pompous

engender   10. The discovery of life on another planet would ___ tremendous excitement among scientists and the general population alike.

       a. deprecate   b. surmise   c. raze   d. engender

tawdry   11. Tanya likes her bleached-blond hair, but her grandmother thinks it makes her look ___. "Nice girls don't dye their hair," she says.

       a. erudite   b. prodigious   c. listless   d. tawdry

(Continues on next page)

_____ *raze* _____ 12. People are arguing about what to do with the beautiful but run-down old town hall: ___ it and build a new one, or spend a lot of money restoring it?

    a. surmise   b. temper   c. engender   d. raze

_____ *paradigm* _____ 13. To many of his students, Professor Oppenheimer was the ___ of a teacher: kind, wise, generous, and insightful.

    a. iconoclast   b. profusion   c. paradigm   d. despot

PART B

Write **C** if the italicized word is used **correctly**. Write **I** if the word is used **incorrectly**.

___I___ 14. Try to get to the refreshment table before my *abstemious* uncle. He'll eat anything that's not nailed down.

___I___ 15. Holidays at Mrs. Miller's house are always exactly the same. She's such an *iconoclast*—everything has to be done according to old family traditions.

___C___ 16. Jaime has very *eclectic* tastes in music. His CD collection contains everything from Mozart to rap to old-time country music to hip-hop to ska.

___C___ 17. I like to order a very spicy curry in my favorite Indian restaurant, but I also like to *temper* its fiery heat with a side order of cool plain yogurt.

___I___ 18. The Wilsons were delighted by their son's engagement to a girl they all loved. "We're not losing a son," said Mr. Wilson. "We're gaining the most *nefarious* daughter we could have ever hoped for."

___I___ 19. The doctor tried to calm the frightened child, but everything he said only *mollified* her, making her shriek and cry all the more.

___C___ 20. The second-grade teacher noticed an *incipient* dislike developing between two boys who sat beside each other, so she changed the seating arrangement to keep the problem from going any further.

___I___ 21. Unlike some flowers, such as marigolds, which are tough and easy to grow, orchids are *hardy* and need very delicate care in order to do well.

___C___ 22. Fans cheered when the boxer knocked his opponent down, but then booed when he delivered a *gratuitous* punch to the fallen man.

___I___ 23. An amusing children's song tells the story of Pierre, a boy whose answer to any question is "I don't care." He responds with the same *fervor*—saying "I don't care"—even when a lion asks "Shall I eat you up?" And so the lion does.

___I___ 24. This morning Roseanne worked silently at her desk, frowning and snapping "Yes" or "No" when anyone asked her a question. I have no idea what's making her so *blithe*.

___C___ 25. It's difficult to be fair and open-minded when a friend's marriage breaks up. It's easy to be *biased* in favor of one's friend and to believe his or her spouse is to blame for everything.

> *Score* (Number correct) _____ × 4 = _____ %

Enter your score above and in the vocabulary performance chart on the inside back cover of the book.

UNIT SIX: Test 2

PART A
Complete each item with a word from the box. Use each word once.

a. **anomaly**	b. **arduous**	c. **ascetic**	d. **astute**	e. **despot**
f. **didactic**	g. **equanimity**	h. **listless**	i. **painstaking**	j. **prodigious**
k. **recalcitrant**	l. **surmise**	m. **unimpeachable**		

unimpeachable   1. Reading through the want ads for live-in baby sitters, Cara was attracted to one that said, "Are you friendly and cheerful? Is your honesty ___? Do you want to become a member of a loving family?"

painstaking   2. Tamika did a(n) ___ job of braiding her sister's hair. Her hours of long, careful work showed—every braid was perfect and beautiful.

listless   3. When a usually energetic child becomes ___, parents often suspect that he or she is getting sick.

prodigious   4. Paul Bunyan, a hero of American folktales, was known for his ___ appetite. Breakfast for Paul might be three dozen eggs, six pounds of bacon, and all the bread a bakery could produce in a day.

recalcitrant   5. I know it's silly to think of a machine as having human motives, but I still believe our office copier is just ___— sometimes it seems to say, "I won't work, and there's nothing you can do to make me."

didactic   6. Children's TV shows like *Sesame Street* are designed to be both entertaining and ___, keeping kids amused as they learn colors, numbers, and ABCs.

arduous   7. Good parenting is ___ work. No one should have a baby without realizing that the job of being a parent is a difficult one.

equanimity   8. As he waited to hear whether he'd gotten a part in a Broadway play, the young actor had trouble maintaining his ___— one minute he'd feel cheerful and confident, and the next he was in despair.

despot   9. Ivan the Terrible was a(n) ___ of sixteenth-century Russia. This ruler was so violent and power-mad that he would slaughter an entire village if he thought one resident was disloyal.

anomaly   10. My father's eyes are a(n) ___—one is brown and the other is blue.

ascetic   11. A(n) ___ person and a person who loves luxury are not suited as housemates. One is trying to scale down his or her standard of living, while the other is trying to raise it.

astute   12. The instructor was so amused by my excuse for not handing in my paper that he gave me a compliment. "Anyone ___ enough to see that I'd enjoy an excuse like that is also smart enough to write a good paper," he said.

surmise   13. We make all kinds of assumptions every day. For instance, when we see the lights on in a friend's house, we ___ that the friend is at home.

(Continues on next page)

PART B
Write **C** if the italicized word is used **correctly**. Write **I** if the word is used **incorrectly**.

_C_ 14. Just before leaving for her job interview, Rita felt *ambivalence* about what she was wearing. She liked her suit but wondered if the skirt was too short. She asked herself if her floral print dress would have been a better choice.

_I_ 15. Although she is behind in the race, the candidate is *resigned* to losing. She will work desperately to earn votes until election day arrives.

_I_ 16. Charles is a writer of such *renown* that hardly anyone has ever heard of him or his books.

_C_ 17. My son's *aversion* to spinach is so great that he can't even bear to see it on the table, much less taste it.

_I_ 18. The dance was a disaster. The guests were so *convivial* that they stood silently against the wall, ignoring one another all evening.

_C_ 19. At present I have just an *abstract* idea of the house I'd like to build some day. To get a more realistic idea of what it would be like, I'd have to work with an architect and draw up some plans.

_I_ 20. The judge spoke sternly to the convicted man. "Your offenses against the community are so *laudable* that I am going to give you the most severe punishment available to me."

_C_ 21. The instructions for the children's new board game were so *abstruse* that the kids gave up in frustration and went outside to ride their bikes.

_C_ 22. You have to be pretty *credulous* to believe some of the stories in the tabloids: "Blind Man Can Smell Colors" or "Aliens Built Mount Rushmore."

_C_ 23. Silver is a beautiful horse, but he is too *intractable* for anyone but the most experienced riders to control.

_I_ 24. Theresa worked hard on her dinner party, and her appreciative guests *deprecated* her efforts, praising the food and decorations to the skies.

_C_ 25. Even on the phone, Wes's depression is obvious. His voice is full of *lassitude*, making him sound sad, tired, and sick.

Score (Number correct) _____ × 4 = _____ %

Enter your score above and in the vocabulary performance chart on the inside back cover of the book.

UNIT SIX: *Test 3*

PART A: Synonyms

PART A: Synonyms
In the space provided, write the letter of the choice that is most nearly the **same** in meaning as the **boldfaced** word.

_a_ 1. **abstract** a) theoretical b) clear c) made up of many parts d) common

_c_ 2. **abstruse** a) brightly colored b) confined c) complicated d) broken

_b_ 3. **anomaly** a) a vegetarian b) an oddity c) a weakness d) a preventive measure

_d_ 4. **astute** a) shy b) recent c) violent d) clever

_a_ 5. **aversion** a) hatred b) explanation c) nuisance d) absence

_a_ 6. **despot** a) a tyrant b) a piece of furniture c) a period of rest d) a comrade

_b_ 7. **didactic** a) intended to deceive b) educational c) cheerful d) sympathetic

_c_ 8. **eclectic** a) handed down over generations b) not provable
c) from multiple sources d) from one source

_c_ 9. **engender** a) to prove b) to force c) to cause d) to defeat

_a_ 10. **equanimity** a) calmness b) aggressiveness c) weight d) vision

_a_ 11. **eulogy** a) a tribute b) a visit c) an excuse d) a loss

_b_ 12. **fervor** a) disturbance b) passion c) illness d) insight

_d_ 13. **lassitude** a) talent b) eagerness c) resistance d) weariness

_c_ 14. **mollify** a) to resent b) to lie to c) to soothe d) to destroy

_c_ 15. **paradigm** a) something abnormal b) a pleasant surprise c) an ideal d) a trick

_a_ 16. **prodigious** a) huge b) perfect c) expert d) annoyed

_d_ 17. **raze** a) to allow b) to rebuild c) to withdraw d) to destroy

_b_ 18. **recalcitrant** a) worthless b) stubborn c) excited d) reckless

_a_ 19. **renown** a) fame b) absence c) location d) waste

_b_ 20. **resigned** a) furious b) unresisting c) valuable d) curious

_d_ 21. **soporific** a) suspicious b) teasing c) amusing d) causing sleep

_b_ 22. **surmise** a) to hide b) to guess c) to refuse d) to attack

_c_ 23. **tawdry** a) useless b) without cause c) vulgar d) lasting a long time

_c_ 24. **temper** a) to excite b) to explain c) to tone down d) to pull back

_a_ 25. **unimpeachable** a) blameless b) bearing fruit c) hairless d) common

(Continues on next page)

PART B: Antonyms
In the space provided, write the letter of the choice that is most nearly the **opposite** in meaning to the **boldfaced** word.

_a_ 26. **abstemious**   **a)** gluttonous   **b)** self-important   **c)** peaceful   **d)** observant

_d_ 27. **ambivalence**   **a)** the ability to use either the left or the right hand   **b)** generosity
      c) acceptance   **d)** decisiveness

_c_ 28. **archaic**   **a)** very large   **b)** hidden   **c)** up-to-date   **d)** violent

_d_ 29. **arduous**   **a)** brief   **b)** graceful   **c)** romantic   **d)** easy

_b_ 30. **ascetic**   **a)** unknown   **b)** self-indulgent   **c)** pleasant   **d)** loose

_a_ 31. **biased**   **a)** open-minded   **b)** normal   **c)** stubborn   **d)** not decorated

_c_ 32. **blithe**   **a)** empty   **b)** easily broken   **c)** depressed   **d)** not complete

_c_ 33. **convivial**   **a)** lazy   **b)** honest   **c)** unsociable   **d)** talented

_d_ 34. **credulous**   **a)** unstable   **b)** respected   **c)** highly educated   **d)** disbelieving

_b_ 35. **deprecate**   **a)** to complain   **b)** to approve of   **c)** to look for   **d)** to reduce

_b_ 36. **diminutive**   **a)** amusing   **b)** huge   **c)** wealthy   **d)** narrow

_b_ 37. **erudite**   **a)** protected   **b)** ignorant   **c)** legal   **d)** jealous

_b_ 38. **extraneous**   **a)** complicated   **b)** essential   **c)** thorough   **d)** frantic

_b_ 39. **gratuitous**   **a)** level   **b)** justified   **c)** proud   **d)** forced

_b_ 40. **hardy**   **a)** varied   **b)** fragile   **c)** bossy   **d)** numerous

_c_ 41. **iconoclast**   **a)** a talkative person   **b)** an athlete   **c)** a traditionalist   **d)** a supervisor

_a_ 42. **incipient**   **a)** fully developed   **b)** badly planned   **c)** without reason   **d)** stubborn

_a_ 43. **intractable**   **a)** obedient   **b)** scarce   **c)** excited   **d)** restless

_d_ 44. **laudable**   **a)** dull   **b)** worried   **c)** careless   **d)** deserving blame

_b_ 45. **listless**   **a)** easily angered   **b)** energetic   **c)** fair   **d)** moist

_d_ 46. **nefarious**   **a)** bored   **b)** well-dressed   **c)** grateful   **d)** saintly

_a_ 47. **painstaking**   **a)** careless   **b)** bad-tempered   **c)** distrustful   **d)** angry

_a_ 48. **pompous**   **a)** humble   **b)** aggressive   **c)** hard-working   **d)** sarcastic

_b_ 49. **profusion**   **a)** lack of interest   **b)** scarcity   **c)** obedience   **d)** arrogance

_d_ 50. **servile**   **a)** sickly   **b)** worried   **c)** faithful   **d)** proud

---

Score   (Number correct) _____ × 2 = _____ %

Enter your score above and in the vocabulary performance chart on the inside back cover of the book.

A. Limited Answer Key

Important Note: Be sure to use this answer key as a learning tool only. You should not turn to this key until you have considered carefully the sentence in which a given word appears.

Used properly, the key will help you to learn words and to prepare for the activities and tests for which answers are not given. For ease of reference, the title of the "Final Check" passage in each chapter appears in parentheses.

Chapter 1 (Blue Jeans)

Sentence Check 1

1. opulence
2. unassailable
3. voluminous
4. sagacious
5. affinity
6. supplant
7. incessant
8. proximity
9. fledgling
10. hackneyed

Chapter 2 (Do Opposites Attract?)

Sentence Check 1

1. brusque
2. indefatigable
3. nonchalance
4. morose
5. stoic
6. effervescent
7. progeny
8. voracious
9. misanthrope
10. dispassionate

Chapter 3 (What Are You Stingy About?)

Sentence Check 1

1. coalesce
2. exemplary
3. incidental
4. parsimonious
5. decadence
6. surreptitious
7. writhe
8. prodigal
9. insolvent
10. exuberance

Chapter 4 (Loony but True)

Sentence Check 1

1. frivolous
2. heist
3. clemency
4. brevity
5. querulous
6. torpor
7. unscathed
8. lampoon
9. respite
10. reproach

Chapter 5 (Writing a Better Paper)

Sentence Check 1

1. jargon
2. levity
3. substantiate
4. eloquent
5. peripheral
6. vacillate
7. dearth
8. meander
9. unobtrusive
10. copious

Chapter 6 (Bad Translations)

Sentence Check 1

1. cognizant
2. hindrance
3. lavish
4. appall
5. negligent
6. commiserate
7. scrutinize
8. kindle
9. expedient
10. ludicrous

Chapter 7 (Memory Aids)

Sentence Check 1

1. Irresolute
2. untenable
3. contract
4. vilify
5. clamor
6. equivocal
7. rescind
8. duplicity
9. stagnant
10. uniform

Chapter 8 (A Formula for Teaching)

Sentence Check 1

1. apocryphal
2. garbled
3. loquacious
4. opaque
5. affable
6. irascible
7. desultory
8. paucity
9. recapitulate
10. obtuse

Chapter 9 (The One-Room Schoolhouse)

Sentence Check 1

1. profane	6. censure
2. cacophony	7. edifice
3. accolade	8. infraction
4. assuage	9. somber
5. gravity	10. diatribe

Chapter 10 (Galileo)

Sentence Check 1

1. languish	6. garner
2. blasphemy	7. heretic
3. renounce	8. incite
4. enmity	9. recluse
5. erroneous	10. peruse

Chapter 11 (Isadora Duncan)

Sentence Check 1

1. virtuoso	6. peerless
2. vitriolic	7. propriety
3. insipid	8. catalyst
4. ingratiate	9. aesthetic
5. disparage	10. whimsical

Chapter 12 (Miles Standish)

Sentence Check 1

1. rebuff	6. dissonance
2. devious	7. amicable
3. efface	8. static
4. garrulous	9. predecessor
5. ponderous	10. immutable

Chapter 13 (Men, Women, and Talk)

Sentence Check 1

1. articulate	6. delineate
2. belittle	7. scanty
3. diffident	8. subjugate
4. laconic	9. conciliatory
5. acquiesce	10. bombastic

Chapter 14 (Is Human Nature Good or Evil?)

Sentence Check 1

1. meager	6. authoritarian
2. salutary	7. turbulence
3. anarchy	8. predilection
4. suppress	9. temerity
5. depravity	10. quixotic

Chapter 15 (The Strange Case of X)

Sentence Check 1

1. steadfast	6. callous
2. desecrate	7. provincial
3. heed	8. usurp
4. indigent	9. supercilious
5. evanescent	10. paragon

Chapter 16 (The Salem Witches)

Sentence Check 1

1. buoyant	6. inexorable
2. marred	7. enervate
3. satirical	8. incorrigible
4. pique	9. partisan
5. irrefutable	10. parochial

Chapter 17 (Fashion Show)

Sentence Check 1

1. capitulate	6. urbane
2. zany	7. Stupor
3. sycophant	8. cajole
4. premonition	9. reverent
5. prestigious	10. egregious

Chapter 18 (Math Anxiety)

Sentence Check 1

1. congenital	6. precocious
2. extol	7. virulent
3. composure	8. elusive
4. inscrutable	9. formidable
5. trepidation	10. aberration

Chapter 19 (The Gypsies)

Sentence Check 1

1. obliterate	6. clairvoyant
2. taciturn	7. spurn
3. stealthy	8. accommodate
4. debilitate	9. preclude
5. contiguous	10. officious

Chapter 20 (The Jonestown Tragedy)

Sentence Check 1

1. discordant	6. thwart
2. indict	7. indoctrinate
3. defame	8. wanton
4. sullen	9. submissive
5. grueling	10. cordial

Chapter 21 (Helen Keller)

Sentence Check 1

1. caustic	6. fallacious
2. chastise	7. elucidate
3. insurgent	8. placid
4. assiduous	9. hypocrisy
5. Trite	10. exalt

Chapter 22 (Figures of Speech)

Sentence Check 1

1. whet	6. crass
2. colloquial	7. tacit
3. hyperbole	8. tactless
4. incisive	9. prerogative
5. discerning	10. judicious

Chapter 23 (When Is a Treatment Therapy?)

Sentence Check 1

1. haphazard	6. assent
2. intangible	7. incontrovertible
3. potent	8. negate
4. rigorous	9. therapeutic
5. spurious	10. ameliorate

Chapter 24 (Hawks and Doves)

Sentence Check 1

1. circumspect	6. deference
2. guile	7. volatile
3. impassive	8. tirade
4. altercation	9. placate
5. pugnacious	10. malevolent

Chapter 25 (New Year's Resolutions)

Sentence Check 1

1. induce	6. ephemeral
2. rectify	7. retract
3. serene	8. phenomenon
4. discrepancy	9. resolution
5. catharsis	10. capricious

Chapter 26 (Weird Facts)

Sentence Check 1

1. hardy	6. soporific
2. intractable	7. extraneous
3. aversion	8. abstemious
4. astute	9. abstruse
5. diminutive	10. eclectic

Chapter 27 (The Scholar)

Sentence Check 1

1. archaic	6. engender
2. erudite	7. painstaking
3. iconoclast	8. pompous
4. fervor	9. renown
5. abstract	10. laudable

Chapter 28 (A Case of Depression)

Sentence Check 1

1. equanimity	6. resigned
2. listless	7. paradigm
3. profusion	8. lassitude
4. convivial	9. mollify
5. recalcitrant	10. surmise

Chapter 29 (Scientific Discoveries)

Sentence Check 1

1. temper	6. biased
2. ambivalence	7. nefarious
3. servile	8. credulous
4. anomaly	9. despot
5. incipient	10. prodigious

Chapter 30 (Saint Francis of Assisi)

Sentence Check 1

1. blithe	6. eulogy
2. didactic	7. tawdry
3. gratuitous	8. raze
4. arduous	9. ascetic
5. unimpeachable	10. deprecate

B. Dictionary Use

It isn't always possible to figure out the meaning of a word from its context, and that's where a dictionary comes in. Following is some basic information to help you use a dictionary.

HOW TO FIND A WORD

A dictionary contains so many words that it can take a while to find the one you're looking for. But if you know how to use guide words, you can find a word rather quickly. *Guide words* are the two words at the top of each dictionary page. The first guide word tells what the first word is on the page. The second guide word tells what the last word is on that page. The other words on a page fall alphabetically between the two guide words. So when you look up a word, find the two guide words that alphabetically surround the word you're looking for.

- Which of the following pair of guide words would be on a page with the word *disparage*?

  disport / dissociate   **disentangle / diskette**   (**dislike / displease**)

The answer to this question and the questions that follow are given on the next page.

HOW TO USE A DICTIONARY LISTING

A dictionary listing includes many pieces of information. For example, here is a typical listing. Note that it includes much more than just a definition.

> **grum•ble** (grŭm′bəl), *v.,* **-bled, -bling.** — *v.* To mutter discontentedly.
> — *n.* A muttered complaint. —**grum′bler,** *n.* —**grum′bly,** *adj.*

Key parts of a dictionary entry are listed and explained below.

Syllables. Dots separate dictionary entry words into syllables. Note that *grumble* has one dot, which breaks the word into two syllables.

- To practice seeing the syllable breakdown in a dictionary entry, write the number of syllables in each word below.

  mis•an•thrope _3_   **res•o•lu•tion** _4_   **in•de•fat•i•ga•ble** _6_

Pronunciation guide. The information within parentheses after the entry word shows how to pronounce the entry word. This pronunciation guide includes two types of symbols: pronunciation symbols and accent marks.

Pronunciation symbols represent the consonant sounds and vowel sounds in a word. The consonant sounds are probably very familiar to you, but you may find it helpful to review some of the sounds of the vowels—*a, e, i, o,* and *u.* Every dictionary has a key explaining the sounds of its pronunciation symbols, including the long and short sounds of vowels.

   Long vowels have the sound of their own names. For example, the *a* in *pay* and the *o* in *no* both have long vowel sounds. Long vowel sounds are shown by a straight line (called a *macron*) above the vowel.

   In many dictionaries, the *short vowels* are shown by a curved line (called a *breve*) above the vowel. Thus the *i* in the first syllable of *grumble* is a short *u.* The pronunciation chart on the inside front cover of this book indicates that the short *i* has the sound of *u* in *up.* It also indicates that the short *a* has the sound of *a* in *hat,* that the short *e* has the sound of *e* in *ten,* and so on.

- Which of the words below have a short vowel sound? Which has a long vowel sound?

  drink _short_   **flight** _long_   **stand** _short_

Another pronunciation symbol is the *schwa* (ə), which looks like an upside-down *e*. It stands for certain rapidly spoken, unaccented vowel sounds, such as the *a* in *above*, the *e* in *item*, the *i* in *easily*, the *o* in *gallop*, and the *u* in *circus*. More generally, it has an "uh" sound, like the "uh" a speaker makes when hesitating. Here are three words that include the schwa sound:

  com•mence•ment (kə-mĕns′mənt) **ex•tro•vert** (ĕk′strə-vûrt) **buoy•ant** (boi′ənt)

• Which syllable in *grumble* contains the schwa sound, the first or the second? _____*second*_____

Accent marks are small black marks that tell you which syllable to emphasize, or stress, as you say a word. An accent mark follows *grum* in the pronunciation guide for *grumble,* which tells you to stress the first syllable of *grumble*. Syllables with no accent mark are not stressed. Some syllables are in between, and they are marked with a lighter accent mark.

• Which syllable has the stronger accent in *supercilious*? _____*third*_____

  su•per•cil•i•ous (soo′pər-sĭl′ē-əs)

Parts of speech. After the pronunciation key and before each set of definitions, the entry word's parts of speech are given. The parts of speech are abbreviated as follows:

  noun—*n.* pronoun—*pron.* adjective—*adj.* adverb—*adv.* verb—*v.*

• The listing for *grumble* shows that it can be two parts of speech. Write them below:

  _____*verb*_____   _____*noun*_____

Definitions. Words often have more than one meaning. When they do, each meaning is usually numbered in the dictionary. You can tell which definition of a word fits a given sentence by the meaning of the sentence. For example, the verb *discriminate* has two definitions: **1.** To make a clear distinction. **2.** To make distinctions on the basis of preference or prejudice.

• Show with a check which definition (1 or 2) applies in each sentence below:

  The directors of X Company have been accused of discriminating against women. 1 ___ 2 ✓

  Colorblind people cannot discriminate between red and green. 1 ✓ 2 ___

Other information. After the definitions in a listing in a hardbound dictionary, you may get information about the *origin* of a word. Such information about origins, also known as *etymology,* is usually given in brackets. And you may sometimes be given one or more synonyms or antonyms for the entry word. *Synonyms* are words that are similar in meaning to the entry word; *antonyms* are words that are opposite in meaning.

WHICH DICTIONARIES TO OWN

You will find it useful to own two recent dictionaries: a small paperback dictionary to carry to class and a hardbound dictionary, which contains more information than a small paperback version. Among the good dictionaries strongly recommended are both the paperback and the hardcover editions of the following:

  The American Heritage Dictionary
  The Random House College Dictionary
  Webster's New World Dictionary

ANSWERS TO THE DICTIONARY QUESTIONS
  Guide words: *dislike/displease*   Accent: stronger accent on third syllable *(cil)*
  Number of syllables: 3, 4, 6   Parts of speech: verb and noun
  Vowels: *drink, stand* (short); *flight* (long) Definitions: 2; 1
  Schwa: second syllable of *grumble*

C. Word List

aberration, 100
abstemious, 148
abstract, 152
abstruse, 148
accolade, 48
accommodate, 104
acquiesce, 72
aesthetic, 64
affable, 44
affinity, 8
altercation, 132
ambivalence, 160
ameliorate, 128
amicable, 68
anarchy, 76
anomaly, 160
apocryphal, 44
appall, 36
archaic, 152
arduous, 164
articulate, 72
ascetic, 164
assent, 128
assiduous, 120
assuage, 48
astute, 148
authoritarian, 76
aversion, 148
belittle, 72
biased, 160
blasphemy, 52
blithe, 164
bombastic, 72
brevity, 20
brusque, 12
buoyant, 92
cacophony, 48
cajole, 96
callous, 80
capitulate, 96
capricious, 136
catalyst, 64
catharsis, 136
caustic, 120

censure, 48
chastise, 120
circumspect, 132
clairvoyant, 104
clamor, 40
clemency, 20
coalesce, 16
cognizant, 36
colloquial, 124
commiserate, 36
composure, 100
conciliatory, 73
congenital, 100
contiguous, 104
contract, 40
convivial, 156
copious, 24
cordial, 108
crass, 124
credulous, 160
dearth, 24
debilitate, 104
decadence, 16
defame, 108
deference, 132
delineate, 72
depravity, 76
deprecate, 164
desecrate, 80
despot, 160
desultory, 44
devious, 68
diatribe, 48
didactic, 164
diffident, 72
diminutive, 148
discerning, 124
discordant, 108
discrepancy, 136
disparage, 64
dispassionate, 12
dissonance, 68
duplicity, 40
eclectic, 148

edifice, 48
efface, 68
effervescent, 12
egregious, 96
eloquent, 24
elucidate, 120
elusive, 100
enervate, 92
engender, 152
enmity, 52
ephemeral, 136
equanimity, 156
equivocal, 40
erroneous, 52
erudite, 152
eulogy, 164
evanescent, 80
exalt, 120
exemplary, 16
expedient, 36
extol, 100
extraneous, 149
exuberance, 16
fallacious, 120
fervor, 152
fledgling, 8
formidable, 100
frivolous, 20
garbled, 44
garner, 52
garrulous, 68
gratuitous, 165
gravity, 49
grueling, 108
guile, 132
hackneyed, 8
haphazard, 128
hardy, 149
heed, 80
heist, 20
heretic, 52
hindrance, 36
hyperbole, 124
hypocrisy, 121

iconoclast, 152
immutable, 68
impassive, 132
incessant, 8
incidental, 16
incipient, 160
incisive, 124
incite, 52
incontrovertible, 128
incorrigible, 92
indefatigable, 12
indict, 108
indigent, 80
indoctrinate, 108
induce, 136
inexorable, 92
infraction, 49
ingratiate, 64
inscrutable, 101
insipid, 64
insolvent, 16
insurgent, 121
intangible, 128
intractable, 149
irascible, 44
irrefutable, 92
irresolute, 40
jargon, 24
judicious, 124
kindle, 36
laconic, 73
lampoon, 20
languish, 53
lassitude, 156
laudable, 153
lavish, 37
levity, 24
listless, 156
loquacious, 44
ludicrous, 37
malevolent, 132
marred, 92
meager, 76
meander, 24
misanthrope, 12
mollify, 156
morose, 12
nefarious, 161
negate, 128
negligent, 37
nonchalance, 13
obliterate, 104
obtuse, 45
officious, 104
opaque, 45
opulence, 8

painstaking, 153
paradigm, 156
paragon, 80
parochial, 93
parsimonious, 17
partisan, 93
paucity, 45
peerless, 64
peripheral, 25
peruse, 53
phenomenon, 136
pique, 93
placate, 133
placid, 121
pompous, 153
ponderous, 69
potent, 129
preclude, 105
precocious, 101
predecessor, 69
predilection, 76
premonition, 96
prerogative, 125
prestigious, 96
prodigal, 17
prodigious, 161
profane, 49
profusion, 157
progeny, 13
propriety, 65
provincial, 81
proximity, 8
pugnacious, 133
querulous, 20
quixotic, 76
raze, 165
rebuff, 69
recalcitrant, 157
recapitulate, 45
recluse, 53
rectify, 137
renounce, 53
renown, 153
reproach, 21
rescind, 40
resigned, 157
resolution, 137
respite, 21
retract, 137
reverent, 96
rigorous, 129
sagacious, 9
salutary, 77
satirical, 93
scanty, 73
scrutinize, 37

serene, 137
servile, 161
somber, 49
soporific, 149
spurious, 129
spurn, 105
stagnant, 41
static, 69
steadfast, 81
stealthy, 105
stoic, 13
stupor, 97
subjugate, 73
submissive, 109
substantiate, 25
sullen, 109
supercilious, 81
supplant, 9
suppress, 77
surmise, 157
surreptitious, 17
sycophant, 97
tacit, 125
taciturn, 105
tactless, 125
tawdry, 165
temerity, 77
temper, 161
therapeutic, 129
thwart, 109
tirade, 133
torpor, 21
trepidation, 101
trite, 121
turbulence, 77
unassailable, 9
uniform, 41
unimpeachable, 165
unobtrusive, 25
unscathed, 21
untenable, 41
urbane, 97
usurp, 81
vacillate, 25
vilify, 41
virtuoso, 65
virulent, 101
vitriolic, 65
volatile, 133
voluminous, 9
voracious, 13
wanton, 109
whet, 125
whimsical, 65
writhe, 17
zany, 97